"No oth[er] ... a pleasu[re] ...

"... Exc[ellent] ... looking f[or] ...
Washington Post

★ ★ ★ ★ ★ (5-star rating) "Crisply written and remarkably personable. Cleverly organized so you can pluck out the minutest fact in a moment. Satisfyingly thorough."
Réalités

"The information they offer is up-to-date, crisply presented but far from exhaustive, the judgments knowledgeable but not opinionated." *New York Times*

"The individual volumes are compact, the prose succinct, and the coverage up-to-date and knowledgeable . . . The format is portable and the index admirably detailed."
John Barkham Syndicate

"... An abundance of excellent directions, diversions, and facts, including perspectives and getting-ready-to-go advice — succinct, detailed, and well organized in an easy-to-follow style." *Los Angeles Times*

"They contain an amount of information that is truly staggering, besides being surprisingly current."
Detroit News

"These guides address themselves to the needs of the modern traveler demanding precise, qualitative information . . . Upbeat, slick, and well put together."
Dallas Morning News

"... Attractive to look at, refreshingly easy to read, and generously packed with information." *Miami Herald*

"These guides are as good as any published, and much better than most." *Louisville* (Kentucky) *Times*

Stephen Birnbaum Travel Guides

Acapulco
Bahamas, Turks & Caicos
Barcelona
Bermuda
Boston
Canada
Cancun, Cozumel, and Isla Mujeres
Caribbean
Chicago
Disneyland
Eastern Europe
Europe
Europe for Business Travelers
Florence
France
Great Britain
Hawaii
Ireland
Italy
Ixtapa & Zihuatanejo
London
Los Angeles
Mexico
Miami & Ft. Lauderdale
New York
Paris
Portugal
Rome
San Francisco
South America
Spain
United States
USA for Business Travelers
Venice
Walt Disney World
Western Europe

CONTRIBUTING EDITORS

Clare Pedrick
Melinda Tang
Faith Willinger

MAPS   Mark Carlson
        Susan Carlson

SYMBOLS   Gloria McKeown

A Stephen Birnbaum Travel Guide

Birnbaum's
FLORENCE
1992

Stephen Birnbaum
Alexandra Mayes Birnbaum
EDITORS

Lois Spritzer
EXECUTIVE EDITOR

Laura L. Brengelman
Managing Editor

Mary Callahan
Ann-Rebecca Laschever
Beth Schlau
Dana Margaret Schwartz
Associate Editors

Gene Gold
Assistant Editor

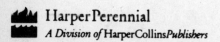

HarperPerennial
A Division of HarperCollins*Publishers*

FIRST EDITION

ISSN: 0749-2561 (Stephen Birnbaum Travel Guides)
ISSN: 1056-4489 (Florence)
ISBN: 0-06-278032-8 (pbk.)

92 93 94 95 96 CC/MPC 10 9 8 7 6 5 4 3 2 1

Contents

USEFUL WORDS AND PHRASES

THE CITY

Thorough, qualitative guide to Florence. This is a comprehensive report on the most compelling attractions and amenities, designed to be used on the spot.

DIVERSIONS

A selective guide to more than a dozen active and/or cerebral theme vacations, including the best places in Florence to pursue them.

For the Experience

For the Body

For the Mind

DIRECTIONS

Nine of the most interesting walking and driving tours in and around Florence.

A Word from the Editor

Look, I was wrong. The conversation had worked its way around to where we should spend the *Christmas* and *New Year* holidays, and Mrs. B. had suggested Florence. I greeted the idea with what can only be described as modified rapture, anticipating a very cold, damp year's end. I couldn't have been less accurate.

For eight of the best days I can recall on the road, the weather in Florence stayed in the 50s and 60s, perfect temperatures for endless strolling along Florentine byways. Florence is, in every way, a perfect city to roam on foot, but the immediate accessibility of its antiquities adds an element to the ambience that no other city can boast. It is as if you awoke each morning and greeted Michelangelo on the way to some Renaissance sight or other, and there is no way to avoid this wonderful pull from the past — as if you would want to.

Late in the afternoon, the setting sun bathed every building in a rosy glow, the sort of light at which we'd just marveled in the paintings at the *Uffizi* and the Pitti Palace. Again, we felt totally immersed in the centuries-old atmosphere of the place. Not at all bad.

In justice to my wife, I should add a word about *Christmas Eve* in the Duomo. Forget for the moment that we arranged to sit in the "box" that originally was reserved for the Medicis, or that combination of the magical entryway (you can manage to pass through the "Gates of Paradise"), the massive interior, and the ritual and music of the evening took us back about 5 centuries. The rest of the congregation was the really memorable part.

Though neatly dressed, they hardly were formally attired, and rather than sit down they mostly stood in the aisles and side sections. Parents and children held hands, chatted amiably with their neighbors, and partook of the ceremony in an informal, thoroughly captivating way. I can't recall a time in my travels when I've felt so much a part of the surrounding scene. What a smart fellow I am for listening to my wife!

My own evolution as a traveler (which happily continues) is mirrored by the evolution of our guidebook series. When we began our series of modern travel guides, we logically began with "area" books, attempting to publish guides that would include the widest possible number of attractive destinations. When the public seemed to accept our new way of delivering travel data, we added titles covering only a single country, and when these became popular we began our newest expansion phase, which centers on a group of books that deal with only a single city. Now we not only can highlight our favorite urban destinations, but can really describe how to get the very most out of a visit.

Such treatment of travel information only mirrors an increasingly pervasive trend among travelers — the frequent return to a treasured foreign travel spot. Once upon a time, even the most dedicated travelers would visit distant parts of the world no more than once in a lifetime — usually as part of that fabled Grand Tour. But greater numbers of would-be sojourners are now availing themselves of the opportunity to visit a favored part of the world over and over again.

So where once it was routine to say you'd "seen" a particular country after a very superficial, once-over-lightly encounter, the more perceptive travelers of today recognize that it's entirely possible to have only skimmed the surface of a specific travel destination even after having visited that place more than a dozen times. Similarly, repeated visits to a single site permit true exploration of special interests, whether they be sporting, artistic, or intellectual.

For those of us who spent the several years working out the special system under which we present information in this series, the luxury of being able to devote nearly as much space as we'd like to just a single city is as close to paradise for guide writers and editors as any of us expects to come. But clearly this is not the first guide to the glories of Florence — one suspects that guides of one sort or another have existed at least since the Medicis began being rude to their neighbors. Guides to Florence have probably existed in one form or another for centuries, so a traveler might logically ask why a new one is suddenly necessary.

Our answer is that the nature of travel to Florence — and even of the travelers who now routinely make the trip — has changed dramatically of late. For the past 2,000 years or so, travel to any foreign address was an extremely elaborate undertaking, one that required extensive advance planning. Even as recently as the 1950s, a person who had actually been to Florence — to say nothing of Venice, Rome, or Milan — could dine out on his or her experiences for years, since such adventures were quite extraordinary and usually the province of the privileged alone.

With the advent of jet air travel in the late 1950s, however, and of increased-capacity, wide-body aircraft during the 1960s, travel to and around once distant destinations became extremely common. In fact, in more than 2 decades of nearly unending inflation, airfares may be the only commodity in the world that has actually gone down in price.

Attitudes as well as costs have also changed significantly in the last couple of decades. Beginning with the so-called flower children of the 1960s, international travel lost much of its aura of mystery. Whereas their parents might have been happy with just a superficial sampling of Florence, these young people simply picked up and settled in various parts of Europe for an indefinite stay. While living as inexpensively as possible, they adapted to the local lifestyle, and generally immersed themselves in things European.

Thus began an explosion of travel. And over the years, the development of inexpensive charter flights and packages fueled and sharpened the new American interest in and appetite for more extensive exploration.

Now, in the 1990s, those same flower children who were in the forefront of the modern travel revolution have undeniably aged. While it may be impolite to point out that they are probably well into their untrustworthy thirties and forties, their original zeal for travel remains undiminished. For them, it's hardly news that the best way to get to the Ponte Vecchio is to walk along the Arno. Such experienced and knowledgeable travelers have decided precisely where they want to go and are more often searching for ideas and insights to expand their already sophisticated travel consciousnesses.

Obviously, any new guidebook to Florence must keep pace with and answer the real needs of today's travelers. That's why we've tried to create a guide that's specifically organized, written, and edited for this more demanding modern audience, travelers for whom qualitative information is infinitely more desirable than mere quantities of unappraised data. We think that this book and the other guides in our series represent a new generation of travel guides, one that is especially responsive to modern needs and interests.

For years, dating back as far as Herr Baedeker, travel guides have tended to be encyclopedic, seemingly much more concerned with demonstrating expertise in geography and history than with making a real analysis of the sorts of things that actually concern a typical modern tourist. But today, when it is hardly necessary to tell a traveler where Florence is located (in many cases, the traveler has been there nearly as often as the guidebook editors), it becomes the responsibility of those editors to provide new perspectives and to suggest new directions in order to make the guide genuinely valuable.

That's exactly what we've tried to do in this series. I think you'll notice a different, more contemporary tone to the text, as well as an organization and focus that are distinctive and more functional. And even a random reading of what follows will demonstrate a substantial departure from the standard guidebook orientation, for not only have we attempted to provide information of a more compelling sort, but we also have tried to present the data in a format that makes it particularly accessible.

Needless to say, it's difficult to decide precisely what to include in a guidebook of this size — and what to omit. Early on, we realized that giving up the encyclopedic approach precluded our listing every single route and restaurant, a realization that helped define our overall editorial focus. Similarly, when we discussed the possibility of presenting certain information in other than strict geographic order, we found that the new format enabled us to arrange data in a way we feel best answers the questions travelers typically ask.

Large numbers of specific questions have provided the real editorial skeleton for this book. The volume of mail I regularly receive emphasizes that modern travelers want very precise information, so we've tried to organize our material in the most responsive way possible. Readers who want to know the best restaurants or the best places to find inexpensive couturier fashions will have no trouble extracting that data from this guide.

Travel guides are, understandably, reflections of personal taste, and putting one's name on a title page obviously puts one's preferences on the line. But I think I ought to amplify just what "personal" means. I don't believe in the sort of personal guidebook that's a palpable misrepresentation on its face. It is, for example, hardly possible for any single travel writer to visit thousands of restaurants (and nearly as many hotels) in any given year and provide accurate appraisals of each. And even if it were physically possible for one human being to survive such an itinerary, it would of necessity have to be done at a dead sprint and the perceptions derived therefrom would probably be less valid than those of any other intelligent individual visiting the same establishments. It is, therefore, impossible (especially in a large, annually revised guidebook *series* such as we offer) to have only one person provide all the data on the entire world.

I also happen to think that such individual orientation is of substantially less value to readers. Visiting a single hotel for just one night or eating one hasty meal in a random restaurant hardly equips anyone to provide appraisals that are of more than passing interest. No amount of doggedly alliterative or oppressively onomatopoeic text can camouflage a technique that is essentially specious. We have, therefore, chosen what I like to describe as the "thee and me" approach to restaurant and hotel evaluation and, to a somewhat more limited degree, to the sites and sights we have included in the other sections of our text. What this really reflects is a personal sampling tempered by intelligent counsel from informed local sources, and these additional friends-of-the-editor are almost always residents of the city and/or area about which they are consulted.

Despite the presence of several editors, writers, researchers, and local correspondents, very precise editing and tailoring keep our text fiercely subjective. So what follows is the gospel according to the Birnbaums, and represents as much of our own taste and instincts as we can manage. It is probable, therefore, that if you like your cities stylish and prefer small hotels with personality to huge high-rise anonymities, we're likely to have a long and meaningful relationship. Readers with dissimilar tastes may be less enraptured.

I also should point out something about the person to whom this guidebook is directed. Above all, he or she is a "visitor." This means that such elements as restaurants have been specifically picked to provide the visitor with a representative, enlightening, stimulating, and, above all, pleasant experience. Since so many extraneous considerations can affect the reception and service accorded a regular restaurant patron, our choices can in no way be construed as an exhaustive guide to resident dining. We think we've listed all the best places, in various price ranges, but they were chosen with a visitor's enjoyment in mind.

Other evidence of how we've tried to tailor our text to reflect modern travel habits is most apparent in the section we call DIVERSIONS. Where once it was common for travelers to spend a foreign visit in a determinedly passive state, the emphasis is far more active today. So we've organized every activity we could reasonably evaluate and presented the material in a way that is especially accessible to activists of either athletic or cerebral bent. It is no longer necessary, therefore, to wade through a pound or two of superfluous prose just to find the very best shop or most palatable pasta within walking distance of the Duomo.

If there is a single thing that best characterizes the revolution in and evolution of current holiday habits, it is that most travelers now consider travel a right rather than a privilege. No longer is a trip to the far corners of the globe necessarily a once-in-a-lifetime thing; nor is the idea of visiting exotic, faraway places in the least worrisome. Travel today translates as the enthusiastic desire to sample all of the world's opportunities, to find that elusive quality of experience that is not only enriching but comfortable. For that reason, we've tried to make what follows not only helpful and enlightening but the sort of welcome companion of which every traveler dreams.

Finally, I also should point out that every good travel guide is a living enterprise; that is, no part of this text is carved in stone. In our annual revisions, we refine, expand, and further hone all our material to serve your travel needs better. To this end, no contribution is of greater value to us than your personal reaction to what we have written, as well as information reflecting your own experiences while using this book. We earnestly and enthusiastically solicit your comments about this guide *and* your opinions and perceptions about places you have recently visited. In this way, we will be able to provide the most current information — including the actual experiences of recent travelers — and to make those experiences more readily available to others. Please write to us at 60 E. 42nd St., New York, NY 10165.

We sincerely hope to hear from you.

STEPHEN BIRNBAUM

How to Use This Guide

A great deal of care has gone into the organization of this guidebook, and we believe it represents a real breakthrough in the presentation of travel material. Our aim is to create a new, more modern generation of travel books and to make this guide the most useful and practical travel tool available today.

Our text is divided into five basic sections in order to present information in the best way on every possible aspect of a Florence vacation. This organization itself should alert you to the vast and varied opportunities available, as well as indicate all the specific data necessary to plan a successful trip. You won't find much of the conventional "swaying palms and shimmering sand" text here; we've chosen instead to deliver more useful and practical information. Prospective itineraries tend to speak for themselves, and with so many diverse travel opportunities, we feel our main job is to highlight what's where and to provide basic information — how, when, where, how much, and what's best — to assist you in making the most intelligent choices possible.

Here is a brief summary of the five basic sections and what you can expect to find in each. We believe that you will find both your travel planning and en route enjoyment enhanced by having this book at your side.

GETTING READY TO GO

This mini-encyclopedia of practical travel facts is a sort of know-it-all companion with all the precise information necessary to create a successful trip to Florence. There are entries on more than 2 dozen separate topics, including how to get where you're going, what preparations to make before leaving, what your trip is likely to cost, and how to avoid prospective problems. The individual entries are specific, realistic, and where appropriate, cost-oriented.

We expect you to use this section most in the course of planning your trip, for its ideas and suggestions are intended to simplify this often confusing period. Entries are intentionally concise, in an effort to get to the meat of the matter with the least extraneous prose. These entries are augmented by extensive lists of specific sources from which to obtain even more specialized data, plus some suggestions for obtaining travel information on your own.

USEFUL WORDS AND PHRASES

Though most hotels and restaurants in Florence have at least one English-speaking staff member, a little knowledge of Italian will go a long way at smaller establishments. This collection of often-used words and phrases will help you to make a hotel or dinner reservation, order a meal, mail a letter — and even buy toothpaste.

THE CITY

The report on Florence has been created with the assistance of researchers, contributors, professional journalists, and experts who live in the city. Although useful at the planning stage, THE CITY is really designed to be taken along and used on the spot. The reports offer a short-stay guide, including an essay introducing the city as a historic entity and as a contemporary place to visit. *At-a-Glance* material is actually a site-by-site survey of the most important, interesting (and sometimes most eclectic) sights to see and things to do. *Sources and Resources* is a concise listing of pertinent information meant to answer a range of potentially pressing questions as they arise — simple things such as the address of the local tourist office, how to get around, which sightseeing tours to take, when special events occur, where to find the best nightspot or to hail a taxi, which are the chic places to shop, and where the best tennis courts and golf courses are to be found. *Best in Town* is our collection of cost-and-quality choices of the best places to eat and sleep on a variety of budgets.

DIVERSIONS

This section is designed to help travelers find the best places in which to pursue a wide range of physical and cerebral activities, without having to wade through endless pages of unrelated text. This very selective guide lists the broadest possible range of activities, including all the best places to pursue them.

We start with a list of possibilities that offer various places to stay and eat, move to those that require some perspiration — sports preferences and other rigorous pursuits — and go on to report on a number of more cerebral and spiritual vacation opportunities. In every case, our suggestion of a particular location — and often our recommendation of a specific hotel — is intended to guide you to that special place where the quality of experience is likely to be the highest. Whether you seek a romantic hostelry or an inspiring cooking school, each category is the equivalent of a comprehensive checklist of the absolute best in Florence.

DIRECTIONS

Here are walking and driving routes that cover the city and its surroundings, along its main thoroughfares and side streets, past its most spectacular landmarks and magnificent parks, into its nearby suburbs, and a bit farther, to towns and cities within easy reach of Florence. This is the only section of the book that is organized geographically; itineraries can be "connected" for longer sojourns or used individually for short, intensive explorations.

Although each of the book's sections has a distinct format and a special function, they have all been designed to be used together to provide a complete inventory of travel information. To use this book to full advantage, take a few minutes to read the table of contents and random entries in each section to get a firsthand feel of how it all fits together.

Pick and choose needed information. Assume, for example, that you have always wanted to make that most fulfilling Florentine visit, an eating tour of the city's bastions of gastronomy — but you never really knew how to organize it or where to go. Choose specific restaurants from the selections offered in "Eating Out" in THE CITY, in each walking tour in DIRECTIONS, and in the roundup of the best in the city called *Buon Appetito: The Best Restaurants in Florence* in the DIVERSIONS section. Then refer to USEFUL WORDS AND PHRASES to help you with everything from deciphering the menu to identifying pasta shapes.

In other words, the sections of this book are building blocks designed to help you put together the best possible trip. Use them selectively as a tool, a source of ideas, a reference work for accurate facts, and a guide to the best buys, the most exciting sights, the most pleasant accommodations, the tastiest food — *the best travel experience* that you can possibly have in Florence.

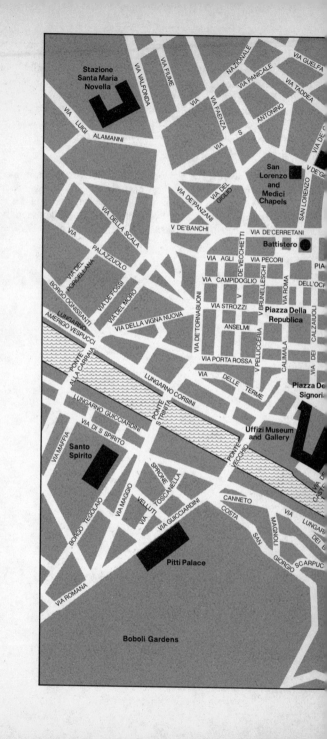

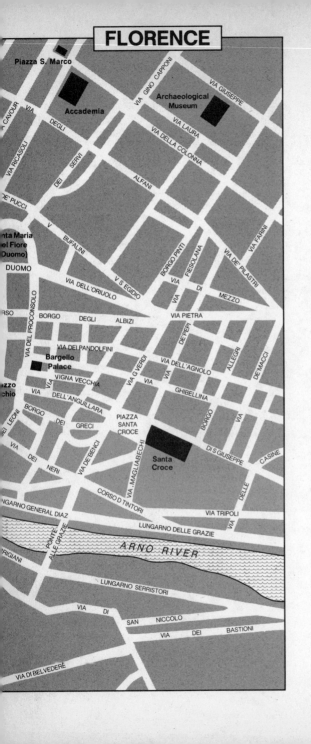

FLORENCE

Piazza S. Marco

VIA GINO CAPPONI

VIA GIUSEPPE

Archaeological
Museum

Accademia

VIA CAVOUR

VIA

DEGLI

VIA LAURA

VIA RICASOLI

VIA DELLA COLONNA

SERVI

DE' PUCCI

DEI

ALFANI

nta Maria
el Fiore
(Duomo)

V

BUFALINI

BORGO PINTI

FIESOLANA

VIA DE' PILASTRI

VIA FARINI

DUOMO

VIA DELL'ORIUOLO

V S EGIDIO

VIA

DI

MEZZO

VIA DEL PROCONSOLO

RSO

BORGO

DEGLI

ALBIZI

VIA PIETRA

DE'PEPI

VIA DEI PANDOLFINI

VIA G VERDI

Bargello
Palace

VIA DELL'AGNOLO

ALLEGRI

DEI MACCI

VIGNA VECCHIA

VIA

azzo
chio

VIA

DELL'ANGUILLARA

GHIBELLINA

BORGO

VIA

EI LEONI

BORGO

DEI

GRECI

PIAZZA
SANTA
CROCE

VIA MAGLIABECHI

DI S GIUSEPPE

CASINE

VIA

DEI

NERI

VIA DE' BENCI

Santa
Croce

DELLE

CORSO D TINTORI

VIA TRIPOLI

VIA

NGARNO GENERAL DIAZ

LUNGARNO DELLE GRAZIE

PONTE

RIGIANI

ALLE GRAZIE

ARNO RIVER

LUNGARNO SERRISTORI

VIA

DI

SAN

NICCOLO

VIA

DEI

BASTIONI

VIA DI BELVEDERE

GETTING READY TO GO

When and How to Go

When to Go

There really isn't a "best" time to visit Florence. For North Americans, as well as Europeans, the period from April to mid-September has long been — and remains — the peak travel period, traditionally the most popular vacation time.

It is important to emphasize that Florence, like the rest of Italy, is hardly a single-season destination; more and more vacationers who have a choice are enjoying the substantial advantages of off-season travel. Though some tourist attractions may close during the off-season — roughly November to March — the major ones remain open and tend to be less crowded. During the off-season, people relax and Italian life proceeds at a more leisurely pace. What's more, travel generally is less expensive.

For some, the most convincing argument in favor of off-season travel is the economic one. Getting there and staying there are less expensive during less popular travel periods, as airfares, hotel rooms, and car rental rates may go down and less expensive package tours become available; the independent traveler can go farther on less, too.

A definite bonus to visiting during the off-season is that even the most basic services are performed more efficiently. In theory, off-season service is identical to that offered during high season, but the fact is that the absence of demanding crowds inevitably begets much more thoughtful and personal attention.

Even during the off-season, high-season rates may prevail because of an important local event. Particularly in the larger cities, and Florence is a major cultural and commercial center, special events and major trade shows held at the time of your visit are sure to affect not only the availability of discounts on accommodations, but the basic availability of a place to stay.

It also should be noted that the months immediately before and after the peak summer months — what the travel industry refers to as shoulder seasons — often are sought out because they offer fair weather and somewhat smaller crowds.

In short, like many other popular places, in Italy and elsewhere, Florence's vacation appeal has become multi-seasonal. But the noted exceptions notwithstanding, most travel destinations are decidedly less heavily trafficked and less expensive during the winter.

CLIMATE: Florence, set in a bowlful of hills, tends to have somewhat more extreme weather than other parts of Italy. Temperatures range from the 60s to the 90s from mid-June to mid-September, and summer can be stifling. In winter, the temperature rarely drops below freezing, ranging from the low 30s to the 50s from December through mid-March, but the cold is damp and often gripping. Still, Florence maintains fairly moderate temperatures year-round. For example, the average temperature is 45F (7C) in January, 60F (15C) in April, 77F (25C) in July, and 63F (17C) in October. Winter is the wettest season; bring your raingear if you're traveling during that time.

Travelers can get current readings and 3-day Accu-Weather forecasts through *American Express Travel Related Services*' Worldwide Weather Report number. By dialing

900-WEATHER and punching in the access code for numerous travel destinations worldwide, an up-to-date recording will provide current temperature, sky conditions, wind speed and direction, heat index, relative humidity, local time, highway reports, and beach and boating reports or ski conditions (where appropriate). For the weather in Florence, punch in FLO. This 24-hour service can be accessed from any touch-tone phone in the US or Canada and costs 95¢ per minute. The charge will show up on your phone bill. For a free list of the areas covered, send a self-addressed, stamped envelope to *1-900-WEATHER,* 261 Central Ave., Farmingdale, NY 11735.

SPECIAL EVENTS: Music lovers from all over the world flock to the *Maggio Musicale Fiorentino,* the most celebrated cultural festival in Florence. It is held each year in *Teatro Comunale* from May to June. However, at press time, the *Teatro Comunale* was closed for asbestos removal, and the *Maggio Musicale* was temporarily moved to *Teatro Verdi.* Orchestras and ballet and opera companies of international fame are featured every year.

Fiesole, a Roman city which was established as early as the 8th century BC, is the setting of *Estate Fiesolana.* Just 5 miles (8 km) northeast of Florence, it can be reached by bus No. 7 from Stazione Santa Maria Novella. In July and August, world-famous orchestras, ballet and opera companies, and various artists perform in *Teatro Romano.* For other cultural and folkloric events, see *Special Events* in THE CITY.

Traveling by Plane

Flying is the most efficient way to get to Florence, and it is the quickest, most convenient means of travel between different parts of Italy once you are there.

The air space between North America and Europe is the most heavily trafficked in the world. It is served by dozens of airlines, almost all of which sell seats at a variety of prices under a vast spectrum of requirements and restrictions. You probably will spend more for your airfare than for any other single item in your travel budget, so try to take advantage of the lowest fares offered by either scheduled airlines or charter companies. You should know what kinds of flights are available, the rules under which air travel operates, and all the special package options.

GATEWAYS: At present, there are no nonstop flights from the US to Florence. Connecting flights are available from Rome and there is nonstop service to Rome departing from New York.

SCHEDULED FLIGHTS: The following airlines have regular nonstop service to Rome: *Alitalia, Delta,* and *TWA.*

A number of other European carriers serve Florence from the US with connecting flights through their main hubs: *Lufthansa* from Chicago and New York via Munich; *Sabena* from Boston and New York via Brussels. *SwissAir*'s subsidiary domestic airline, *Crossair,* flies from Lugano to Florence. However, there are no direct flights between the US and Lugano. Connecting flights are available from Geneva or Zurich. The US gateways for both cities are Atlanta, Boston, Chicago, Los Angeles, and New York.

However, since the airport at Florence is quite small and mostly for domestic traffic, a more popular way of reaching the city is via the international airport in Pisa. A 1-hour train service runs between Pisa and Florence.

The following European airlines provide service between the US and Pisa through their main hubs: *Air France* from Anchorage, Boston, Chicago, Houston, Los Angeles, Miami, Newark, New York, San Francisco, and Washington, DC, via Paris; *British*

Airways via [...] n numerous US gateways); and *Lufthansa* from Atlan[...]es, Miami, New York, Philadelphia, San Francisco, [...]art. *Crossair* also flies to Pisa from Lugano.

Tickets [...] many regularly scheduled flights, a full-fare ticket pro[...] (although at considerable expense) because there are[...]ts. A prospective passenger can buy a ticket for a flig[...]eoff — if a seat is available. If your ticket is for a ro[...]rn reservation whenever you wish — months before y[...]eturn. Assuming foreign immigration require-ments [...] destination for as long as you like. (Tickets genera[...] renewed if not used.) You also can cancel your flight[...]wever, while it is true that this category of ticket can b[...]t is advisable to reserve well in advance during pop[...] holiday times.

F[...] [...]ge so rapidly that even experts find it difficult to kee[...]ng situation is due to a number of factors, including air[...]elations, increasing fuel costs, and vastly increased co[...]

[...]conception about fares on scheduled airlines is that th[...]ow much service will be provided on the flight. This i[...]far more realistic rule of thumb is that the less you [...]rictions and qualifications are likely to come into play [...]ell as after you get off). These qualifying aspects relate [...] the week) during which you must travel, how far in [...]ur ticket, the minimum and maximum amount of time [...], your willingness to decide on a return date at the time [...] to stick to that decision. It is not uncommon for passen-ge[...] the same wide-body jet to have paid fares varying by hundreds of do[...] oo often the traveler paying more would have been equally willing (and able) to accep the terms of the far less expensive ticket.

In general, the great variety of fares between the US and Florence can be reduced to four basic categories — first class, business class, coach (also called economy or tourist class), and excursion or discount fares. In addition, Advance Purchase Excur-sion (APEX) fares offer savings under certain conditions.

In a class by itself is the *Concorde,* the supersonic jet developed jointly by France and Great Britain that cruises at speeds of 1,350 miles per hour (about twice the speed of sound) and makes transatlantic crossings in half the time (3¾ hours from New York to Paris) of conventional, subsonic jets. *Air France* offers *Concorde* service to Paris from New York; *British Airways* flies from Miami, Washington, DC, and New York to London. Service is "single" class (with champagne and caviar all the way), and the fare is expensive, about 20% more than a first class ticket on a subsonic aircraft. Some discounts have been offered, but time is the real gift of the *Concorde.* For travelers to European destinations other than Paris or London, this "gift" may be more or less valuable as compared to a direct flight when taking connecting flights into account.

A **first class** ticket admits you to the special section of the aircraft with larger seats, more legroom, better (or more elaborately served) food, free drinks and headsets for movies and music channels, and above all, personal attention. First class fares are about twice those of full-fare (often called "regular") economy.

Behind first class often lies **business class**, usually a separate cabin or cabins. While standards of comfort and service are not as high as in first class, they represent a considerable improvement over conditions in the rear of the plane, with roomier seats, more leg and shoulder space between passengers, and fewer seats abreast. Free liquor and headsets, a choice of meal entrées, and a separate counter for speedier check-in are other inducements. Note that airlines often have their own names for their business class service — such as Le Club on *Air France,* and Ambassador Class on *TWA.*

The terms of the **coach** or **economy** fare may vary slightly from airline to airline; from time to time airlines may be selling more than one type of economy fare. Coach or economy passengers sit more snugly, as many as 10 in a single row on a wide-body jet, behind the first class and business class sections. Normally, alcoholic drinks are not free, nor are the headsets.

In first, business, and economy class, passengers are entitled to reserve seats and are sold tickets on an open reservation system, with tickets sold up to the last minute if seats are available. The passengers may travel on any scheduled flight they wish, buy a one-way or round-trip ticket, and have the ticket remain valid for a year. There are no requirements for a minimum or maximum stay or for advance booking and no cancellation penalties. The first class and business tickets also allow free stopover privileges; limited free stopovers often are permitted in some economy fares, while with others a surcharge may apply. The cost of economy and business class tickets between the US and Italy does not vary much in the course of the year.

Excursion and other **discount** fares are the airlines' equivalent of a special sale and usually apply to round-trip bookings only. These fares generally differ according to the season and the number of travel days permitted. They are only a bit less flexible than full-fare economy tickets, and are, therefore, often useful for both business and holiday travelers. Most round-trip excursion tickets include strict minimum and maximum stay requirements and can be changed only within prescribed time limits. So don't count on extending a ticket beyond the specified time of return or staying less time than required. Different airlines may have different regulations concerning the number of stopovers permitted, and sometimes excursion fares are less expensive during midweek. The availability of these reduced-rate seats is most limited at busy times such as holidays. Discount or excursion fare ticket holders sit with the coach passengers and, for all intents and purposes, are indistinguishable from them. They receive all the same basic services, even though they may have paid anywhere between 30% and 55% less for the trip. Obviously, it's wise to make plans early enough to qualify for this less expensive transportation if possible.

These discount or excursion fares may masquerade under a variety of names and invariably have strings attached. A common requirement is that the ticket be purchased a certain number of days — usually no fewer than 7 or 14 days — in advance of departure, though it may be booked weeks or months in advance (it has to be "ticketed," or paid for, shortly after booking, however). The return reservation usually has to be made at the time of the original ticketing and cannot be changed later than a certain number of days (again, usually 7 or 14) before the return flight. If events force a passenger to change the return reservation after the date allowed, the difference between the round-trip excursion rate and the round-trip coach rate probably will have to be paid, though most airlines allow passengers to use their discounted fares by standing by for an empty seat, even if the carrier doesn't otherwise have standby fares. Another common condition is the minimum and maximum stay requirement; for example, 1 to 6 days or 6 to 14 days (but including a Saturday night). Last, cancellation penalties of up to 50% of the full price of the ticket have been assessed — check the specific penalty in effect when you purchase your discount/excursion ticket — so careful planning is imperative.

Of even greater risk — and bearing the lowest price of all the current discount fares — is the ticket where no change at all in departure and/or return flights is permitted, and where the ticket price is totally nonrefundable. If you do buy a non-refundable ticket, you should be aware of a new policy followed by many airlines that may make it easier to change your plans if necessary. For a fee — set by each airline and payable at the airport when checking in — you *may* be able to change the time or date of a return flight on a nonrefundable ticket. However, if the nonrefundable ticket price for the replacement flight is higher than that of the original (as often is the case when trading in a weekday for a weekend flight), you also will have to pay the difference. Any such change must be made a certain number of days in advance — in some cases as little as 2 days — of either the original or the replacement flight, whichever is earlier; restrictions are set by the individual carrier. (Travelers holding a nonrefundable or other restricted ticket who must change their plans due to a family emergency should know that some carriers may make special allowances in such situations; see *Medical and Legal Aid and Consular Services,* in this section.)

One excursion fare available for travel between the US and Florence, but not to the majority of other European destinations, comes unencumbered by advance booking requirements and cancellation penalties, permits one stopover (for a fee) in each direction, and has "open jaws," meaning that you can fly to one city and depart from another, arranging and paying for your own transportation between the two. The ticket costs about a third less than economy — during the off-season. High-season prices may be less attractive. The ticket currently is good for a minimum of 7 days and a maximum of 6 months abroad.

There also is a newer, often less expensive, type of excursion fare, the **APEX**, or **Advanced Purchase Excursion** fare. (In the case of flights to Europe, this type of fare also may be called a "Eurosaver" fare.) As with traditional excursion fares, passengers paying an APEX fare sit with and receive the same basic services as any other coach or economy passengers, even though they may have paid up to 50% less for their seats. In return, they are subject to certain restrictions. In the case of flights to Florence, the ticket usually is good for a minimum of 7 days abroad and a maximum, currently, of 2 months (depending on the airline and the destination); and as its name implies, it must be "ticketed," or paid for in its entirety, a certain period of time before departure — usually 21 days, although in the case of Florence it may be as little as 14 days.

The drawback to an APEX fare is that it penalizes travelers who change their minds — and travel plans. The return reservation must be made at the time of the original ticketing, and if for some reason you change your schedule, you will have to pay a penalty of $100 or 10% of the ticket value, whichever is greater, as long as you travel within the validity period of your ticket. But if you change your return to a date less than the minimum stay or more than the maximum stay, the difference between the round-trip APEX fare and the full round-trip coach rate will have to be paid. There also is a penalty of anywhere from $75 to $125 or more for canceling or changing a reservation *before* travel begins — check the specific penalty in effect when you purchase your ticket. No stopovers are allowed on an APEX ticket, but it is possible to create an open-jaw effect by buying an APEX on a split ticket basis; for example, flying to Rome (and then continuing on to Florence) and returning from Milan. The total price would be half the price of an APEX to Rome plus half the price of an APEX to Milan. APEX tickets to Florence are sold at basic and peak rates (peak season is roughly May through September) and may include surcharges for weekend flights.

There also is a Winter or Super APEX, which may go under different names for different carriers. Similar to the regular APEX fare, it costs slightly less but is more restrictive. Depending on the airline and destination, it usually is available only for off-peak winter travel and is limited to a stay of between 7 and 21 days. Advance purchase still is required (currently, 30 days prior to travel), and ticketing must be completed within 48 hours of reservation. The fare is nonrefundable, except in cases of hospitalization or death.

At the time of this writing, *Alitalia* offered Super APEX on transatlantic flights to most destinations in Italy during the off-season.

Another type of fare that sometimes is available is the youth fare. At present, most

US airlines and *Alitalia* are using a form of APEX fare as a youth fare — offered to travelers through age 24, in the case of *Alitalia;* for some other airlines, it may be up to age 26. The maximum stay is extended to a year. Seats can be reserved no more than 3 days before departure, and tickets must be purchased when the reservation is made. The return is booked at time of reservation, or it can be left open. There is no cancellation penalty, but the fare is subject to availability, so it may be difficult to book a return during peak travel periods, and as with the regular APEX fare, it may not even be available for travel to or from Florence during high season, especially if you have a strict traveling schedule.

The major airlines serving Florence from the US also may offer individual excursion fares in conjunction with ground accommodation packages. Previously called ITX, and sometimes referred to as individual tour-basing fares, these fares generally are offered as part of "air/hotel/car/transfer packages," and can reduce the cost of an economy fare by more than a third. The packages are booked for a specific length of time, with return dates specified; rescheduling and cancellation restrictions and penalties vary from carrier to carrier. At the time of this writing, airlines that offer this type of fare to Italy include *Air France, Alitalia, British Airways, Delta,* and *TWA.* Note that their offerings may or may not represent substantial savings over standard economy fares, so check at the time you plan to travel. (For further information on package options, see *Package Tours,* in this section.)

Travelers looking for the least expensive possible airfares should, finally, scan the travel pages of their hometown newspapers (especially the Sunday travel sections) for announcements of special promotional fares. Most airlines traditionally have offered their most attractive special fares to encourage travel during slow seasons, and to inaugurate and publicize new routes. Even if none of these factors apply, prospective passengers can be fairly sure that the number of discount seats per flight at the lowest price is strictly limited, or that the fare offering includes a set expiration date — which means it's absolutely necessary to move fast to enjoy the lowest possible price.

It's always wise to ask about discount or promotional fares and about any conditions that might restrict booking, payment, cancellation, and changes in plans. Check the prices from other neighboring cities. A special rate may be offered in a nearby city but not in yours, and it may be enough of a bargain to warrant your leaving from that city. Ask if there is a difference in price for midweek versus weekend travel, or if there is a further discount for traveling early in the morning or late at night. Also be sure to investigate package deals, which are offered by virtually every airline. These may include a car rental, accommodations, and dining and/or sightseeing features in addition to the basic airfare, and the combined cost of packaged elements usually is considerably less than the cost of the exact same elements when purchased separately.

If in the course of your research you come across a deal that seems too good to be true, keep in mind that logic may not be a component of deeply discounted airfares — there's not always any sane relationship between miles to be flown and the price to get there. More often than not, the level of competition on a given route dictates the degree of discount, and don't be dissuaded from accepting an offer that sounds irresistible just because it also sounds illogical. Better to buy that inexpensive fare while it's being offered and worry about the sense — or absence thereof — while you're flying to your desired destination.

When you're satisfied that you've found the lowest possible price for which you can conveniently qualify, make your booking. You may have to call the airline more than once, because different airline reservations clerks have been known to quote different prices, and different fares will be available at different times for the same flight because of a relatively new computerized airline practice called yield management, which adds or subtracts low-fare seats to a given flight depending on how well it is selling.

To protect yourself against fare increases, purchase and pay for your ticket as soon as possible after you've received a confirmed reservation. Airlines generally will honor their tickets, even if the operative price at the time of your flight is higher than the price you paid; if fares go up between the time you *reserve* a flight and the time you *pay* for it, you likely will be out of luck. Finally, with excursion or discount fares, it is important to remember that when a reservation clerk says that you must purchase a ticket by a specific date, this is an absolute deadline. Miss it and the airline may automatically cancel your reservation without telling you. Once you are signed up for such a program, if flying to Europe on *Air France, Alitalia, Lufthansa,* or another Europe-based airline, ask if the miles to be flown may be applied toward your collective bonus mileage account with a US carrier. For example, miles flown on *Alitalia* can be applied to *Continental, United,* and *USAir* frequent flyer mileage programs.

Frequent Flyers – Among the leading carriers serving Italy, *Air France, British Airways, Delta,* and *TWA* offer a bonus system to frequent travelers. After the first 10,000 miles, for example, a passenger might be eligible for a first class seat for the coach fare; after another 10,000 miles, he or she might receive a discount on his or her next ticket purchase. The value of the bonuses continues to increase as more miles are logged. Once you are signed up for such a program, if flying to Europe on *Air France, Alitalia, Lufthansa, Sabena, SwissAir,* or another Europe-based airline, ask if the miles to be flown may be applied toward your collective bonus mileage account with a US carrier. For example, miles flown on *Alitalia* can be applied to *Continental, United,* and *USAir* frequent flyer mileage programs.

Bonus miles also may be earned by patronizing affiliated car rental companies or hotel chains, or by using one of the credit cards that now offers this reward. In deciding whether to accept such a credit card from one of the issuing organizations that tempt you with frequent flyer mileage bonuses on a specific airline, first determine whether the interest rate charged on the unpaid balance is the same as (or less than) possible alternate credit cards, and whether the annual "membership" fee also is equal or lower. If these charges are slightly higher than those of competing cards, weigh the difference against the potential value in airfare savings. Also ask about any bonus miles awarded just for signing up — 1,000 is common, 5,000 generally the maximum.

For the most up-to-date information on frequent flyer bonus options, you may want to send for the monthly newsletter *Frequent.* Issued by Frequent Publications, it provides current information about frequent flyer plans in general, as well as specific data about promotions, awards, and combination deals to help you keep track of the profusion — and confusion — of current and upcoming availabilities. For a year's subscription, send $33 to Frequent Publications, 4715-C Town Center Dr., Colorado Springs, CO 80916 (phone: 800-333-5937).

There also is a monthly magazine called *Frequent Flyer,* but unlike the newsletter mentioned above, its focus is primarily on newsy articles of interest to business travelers and other frequent flyers. Published by Official Airline Guides (PO Box 58543, Boulder, CO 80322-8543; phone: 800-323-3537), *Frequent Flyer* is available for $24 for a 1-year subscription.

Low-Fare Airlines – Increasingly, the stimulus for special fares is the appearance of airlines associated with bargain rates. On these airlines, all seats on any given flight generally sell for the same price, which is somewhat below the lowest discount fare offered by the larger, more established airlines. It is important to note that tickets offered by the smaller airlines specializing in low-cost travel frequently are not subject to the same restrictions as the lowest-priced ticket offered by the more established carriers. They may not require advance purchase or minimum and maximum stays, may involve no cancellation penalties, and may be available one way or round trip. A disadvantage to low-fare airlines, however, is that when something goes wrong, such as delayed baggage or a flight cancellation due to equipment breakdown, their smaller fleets and fewer flights mean that passengers may have to wait longer for a solution than they would on one of the equipment-rich major carriers.

At press time, one of the few airlines offering a consistently low fare to Europe was *Virgin Atlantic* (phone: 800-862-8621 or 212-242-1330), which flies daily from New York (Newark) to London's Gatwick Airport. The airline sells tickets in several categories, including business or "upper" class, economy, APEX, and nonrefundable variations on standby. Fares from New York to London include Late Saver fares — which must be purchased not less than 7 days prior to travel — and Late Late Saver fares — which are purchased no later than 1 day prior to travel. Travelers to Florence have to take a second flight there from London, but still may save money. To determine the potential savings, add the cost of these transatlantic fares and the cost of connecting flights to come up with the total ticket price.

In a class by itself is *Icelandair,* which always has been a scheduled airline but long has been known as a good source of low-cost flights to Europe. *Icelandair* flies from Baltimore/Washington, DC, New York, and Orlando to Copenhagen (Denmark), Glasgow and London (Great Britain), Gothenburg and Stockholm (Sweden), Helsinki (Finland), Luxembourg (in the country of the same name), Oslo (Norway), Paris (France), and Reykjavik (Iceland). In addition, the airline increases the options for its passengers by offering "thru-fares" on connecting flights to other European cities. (The price of the intra-European flights — aboard Luxembourg's *Luxair* — is included in the price *Icelandair* quotes for the transatlantic portion of the travel to these additional destinations.)

Icelandair sells tickets in a variety of categories, from unrestricted economy fares to a sort of standby "3-days-before" fare (which functions just like the youth fares described above but has no age requirement). Travelers should be aware, however, that most *Icelandair* flights stop in Reykjavik for 45 minutes — a minor delay for most, but one that further prolongs the trip for passengers who will wait again to board connecting flights to their ultimate destination of Florence. It may be a better choice for travelers intending to visit *other* destinations on the Continent when taking both this delay and the cost of connections into account. For reservations and tickets, contact a travel agent or *Icelandair* (phone: 800-223-5500 or 212-967-8888).

Intra-European Fares – The cost of the round trip across the Atlantic is not the only expense to consider, for flights between European cities can be quite expensive. But discounts have recently been introduced on routes between some European cities, and other discounts do exist.

Recent Common Market moves toward airline deregulation are expected to lead gradually to a greater number of budget fares. In the meantime, however, the high cost of fares between most European cities can be avoided by careful use of stopover rights on the higher-priced transatlantic tickets — first class, business class, and full-fare economy. If your ticket doesn't allow stopovers, ask about excursion fares such as PEX and Super PEX, APEX for round trips, and other excursion fares for one-way trips. If you are able to comply with applicable restrictions and can use them, you may save as much as 35% to 50% off full-fare economy. Note that these tickets, which once could be bought only after arrival in Europe, now are sold in the US and can be bought before departure.

Both *Alitalia* and its subsidiary, *Aero Transporti Italiano* (a domestic airline), offer discount fares for round-trip travel within Italy. These must be purchased with a transatlantic flight on board *Alitalia.*

At press time, *Alitalia* was offering a program called Visit Italy for travel within Italy. Passengers can take two flights to any destinations on board either *Alitalia* or *Aero Transporti Italiano* for $100. Visit Italy must be purchased in the US together with a transatlantic flight, and each portion of the domestic flights must also be booked while in the US. Check with *Alitalia* at the time you plan to travel to see if this program is still available.

Taxes and Other Fees – Travelers who have shopped for the best possible flight at the lowest possible price should be warned that a number of extras will be added to that price and collected by the airline or travel agent who issues the ticket. These taxes *usually* (but not always) are included in the prices quoted by airline reservations clerks.

The $6 International Air Transportation Tax is a departure tax paid by all passengers flying from the US to a foreign destination. A $10 US Federal Inspection Fee is levied on all air and cruise passengers who arrive in the US from outside North America. Still another fee is charged by some airlines to cover more stringent security procedures, prompted by recent terrorist incidents. The 8% federal US Transportation Tax applies to travel within the US or US territories, as well as to passengers flying between US cities en route to a foreign destination if the trip includes a stopover of more than 12 hours at a US point. Someone flying from Los Angeles to New York and stopping in New York for more than 12 hours before boarding a flight to Italy, for instance, would pay the 8% tax on the domestic portion of the trip.

Reservations – For those who don't have the time or patience to investigate personally all possible air departures and connections for a proposed trip, a travel agent can be of inestimable help. A good agent should have all the information on which flights go where and when, and which categories of tickets are available on each. Most have computerized reservation links with the major carriers, so that a seat can be reserved and confirmed in minutes. An increasing number of agents also possess fare-comparison computer programs, so they often are very reliable sources of detailed competitive price data. (For more information, see *How to Use a Travel Agent,* in this section.)

When making reservations through a travel agent, ask the agent to give the airline your home phone number, as well as your daytime business phone number. All too often the agent uses the agency number as the official contact for changes in flight plans. Especially during the winter, weather conditions hundreds or even thousands of miles away can wreak havoc with flight schedules. Aircraft are constantly in use, and a plane delayed in the Orient or on the West Coast can miss its scheduled flight from the East Coast the next morning. The airlines are fairly reliable about getting this sort of information to passengers if they can reach them; diligence does little good at 10 PM if the airline has only the agency's or an office number.

Reconfirmation is strongly recommended for all international flights, and in the case of flights to Florence, it is a good idea to confirm your round-trip reservations — especially the return leg — as well as any point-to-point flights within Europe. Some (though increasingly fewer) reservations to and from international destinations are automatically canceled after a required reconfirmation period (typically 72 hours) has passed — even if you have a confirmed, fully paid ticket in hand. It always is wise to call ahead to make sure that the airline did not slip up in entering your original reservation, or in registering any changes you may have made since, and that it has your seat reservation and/or special meal request in the computer. If you look at the printed information on the ticket, you'll see the airline's reconfirmation policy stated explicitly. Don't be lulled into a false sense of security by the "OK" on your ticket next to the number and time of the return flight. This only means that a reservation has been entered; a reconfirmation still may be necessary. If in doubt — call.

If you plan not to take a flight on which you hold a confirmed reservation, by all means inform the airline. Because the problem of "no-shows" is a constant expense for airlines, they are allowed to overbook flights, a practice that often contributes to the threat of denied boarding for a certain number of passengers (see "Getting Bumped," below).

Seating – For most types of tickets, airline seats usually are assigned on a first-come, first-served basis at check-in, although some airlines make it possible to reserve a seat at the time of ticket purchase. Always check in early for your flight, even with advance seat assignments. A good rule of thumb for international flights is to arrive at the airport *at least* 2 hours before the scheduled departure to give yourself plenty of time in case there are long lines.

Most airlines furnish seating charts, which make choosing a seat much easier, but there are a few basics to consider. You must decide whether you prefer a window, aisle, or middle seat. On flights where smoking is permitted, you also should specify if you prefer the smoking or nonsmoking section. There is a useful quarterly publication called the *Airline Seating Guide* that publishes seating charts for most major US airlines and many foreign carriers as well. Your travel agent should have a copy, or you can buy the US edition for $39.95 per year and the international edition for $44.95. Order from Carlson Publishing Co., Box 888, Los Alamitos, CA 90720 (phone: 800-728-4877 or 213-493-4877).

Simply reserving an airline seat in advance, however, actually may guarantee very little. Most airlines require that passengers arrive at the departure gate at least 45 minutes (sometimes more) ahead of time to hold a seat reservation. Some US airlines may cancel seat assignments and may not honor reservations of passengers not "checked in" 45 minutes before the scheduled departure time, and they *ask* travelers to check in at least 2 hours before all international flights. It pays to read the fine print on your ticket carefully and plan ahead.

A far better strategy is to visit an airline ticket office (or one of a select group of travel agents) to secure an actual boarding pass for your specific flight. Once this has been issued, airline computers show you as checked in, and you effectively own the seat you have selected (although some carriers may not honor boarding passes of passengers arriving at the gate less than 10 minutes before departure). This also is good — but not foolproof — insurance against getting bumped from an overbooked flight and is, therefore, an especially valuable tactic at peak travel times.

Smoking – For information on airplane smoking regulations, there is a wallet-size guide that notes in detail the rights of smokers and nonsmokers according to current US regulations. It is available by sending a self-addressed, stamped envelope to *ASH (Action on Smoking and Health),* Airline Card, 2013 H St. NW, Washington, DC 20006 (phone: 202-659-4310).

Meals – If you have specific diet requirements, be sure to let the airline know well before departure time. The available meals include vegetarian, seafood, kosher, Muslim, Hindu, high-protein, low-calorie, low-cholesterol, low-fat, low-sodium, diabetic, bland, and children's menus. There is no extra charge for this option. It usually is necessary to request special meals when you make your reservations — check-in time is too late. It's also wise to reconfirm that your request for a special meal has made its way into the airline's computer — the time to do this is 24 hours before departure. (Note that special meals generally are not available on intra-European flights on small local carriers. If this poses a problem, try to eat before you board, or bring a snack with you.)

Baggage – When you fly on a US airline or on a major international carrier such as *Alitalia,* US baggage regulations will be in effect. Though airline baggage allowances vary slightly, in general all passengers are allowed to carry on board, without charge, one piece of luggage that will fit easily under a seat of the plane or in an overhead bin and whose combined dimensions (length, width, and depth) do not exceed 45 inches. A reasonable amount of reading material, camera equipment, and a handbag also are allowed. In addition, all passengers are allowed to check two bags in the cargo hold: one usually not to exceed 62 inches when length, width, and depth are combined, the other not to exceed 55 inches in combined dimensions. Generally no single bag may weigh more than 70 pounds.

Airline Clubs – US carriers often have clubs for travelers who pay for membership. These clubs are not solely for first class passengers, although a first class ticket *may* entitle a passenger to lounge privileges. Membership (which, by law, requires a fee) entitles the traveler to use the private lounges at airports along their route, to refreshments served in these lounges, and to check-cashing privileges at most of their counters. Extras include special telephone numbers for individual reservations, embossed luggage tags, and a membership card for identification. Airlines serving Italy that offer membership in such clubs include the following:

British Airways: The *Executive Club.* Single yearly membership £125 (about $200 at press time). Note that there is no discounted rate for a spouse.
Delta: The *Crown Club.* Single yearly membership $150; spouse an additional $50 per year.
TWA: The *Ambassador Club.* Single yearly membership $150, spouse an additional $25; lifetime memberships also available.

Note that such companies do not have club facilities in all airports. Other airlines also offer a variety of special services in many airports.

CHARTER FLIGHTS: By booking a block of seats on a specially arranged flight, charter operators offer travelers air transportation for a substantial reduction over the full coach or economy fare. These operators may offer air-only charters (selling transportation alone) or charter packages (the flight plus a combination of land arrangements such as accommodations, meals, tours, or car rentals). Charters are especially attractive to people living in smaller cities or out-of-the-way places, because they frequently leave from nearby airports, saving travelers the inconvenience and expense of getting to a major gateway.

From the consumer's standpoint, charters differ from scheduled airlines in two main respects: You generally need to book and pay in advance, and you can't change the itinerary or the departure and return dates once you've booked the flight. In practice, however, these restrictions don't always apply. Today, although most charter flights still require advance reservations, some permit last-minute bookings (when there are unsold seats available), and some even offer seats on a standby basis.

Though charters almost always are round-trip, and it is unlikely that you would be sold a one-way seat on a round-trip flight, on rare occasions one-way tickets on charters are offered. Although it may be possible to book a one-way charter in the US, giving you more flexibility in scheduling your return, note that US regulations pertaining to charters may be more permissive than the charter laws of other countries. For example, if you want to book a one-way foreign charter back to the US, you may find advance booking rules in force.

Some things to keep in mind about charter travel:

1. It cannot be repeated often enough that if you are forced to cancel your trip, you can lose much (and possibly all) of your money unless you have cancellation insurance, which is a *must* (see *Insurance,* in this section). Frequently, if the cancellation occurs far enough in advance (often 6 weeks or more), you may forfeit only a $25 or $50 penalty. If you cancel only 2 or 3 weeks before the flight, there may be no refund at all unless you or the operator can provide a substitute passenger.
2. Charter flights may be canceled by the operator up to 10 days before departure for any reason, usually underbooking. Your money is returned in this event, but there may be too little time for you to make new arrangements.
3. Most charters have little of the flexibility of regularly scheduled flights regarding refunds and the changing of flight dates, if you book a return flight, you must be on it or lose your money.

4. Charter operators are permitted to assess a surcharge, if fuel or other costs warrant it, of up to 10% of the airfare up to 10 days before departure.

5. Because of the economics of charter flights, your plane almost always will be full, so you will be crowded, though not necessarily uncomfortable. (There is, however, a new movement among charter airlines to provide flight accommodations that are more comfort-oriented, so this situation may change in the near future.)

To avoid problems, *always* choose charter flights with care. When you consider a charter, ask your travel agent who runs it and carefully check the company. The Better Business Bureau in the company's home city can report on how many complaints, if any, have been lodged against it in the past. Protect yourself with trip cancellation and interruption insurance, which can help safeguard your investment if you or a traveling companion is unable to make the trip and must cancel too late to receive a full refund from the company providing your travel services. (This is advisable whether you're buying a charter flight alone or a tour package for which the airfare is provided by charter or scheduled flight.)

Bookings – If you do take a charter, read the contract's fine print carefully and pay particular attention to the following:

Instructions concerning the payment of the deposit and its balance and to whom the check is to be made payable. Ordinarily, checks are made out to an escrow account, which means the charter company can't spend your money until your flight has safely returned. This provides some protection for you. To ensure the safe handling of your money, make out your check to the escrow account, the number of which must appear by law on the brochure, though all too often it is on the back in fine print. Write the details of the charter, including the destination and dates, on the face of the check; on the back, print "For Deposit Only." Your travel agent may prefer that you make out your check to the agency, saying that it will then pay the tour operator the fee minus commission. It is perfectly legal to write the check as we suggest, however, and if your agent objects too vociferously (he or she should trust the tour operator to send the proper commission), consider taking your business elsewhere. If you don't make your check out to the escrow account, you lose the protection of that escrow should the trip be canceled. Furthermore, recent bankruptcies in the travel industry have served to point out that even the protection of escrow may not be enough to safeguard a traveler's investment. More and more, insurance is becoming a necessity. The charter company should be bonded (usually by an insurance company), and if you want to file a claim against it, the claim should be sent to the bonding agent. The contract will set a time limit within which a claim must be filed.

Specific stipulations and penalties for cancellations. Most charters allow you to cancel up to 45 days in advance without major penalty, but some cancellation dates are 50 to 60 days before departure.

Stipulations regarding cancellation and major changes made by the charterer. US rules say that charter flights may not be canceled within 10 days of departure except when circumstances — such as natural disasters or political upheavals — make it impossible to fly. Charterers may make "major changes," however, such as in the date or place of departure or return, but you are entitled to cancel and receive a full refund if you don't wish to accept these changes. A price increase of more than 10% at any time up to 10 days before departure is considered a major change; no price increase at all is allowed during the last 10 days immediately before departure.

At press time, only one charter company, *Tower Air,* regularly offered charter service to Italy. During high season, there are two flights weekly leaving for Rome (where connections can be made to Florence) from New York's Kennedy Airport. For reservations, call *Fantasy Holidays,* 400 Jericho Turnpike, Suite 301, Jericho, NY 11563 (phone: 800-645-2555 or 516-935-8500).

For the full range of possibilities at the time you plan to travel, you may want to subscribe to the travel newsletter *Jax Fax*, which regularly features a list of charter companies and packagers offering seats on charter flights and may be a source for other possible charter flights to Florence. For a year's subscription, send a check or money order for $12 to *Jax Fax* (397 Post Rd., Darien, CT 06820; phone: 203-655-8746).

DISCOUNTS ON SCHEDULED FLIGHTS: Promotional fares often are called discount fares because they cost less than what used to be the standard airline fare — full-fare economy. Nevertheless, they cost the traveler the same whether they are bought through a travel agent or directly from the airline. Tickets that cost less if bought from some outlet other than the airline do exist, however. While it is likely that the vast majority of travelers flying to Florence in the near future will be doing so on a promotional fare or charter rather than on a "discount" air ticket of this sort, it still is a good idea for cost-conscious consumers to be aware of the latest developments in the budget airfare scene. Note that the following discussion makes clear-cut distinctions among the types of discounts available based on how they reach the consumer; in actual practice, the distinctions are not nearly so precise.

Net Fare Sources – The newest notion for reducing the costs of travel services comes from travel agents who offer individual travelers "net" fares. Defined simply, a net fare is the bare minimum amount at which an airline or tour operator will carry a prospective traveler. It doesn't include the amount that normally would be paid to the travel agent as a commission. Traditionally, such commissions amount to about 10% on domestic fares and from 10% to 20% on international fares — not counting significant additions to these commission levels that are paid retroactively when agents sell more than a specific volume of tickets or trips for a single supplier. At press time, at least one travel agency in the US was offering travelers the opportunity to purchase tickets and/or tours for a net price. Instead of making its income from individual commissions, this agency assesses a fixed fee that may or may not provide a bargain for travelers; it requires a little arithmetic to determine whether to use the services of a net travel agent or those of one who accepts conventional commissions. One of the potential drawbacks of buying from agencies selling travel services at net fares is that some airlines refuse to do business with them, thus possibly limiting your flight options.

Travel Avenue is a fee-based agency that rebates its ordinary agency commission to the customer. For domestic flights, they will find the lowest retail fare, then rebate 7% to 10% (depending on the airline selected) of that price minus a $10 ticket-writing charge. The rebate percentage for international flights varies from 5% to 16% (again depending on the airline), and the ticket-writing fee is $25. The ticket-writing charge is imposed per ticket; if the ticket includes more than eight separate flights, an additional $10 or $25 fee is charged. Customers using free flight coupons pay the ticket-writing charge, plus an additional $5 coupon processing fee.

Travel Avenue will rebate its commissions on all tickets, including heavily discounted fares and senior citizen passes. Available 7 days a week, reservations should be made far enough in advance to allow the tickets to be sent by first class mail, since extra charges accrue for special handling. It's possible to economize further by making your own airline reservation, then asking *Travel Avenue* only to write/issue your ticket. For travelers outside the Chicago area, business may be transacted by phone and purchases charged to a credit card. For further information, contact *Travel Avenue* at 641 W. Lake St., Suite 201, Chicago, IL 60606-1012 (phone: 312-876-1116 in Illinois; 800-333-3335 elsewhere in the US).

Consolidators and Bucket Shops – Other vendors of travel services can afford to sell tickets to their customers at an even greater discount because the airline has sold the tickets to them at a substantial discount (usually accomplished by sharply increasing commissions to that vendor), a practice in which many airlines indulge, albeit discreetly, preferring that the general public not know they are undercutting their own "list" prices. Airlines anticipating a slow period on a particular route sometimes sell off a certain portion of their capacity to a wholesaler or consolidator. The wholesaler sometimes is a charter operator who resells the seats to the public as though they were charter seats, which is why prospective travelers perusing the brochures of charter operators with large programs frequently see a number of flights designated as "scheduled service." As often as not, however, the consolidator, in turn, sells the seats to a travel agency specializing in discounting. Airlines also can sell seats directly to such an agency, which thus acts as its own consolidator. The airline offers the seats either at a net wholesale price, but without the volume-purchase requirement that would be difficult for a modest retail travel agency to fulfill, or at the standard price, but with a commission override large enough (as high as 50%) to allow both a profit and a price reduction to the public.

Travel agencies specializing in discounting sometimes are called "bucket shops," a term fraught with connotations of unreliability in this country. But in today's highly competitive travel marketplace, more and more conventional travel agencies are selling consolidator-supplied tickets, and the old bucket shops' image is becoming respectable. Agencies that specialize in discounted tickets exist in most large cities, and usually can be found by studying the smaller ads in the travel sections of Sunday newspapers.

Before buying a discounted ticket, whether from a bucket shop or a conventional, full-service travel agency, keep the following considerations in mind: To be in a position to judge how much you'll be saving, first find out the "list" prices of tickets to your destination. Then, do some comparison shopping among agencies. Also bear in mind that a ticket that may not differ much in price from one available directly from the airline may, however, allow the circumvention of such things as the advance purchase requirement. If your plans are less than final, be sure to find out about any other restrictions, such as penalties for canceling a flight or changing a reservation. Most discount tickets are non-endorsable, meaning that they can be used only on the airline that issued them, and they usually are marked "nonrefundable" to prevent their being cashed for a list price refund.

A great many bucket shops are small businesses operating on a thin margin, so it's a good idea to check the local Better Business Bureau for any complaints registered against the one with which you're dealing — before parting with any money. If you still do not feel reassured, consider buying discounted tickets only through a conventional travel agency, which can be expected to have found its own reliable source of consolidator tickets — some of the largest consolidators, in fact, sell only to travel agencies.

A few bucket shops require payment in cash or by certified check or money order, but if credit cards are accepted, use that option. Note, however, if buying from a charter operator selling seats for both scheduled and charter flights, that the scheduled seats are not protected by the regulations — including the use of escrow accounts — governing the charter seats. Well-established charter operators, nevertheless, may extend the same protections to their scheduled flights, and when this is the case, consumers should be sure that the payment option selected directs their money into the escrow account.

The following are among the numerous consolidators offering discount fares to Europe. Available flights and destinations vary from time to time. Check at the time you plan to travel whether they offer any flights to Florence.

Bargain Air (655 Deep Valley Dr., Suite 355, Rolling Hills, CA 90274; phone: 800-347-2345 or 213-377-2919).

Maharaja/Consumer Wholesale (393 Fifth Ave., 2nd Floor, New York, NY 10016; phone: 212-391-0122 in New York; 800-223-6862 elsewhere in the US).

TFI Tours International (34 W. 37th St., 12th Floor, New York, NY 10001; phone: 212-736-1140).

Travac Tours and Charters (989 Sixth Ave., New York, NY 10018; phone: 212-563-3303).

25 West Tours (2490 Coral Way, Miami, FL 33145; phone: 305-856-0810; 800-423-6954 in Florida; 800-252-5052 elsewhere in the US).

Unitravel (1177 N. Warson Rd., St. Louis, MO 63132; phone: 314-569-0900 in Missouri; 800-325-2222 elsewhere in the US).

The newsletter *Jax Fax* (see "Charter Flights," above) also is a good source of information on consolidators.

■**Note:** Although rebating and discounting are becoming increasingly common, there is some legal ambiguity concerning them. Strictly speaking, it is legal to discount domestic tickets, but not international tickets. On the other hand, the law that prohibits discounting, the Federal Aviation Act of 1958, is ignored consistently these days, in part because consumers benefit from the practice and in part because many illegal arrangements are indistinguishable from legal ones. Since the line separating the two is so fine that even the authorities can't always tell the difference, it is unlikely that most consumers would be able to do so, and in fact it is not illegal to *buy* a discounted ticket. If the issue of legality bothers you, ask the agency whether any ticket you're about to buy would be permissible under the above-mentioned act.

OTHER DISCOUNT TRAVEL SOURCES: An excellent source of information on economical travel opportunities is the *Consumer Reports Travel Letter,* published monthly by Consumers Union. It keeps abreast of the scene on a wide variety of fronts, including package tours, rental cars, insurance, and more, but it is especially helpful for its comprehensive coverage of airfares, offering guidance on all the options from scheduled flights on major or low-fare airlines to charters and discount sources. For a year's subscription, send $37 ($57 for 2 years) to *Consumer Reports Travel Letter* (PO Box 53629, Boulder, CO 80322-3629; phone: 800-999-7959). For information on other travel newsletters, see *Sources and Resources,* in this section.

Last-Minute Travel Clubs – Still another way to take advantage of bargain airfares is open to those who have a flexible schedule. A number of organizations, usually set up as last-minute travel clubs and functioning on a membership basis, routinely keep in touch with travel suppliers to help them dispose of unsold inventory at discounts of between 15% and 60%. A great deal of the inventory consists of complete tour packages and cruises, but some clubs offer air-only charter seats and, occasionally, seats on scheduled flights.

Members generally pay an annual fee and receive a toll-free hotline number to call for information on imminent trips. In some cases, they also receive periodic mailings with information on bargain travel opportunities for which there is more advance notice. Despite the suggestive names of the clubs providing these services, last-minute travel does not necessarily mean that you cannot make plans until literally the last minute. Trips can be announced as little as a few days or as much as 2 months before departure, but the average is from 1 to 4 weeks' notice.

Among the organizations regularly offering such discounted travel opportunities to Florence are the following:

Discount Club of America (61-33 Woodhaven Blvd., Rego Park, NY 11374; phone: 800-321-9587 or 718-335-9612). Annual fee: $39 per family.

Encore Short Notice (4501 Forbes Blvd., Lanham, MD 20706; phone: 800-242-9913). Annual fee: $48 per family.

Traveler's Advantage (3033 S. Parker Rd., Suite 1000, Aurora, CO 80014; phone: 800-548-1116). Annual fee: $49 per family.

Worldwide Discount Travel Club (1674 Meridian Ave., Miami Beach, FL 33139; phone: 305-534-2082). Annual fee: $40 per person; $50 per family.

Generic Air Travel – Organizations that apply the same flexible-schedule idea to air travel only and sell tickets at literally the last minute also exist. The service they provide sometimes is known as "generic" air travel, and it operates somewhat like an ordinary airline standby service, except that the organizations running it offer seats on not one but several scheduled and charter airlines.

One pioneer of generic flights is *Airhitch* (2790 Broadway, Suite 100, New York, NY 10025; phone: 212-864-2000), which arranges flights to Italy from various US gateways. Prospective travelers register by paying a fee (applicable toward the fare) and stipulate a range of acceptable departure dates and their desired destination, along with alternate choices. The week before the date range begins, they are notified of at least two flights that will be available during the time period, agree on one, and remit the balance of the fare to the company. If they do not accept any of the suggested flights, they lose their deposit; if, through no fault of their own, they do not ultimately get on any agreed-on flight, all of their money is refunded. Return flights are arranged the same way.

Bartered Travel Sources – Suppose a hotel buys advertising space in a newspaper. As payment, the hotel gives the publishing company the use of a number of hotel rooms in lieu of cash. This is barter, a common means of exchange among hotels, airlines, car rental companies, cruise lines, tour operators, restaurants, and other travel service companies. When a bartering company finds itself with empty airline seats (or excess hotel rooms, or cruise ship cabin space, and so on) and offers them to the public, considerable savings can be enjoyed.

Bartered-travel clubs often offer discounts of up to 50% to members who pay an annual fee (approximately $50 at press time) which entitles them to select from the flights, cruises, hotel rooms, or other travel services that the club obtained by barter. Members usually present a voucher, club credit card, or scrip (a dollar-denomination voucher negotiable only for the bartered product) to the hotel, which in turn subtracts the dollar amount from the bartering company's account.

Selling bartered travel is a perfectly legitimate means of retailing. One advantage to club members is that they don't have to wait until the last minute to obtain flight or room reservations.

Among the companies specializing in bartered travel, several that frequently offer members travel services to Florence include the following:

IGT (In Good Taste) Services (1111 Lincoln Rd., 4th Floor, Miami Beach, FL 33139; phone: 800-444-8872 or 305-534-7900). Annual fee: $48 per family.
Travel Guide (18210 Redmond Way, Redmond, WA 98052; phone: 206-885-1213). Annual fee: $48 per family.
Travel World Leisure Club (225 W. 34th St., Suite 2203, New York, NY 10122; phone: 800-444-TWLC or 212-239-4855). Annual fee: $50 per family.

On Arrival

FROM THE AIRPORT TO THE CITY: Florence's Peretola Civic Airport is mostly for domestic traffic, with some flights coming from major European cities. It is located about 8 miles (about 13 km) northwest of the city. Foreign visitors more often arrive in Galileo Galilei Airport in Pisa, about 60 miles (about 100 km) west of Florence.

Taxi – From Peretola to central Florence, the ride can take anywhere between 10 and 40 minutes; the taxi fare is about 25,000 lire (about $19). There is a nighttime surcharge.

Public Transportation – There is a bus service that runs between Peretola and central Florence. Take No. 23C from the airport to the city's main railway station, Stazione Centrale Santa Maria Novella, where you can transfer to other buses or take a taxi. The most convenient way to commute between Pisa's airport and Florence is by train. The one-hour train ride takes you into Stazione Centrale Santa Maria Novella. Buy your ticket at the airport; it costs about 6,000 lire (about $5). The price more than doubles if you buy it on the train. More information on the public transportation system appears in THE CITY.

CAR RENTAL: While cars are useful for day trips outside Florence, they are usually more trouble than they are worth for touring within the city. A visitor to Florence and the rest of Italy needs to know, however, how to drive in the country and how to rent a car; there are differences from what you are used to at home.

Renting a car in Florence is not inexpensive, but it is possible to economize by determining your own needs and then shopping around among the car rental companies until you find the best deal. It might be less expensive to rent a car in the center of Florence rather than at the airport. Ask about special rates or promotional deals, such as weekend or weekly rates, bonus coupons for airline tickets, or 24-hour rates that include gas and unlimited mileage.

Renting from the US – Travel agents can arrange foreign rentals for clients, but it is just as easy to call and rent a car yourself. Listed below are some of the major international rental companies that have representation in Florence and have information and reservations numbers that can be dialed toll-free from the US:

Avis (phone: 800-331-1084). Has representatives at Pisa's Galileo Galilei Airport, and in Florence at Peretola and 2 other city locations.

Budget (phone: 800-527-0700). Has representatives at Pisa's Galileo Galilei Airport and 1 location in Florence.

Dollar Rent-a-Car (known in Europe as *Eurodollar;* phone: 800-800-4000). Has representatives at Pisa's Galileo Galilei Airport and 1 location in Florence.

Hertz (phone: 800-654-3001). Has representatives at Pisa's Galileo Galilei Airport and 2 locations in Florence.

National (known in Europe as *Europcar;* phone: 800-CAR-EUROPE). Has representatives at Pisa's Galileo Galilei Airport, and in Florence at Peretola and 1 other city location.

It also is possible to rent a car before you go by contacting any number of smaller or less well known US companies that do not operate worldwide. These organizations specialize in European auto travel, including leasing and car purchase in addition to car rental, or actually are tour operators with well-established European car rental programs. These firms, whose names and addresses are listed below, act as agents for a variety of European suppliers, offer unlimited mileage almost exclusively, and frequently manage to undersell their larger competitors by a significant margin.

Auto Europe (PO Box 1097, Camden, ME 04843; phone: 207-236-8235; 800-223-5555 throughout the US; 800-458-9503 in Canada).

Europe by Car (One Rockefeller Plaza, New York, NY 10020; phone: 212-581-3040 in New York State; 800-223-1516 elsewhere in the US; and 9000 Sunset Blvd., Los Angeles, CA 90069; phone: 800-252-9401 or 213-272-0424).

European Car Reservations (349 W. Commercial St., Suite 2950, East Rochester, NY 14445; phone: 800-535-3303).

Foremost Euro-Car (5430 Van Nuys Blvd., Suite 306, Van Nuys, CA 91401;

phone: 818-786-1960 or 800-272-3299 in California; 800-423-3111 elsewhere in the US).

Kemwel Group Inc. (106 Calvert St., Harrison, NY 10528; phone: 800-678-0678 or 914-835-5555).

Meier's World Travel, Inc. (6033 W. Century Blvd., Suite 1080, Los Angeles, CA 90045; phone: 800-937-0700). In conjunction with major car rental companies, arranges economical rentals throughout Europe, including Florence.

One of the ways to keep the cost of car rentals down is to deal with a car rental consolidator, such as *Connex International* (23 N. Division St., Peekskill, NY 10566; phone: 800-333-3949 or 914-739-0066). *Connex's* main business is negotiating with virtually all of the major car rental agencies for the lowest possible prices for its customers. This company arranges rentals throughout Europe, including Florence.

Local Rentals – It long has been common wisdom that the most expensive way to rent a car is to make arrangements in Europe. This is less true today than it used to be. Many medium to large European car rental companies have become the overseas suppliers of stateside companies such as those mentioned previously, and often the stateside agency, by dint of sheer volume, has been able to negotiate more favorable rates for its US customers than the European firm offers its own. Still lower rates may be found by searching out small, strictly local rental companies overseas, whether at less than prime addresses in major cities or in more remote areas. But to find them you must be willing to invest a sufficient amount of vacation time comparing prices on the scene. You also must be prepared to return the car to the location that rented it; drop-off possibilities are likely to be limited.

There is not a wide choice of local car rental companies in Florence; however, branches of the Italian Government Travel Office may be able to supply the names of Italian car rental companies. The local yellow pages is another good place to begin. Also see *Getting Around* in THE CITY.

Requirements – Whether you decide to rent a car in advance from a large international rental company with European branches or wait to rent from a local company, you should know that renting a car is rarely as simple as signing on the dotted line and roaring off into the night. To drive in Italy, you need only a valid US driver's license; however, if you plan to rent from a local company, you might be asked for an International Driving Permit (see below), and will have to convince the renting agency that (1) you are personally creditworthy, and (2) you will bring the car back at the stated time. This will be easy if you have a major credit card; most rental companies accept credit cards in lieu of a cash deposit, as well as for payment of your final bill. If you prefer to pay in cash, leave your credit card imprint as a "deposit," then pay your bill in cash when you return the car.

If you are planning to rent a car once you're in Florence, *Avis, Budget, Hertz,* and other US rental companies usually *will* rent to travelers paying in cash and leaving either a credit card imprint or a substantial amount of cash as a deposit. This is not necessarily standard policy, however, as other international chains and a number of local and regional European companies will *not* rent to an individual who doesn't have a valid credit card. In this case, you may have to call around to find a company that accepts cash.

Also keep in mind that although the minimum age to drive a car in Italy is 18, the minimum age to rent a car is set by the rental company. (Restrictions vary from company to company, as well as at different locations.) Many firms have a minimum age requirement of 21, some raise that to 23 or 25, and for some models of cars it rises to 30. The upper age limit at many companies is between 69 and 75; others have no upper limit or may make drivers above a certain age subject to special conditions.

Don't forget that all car rentals are subject to value added tax. This tax rarely is included in the rental price that's advertised or quoted, but it always must be paid — whether you pay in advance in the US or pay it when you drop off the car. In Italy, the VAT rate on car rentals is 19%.

Driving Documents – A valid driver's license from his or her own state of residence is required for a US citizen to drive in Italy. In addition, an International Driving Permit (IDP), which is a translation of the US license in 9 languages, may be required if you plan to rent a car from a local firm.

You can obtain your IDP, before you leave, from most branches of the *American Automobile Association (AAA).* Applicants must be at least 18 years old, and the application must be accompanied by two passport-size photos (some *AAA* branches have a photo machine available), a valid US driver's license, and a fee of $10. The IDP is good for 1 year and must be accompanied by your US license to be valid.

Proof of liability insurance also is required and is a standard part of any car rental contract. (To be sure of having the appropriate coverage, let the rental staff know in advance about any national borders you plan to cross.) Car rental companies also make provisions for breakdowns, emergency service, and assistance; ask for a number to call when you pick up the vehicle.

Rules of the Road – Contrary to first impressions, Italian drivers generally are careful and quite patient, and rules of the road do exist in Florence. Driving in Italy is on the right side of the road, as in most of Europe. Passing is on the left; the left turn signal must be flashing before and while passing, and the right indicator must be used when pulling back to the right. Also, don't be intimidated by tailgaters — everyone does it.

According to law, those coming from the right at intersections have the right of way, as in the US, and pedestrians, provided they are in marked crosswalks, have priority over all vehicles. In many areas, though, signposting is meager, and traffic at intersections converges from all directions, resulting in a proceed-at-your-own-risk flow.

Throughout Italy the city speed limits usually are 50 kph (about 30 mph). Outside the city, the speed limit is 90 kph (about 55 mph) on main roads and 130 kph (about 80 mph) on major highways (autostrade). However, the speed limit on autostrade is reduced to 110 kph (about 80 mph) on weekends, public holidays, and from mid-July to early-September.

■ **Note:** Finding a parking spot in Florence can be a major hassle. Street parking in central Florence is forbidden during the day. Drivers who park there risk having their cars towed and paying a heavy fine. There are a few parking garages scattered throughout the city. In addition, parts of the downtown area are sealed off to all traffic during weekdays. You would probably save yourself some major headaches if you try to discover Florence on foot, since most of the major attractions are within walking distance of each other.

Gasoline – In Italy, gasoline (*benzina*) is sold by the liter (which is slightly more than 1 quart; approximately 3.8 liters equal 1 US gallon). Regular or leaded gas (also called *benzina*) generally is sold in two grades — called *normale* and *super.* Diesel fuel is widely available (diesel fuel pumps normally carry a sign for *gasolio*). Unleaded fuel (*benzina verde* or *benzina senza piombo*) is available in some gas stations outside Florence. However, since unleaded gas is still a rarity in some parts of Europe, your safest bet if you're planning to drive outside the city is to rent a car that takes leaded gasoline.

Gas prices everywhere rise and fall depending on the world supply of oil, and an American traveling overseas is further affected by the prevailing rate of exchange, so it is difficult to say exactly how much fuel will cost when you travel. It is not difficult to predict, however, that gas prices will be much higher in Italy than you are accustomed to paying in the US.

Package Tours

 If the mere thought of buying a package for visiting Florence conjures up visions of a march through the city in lockstep with a horde of frazzled fellow travelers, remember that packages have come a long way. For one thing, not all packages necessarily are escorted tours, and the one you buy does not have to include any organized touring at all — nor will it necessarily include traveling companions. If it does, however, you'll find that people of all sorts — many just like yourself — are taking advantage of packages today because they are economical and convenient, save you an immense amount of planning time, and exist in such variety that it's virtually impossible not to find one that suits at least the majority of your travel preferences. Given the high cost of travel these days, packages have emerged as a particularly wise buy.

In essence, a package is just an amalgam of travel services that can be purchased in a single transaction. A Florence package (tour or otherwise) may include any or all of the following: round-trip transatlantic transportation, transfers between the airport and the hotel, local transportation (and/or car rentals), accommodations, some or all meals, sightseeing, entertainment, taxes, tips, escort service, and a variety of incidental features that might be offered as options at additional cost. Its principal advantage is that it saves money: The cost of the combined arrangements invariably is well below the price of all of the same elements if bought separately, and, particularly if transportation is provided by charter or discount flight, the whole package could cost less than just a round-trip economy airline ticket on a regularly scheduled flight. A package provides more than economy and convenience: It releases the traveler from having to make individual arrangements for each separate element of a trip.

Tour programs generally can be divided into two categories — "'escorted" (or locally hosted) and "independent." An escorted tour means that a guide will accompany the group from the beginning of the tour through to the return flight; a locally hosted tour means that the group will be met upon arrival at each location by a different local host. On independent tours (which are the ones generally available for visiting cities, such as Florence), there usually is a choice of hotels, meal plans, and sightseeing trips in each city, as well as a variety of special excursions. The independent plan is for travelers who do not want a totally set itinerary, but who do prefer confirmed hotel reservations. Always bring along complete contact information for your tour operator in case a problem arises, although US tour operators often have European affiliates who can give additional assistance or make other arrangements on the spot.

To determine whether a package — or, more specifically, *which* package — fits your travel plans, start by evaluating your interests and needs, deciding how much and what you want to spend, see, and do. Gather whatever package tour information is available for your schedule. Be sure that you take the time to read the brochure *carefully* to determine precisely what is included. Keep in mind that travel brochures are written to entice you into signing up for a package tour. Often the language is deceptive and devious. For example, a brochure may quote the lowest prices for a package tour based on facilities that are unavailable during the off-season, undesirable at any season, or just plain nonexistent. Information such as "breakfast included" (as it often is in packages to Italy) or "plus tax" (which can add up) should be taken into account. Note, too, that the prices quoted in brochures almost always are based on double occupancy: The rate listed is for each of two people sharing a double room, and if you travel alone, the supplement for single accommodations can raise the price considerably (see *Hints for Single Travelers,* in this section).

In this age of erratic airfares, the brochure most often will *not* include the price of an airline ticket in the price of the package, though sample fares from various gateway cities usually will be listed separately, to be added to the price of the ground arrangements. Before figuring your actual cost, check the latest fares with the airlines, because the samples invariably are out of date by the time you read them. If the brochure gives more than one category of sample fares per gateway city — such as an individual tour-basing fare, a group fare, an excursion, APEX, or other discount ticket — your travel agent or airline tour desk will be able to tell you which one applies to the package you choose, depending on when you travel, how far in advance you book, and other factors. (An individual tour-basing fare is a fare computed as part of a package that includes land arrangements, thereby entitling a carrier to reduce the air portion almost to the absolute minimum. Though it always represents a savings over full-fare coach or economy, lately the individual tour-basing fare has not been as inexpensive as the excursion and other discount fares that also are available to individuals. The group fare usually is the least expensive fare, and it is the tour operator, not you, who makes up the group.) When the brochure does include round-trip transportation in the package price, don't forget to add the cost of round-trip transportation from your home to the departure city to come up with the total cost of the package.

Finally, read the general information regarding terms and conditions and the responsibility clause (usually in fine print at the end of the descriptive literature) to determine the precise elements for which the tour operator is — and is not — liable. Here the tour operator frequently expresses the right to change services or schedules as long as equivalent arrangements are offered. This clause also absolves the operator of responsibility for circumstances beyond human control, such as floods, or injury to you or your property. While reading, ask the following questions:

1. Does the tour include airfare or other transportation, sightseeing, meals, transfers, taxes, baggage handling, tips, or any other services? Do you want all these services?
2. If the brochure indicates that "some meals" are included, does this mean a welcoming and farewell dinner, two breakfasts, or every evening meal?
3. What classes of hotels are offered? If you will be traveling alone, what is the single supplement?
4. Does the tour itinerary or price vary according to the season?
5. Are the prices guaranteed; that is, if costs increase between the time you book and the time you depart, can surcharges unilaterally be added?
6. Do you get a full refund if you cancel? If not, be sure to obtain cancellation insurance.
7. Can the operator cancel if too few people join? At what point?

One of the consumer's biggest problems is finding enough information to judge the reliability of a tour packager, since individual travelers seldom have direct contact with the firm putting the package together. Usually, a retail travel agent is interposed between customer and tour operator, and much depends on his or her candor and cooperation. So ask a number of questions about the tour you are considering. For example:

- Has the travel agent ever used a package provided by this tour operator?
- How long has the tour operator been in business? Check the Better Business Bureau in the area where the tour operator is based to see if any complaints have been filed against it.
- Is the tour operator a member of the *United States Tour Operators Association* (*USTOA;* 211 E. 51st St., Suite 12B, New York, NY 10022; phone: 212-944-5727)? *USTOA* will provide a list of its members upon request; it also offers a useful brochure, *How to Select a Package Tour.*

- How many and which companies are involved in the package?
- If air travel is by charter flight, is there an escrow account in which deposits will be held; if so, what is the name of the bank?

This last question is very important. US law requires that tour operators place every charter passenger's deposit and subsequent payment in a proper escrow account (see "Charter Flights," above).

■ **A word of advice:** Purchasers of vacation packages who feel they're not getting their money's worth are more likely to get a refund if they complain in writing to the operator — and bail out of the whole package immediately. Alert the tour operator or resort manager to the fact that you are dissatisfied, that you will be leaving for home as soon as transportation can be arranged, and that you expect a refund. They may have forms to fill out detailing your complaint; otherwise, state your case in a letter. Even if difficulty in arranging immediate transportation home detains you, your dated, written complaint should help in procuring a refund from the operator.

SAMPLE PACKAGES: Generally speaking, escorted tours cover whole countries or sections of countries. For stays that feature Florence only, you would be looking at an independent city package, sometimes known at a "stay-put" program. Basically the city package includes round-trip transfer between airport and hotel, a choice of hotel accommodations (usually including breakfast) in several price ranges, plus any number of other features you may not need or want but would lose valuable time arranging if you did. Common package features are 1 or 2 half-day guided tours of the city; a boat cruise; passes for unlimited local travel by bus or train; discount cards for shops, museums, and restaurants; temporary membership in and admission to clubs, discotheques, or other nightspots; and car rental for some or all of your stay. Other features may include anything from a souvenir travel bag to a tasting of local wines, dinner, and a show. The packages usually are a week long — although 4-day and 14-day packages also are available, and most packages can be extended by extra days — and often are hosted; that is, a representative of the tour company may be available at a local office or even in the hotel to answer questions, handle problems, and assist in arranging activities and option excursions.

Among companies offering tour packages to and including Florence are the following:

American Express Travel Related Services (offices throughout the US; phone: 800-241-1700 for information and local branch offices). Offers Florence city packages and an individual 14-day rail package that visit Florence, as well as Milan, Rome, and Venice. Other Italian itineraries, ranging from 12 to 18 days, all include a 1- or 2-day excursion in Florence.

American Jewish Congress (15 E. 84th St., New York, NY 10028; phone: 212-879-4588 in New York State; 800-221-4684 elsewhere in the US). This group arranges tours for Jewish travelers. Among their recent itineraries was a 16-day Grand Tour that included a visit to Florence.

Bennett (270 Madison Ave., New York, NY 10016; phone: 800-221-2420 or 212-532-5060). Offers 3-night or longer Florence city packages.

Contiki Holidays (1432 E. Katella Ave., Anaheim, CA 92805; phone: 714-937-0611). Specializing in packages for younger travelers, this operator offers 17- to 55-day motorcoach tours in Europe that include excursions in Florence. There's also a 13-day Italian tour that visits Florence.

Dailey-Thorp Travel (315 W. 57th St., New York, NY 10019; phone: 212-307-1555). This music and opera specialist offers a 12-day tour of Italy, visiting and attending performances at famous theaters in Florence, as well as Milan, Rome, and Venice, and a 13-day Grand Opera tour of Europe also stopping in Florence. Their roster is always changing, but the company regularly sends a group to Florence's *Maggio Musicale* and performances at the *Teatro Comunale.*

David B. Mitchell & Company (200 Madison Ave., New York, NY 10016; phone: 800-372-1323 or 212-889-4822). Also offers luxurious self-drive or chauffeured tours, including a 14-day La Terra Cotta package that visits Florence, as well as Rome, Siena, and Venice. Also arranges customized tours for 7-days or longer.

DER Tours (11933 Wilshire Blvd., Los Angeles, CA 90025; phone: 800-937-123 or 213-479-4411). Offers 3-night or longer Florence city packages.

Donna Franca Tours (470 Commonwealth Ave., Boston, MA 02215; phone: 617-227-3111 in Massachusetts; 800-225-6290 elsewhere in the US). Offers escorted motorcoach tours of Italy that include visits to Florence. This tour operator prefers that bookings be made through travel agents.

Europe Express (588 Broadway, Suite 505, New York, NY 10012; phone: 800-927-3876 or 212-334-0836). Offers 3-night or longer city packages to Florence, as well as Milan, Rome, and Venice.

Globus-Gateway and Cosmos (95-25 Queens Blvd., Rego Park, NY 11374; phone: 800-221-0090; or 150 S. Los Robles Ave., Pasadena, CA 91101; phone: 800-556-5454 or 818-449-2019). These affiliated agencies offer 15- to 28-day escorted trips in Europe that include excursions in Florence. There are also 9-, 14-, and 16-day itineraries in Italy covering its major cities, including Florence. Note that bookings must be made through a travel agent.

Insight International Tours (745 Atlantic Ave., Suite 720, Boston, MA 02111; phone: 800-582-8380 or 617-426-6666). Offers 14- to 38-day escorted packages that include 1- or 2-day stops in Florence. As this tour operator is a wholesaler, bookings must be made through a travel agent.

Jet Vacations (1775 Broadway, New York, NY 10019; phone: 800-JET-0999 or 212-247-0999). Offers city packages to Florence, as well as Milan, Rome, and Venice.

Marsans International (19 W. 34th St., Suite 302, New York, NY 10001; phone: 212-239-3880 in New York State; 800-223-6114 elsewhere in the US). Offers independent city packages.

Meier's World Travel (6033 W. Century Blvd., Suite 1080, Los Angeles, CA 90045; phone: 800-937-0700). Arranges 3-night customized city packages throughout Italy, including Florence.

Perillo Tours (577 Chestnut Ridge Rd., Woodcliff Lake, NJ 07675; phone: 800-431-1515). Offers escorted motorcoach tours of Italy, visiting Florence, as well as Rome and Venice.

Petrabax Tours ((97-45 Queens Blvd., Suite 505, Rego Park, NY 11374; phone: 718-897-7272 in New York State; 800-367-6611 elsewhere). Offers 4-day or longer Florence city packages. Note that this operator caters to Spanish-speaking clientele.

Saga Holidays (120 Boylston St., Boston, MA 02116-9719; phone: 800-343-0273 or 617-451-6808). Specializing in older travelers, this company offers an 18-day multi-country tour that stops in Florence.

SuperCities (7855 Haskell Ave., Van Nuys, CA 91406; phone: 800-633-3000 or 818-988-7844). Offers Florence city packages. This tour operator is a wholesaler, so use a travel agent.

Travcoa (PO Box 2630, Newport Beach, CA 92658-2630; phone: 800-992-2004). Offers a 16-day trip in Italy, visiting Florence, as well as Naples, Rome, and Venice.

Travel Bound (599 Broadway, Penthouse, New York, NY 10012; phone: 800-456-8656 or 212-334-1350). Offers customized city packages to Florence. This tour operator is a wholesaler, so use a travel agent.

World of Oz (211 E. 43rd St., New York, NY 10017; phone: 800-248-0234 or 212-661-0580). Offers customized city packages to Florence for a minimum of 3 nights.

For the gastronome, *Cucina Toscana* (7 Via della Chiesa, Florence 50125; phone and fax: 55-233-7014) organizes trips in Florence, through Tuscany, and beyond. Customized excursions of 1 day to 1 month focus on food, wine, and interesting between-meal activities, including visits to wine makers, chocolate dippers, bread bakers, salami stuffers, and more. Rustic *trattorie* and elegant restaurants are the scenes of the dining experiences.

For the golfer — there are a number of courses around the city — customized golf packages to Italy are offered by *Golfing Holidays* (231 E. Millbrae Ave., Millbrae, CA 94030; phone: 415-697-0230) and *ITC Golf Tours* (4439 Atlantic Ave., Suite 205, Long Beach, CA 90807; phone: 800-257-4981 or 213-595-6905). These companies can arrange a golf packages anywhere and any way you want it, including in and around Florence.

And horseback riding holidays are the province of *Equitour* (P.O. Box 807, Dubois, WY; phone: 307-455-3363 in Wyoming; 800-545-0019 elsewhere in the US), which offers 8-day riding packages near Florence and Rome.

Many of the major air carriers maintain their own tour departments or subsidiaries to stimulate vacation travel to the cities they serve. In all cases, the arrangements may be booked through a travel agent or directly with the company. Airlines that may offer city packages to Florence include the following:

Alitalia (Tour Department; 666 Fifth Ave., 6th Floor, New York, NY 10103; phone: 800-442-5860 or 212-582-8900).

British Airways (Tour Department; 530 Fifth Ave., New York, NY 10036; phone: 800-AIRWAYS).

TWA Getaways (10 E. Stow Rd., Marlton, NJ 08053; phone: 800-GETAWAY).

■ **Note:** Frequently, the best city packages are offered by the hotels, which are trying to attract guests during the weekends, when business travel drops off, and during other off periods. These packages often are advertised in the local newspapers and sometimes in the travel sections of big metropolitan papers, such as *The New York Times.* It's worth asking about packages, especially family and special-occasion offerings, when you call to make a hotel reservation. Calling several hotels can garner you a variety of options from which to choose.

Preparing

How to Use a Travel Agent

 A reliable travel agent remains the best source of service and information for planning a trip abroad, whether you have a specific itinerary and require an agent only to make reservations or you need extensive help in sorting through the maze of airfares, tour offerings, hotel packages, and the scores of other arrangements that may be involved in a trip to Florence.

Know what you want from a travel agent so that you can evaluate what you are getting. It is perfectly reasonable to expect your agent to be a thoroughly knowledgeable travel specialist, with information about your destination and, even more crucial, a command of current airfares, ground arrangements, and other wrinkles in the travel scene.

Most travel agents work through computer reservations systems (CRS). These are used to assess the availability and cost of flights, hotels, and car rentals, and through them they can book reservations. Despite reports of "computer bias," in which a computer may favor one airline over another, the CRS should provide agents with the entire spectrum of flights available to a given destination, as well as the complete range of fares, in considerably less time than it takes to telephone the airlines individually — and at no extra charge to the client.

Make the most intelligent use of a travel agent's time and expertise; understand the economics of the industry. As a client, traditionally you pay nothing for the agent's services; with few exceptions, it's all free, from hotel bookings to advice on package tours. Any money the travel agent makes on the time spent arranging your itinerary — booking hotels or flights, or suggesting activities — comes from commissions paid by the suppliers of these services — the airlines, hotels, and so on. These commissions generally run from 10% to 15% of the total cost of the service, although suppliers often reward agencies that sell their services in volume with an increased commission, called an override. In most instances, you'll find that travel agents make their time and experience available to you at no cost, and you do not pay more for an airline ticket, package tour, or other product bought from a travel agent than you would for the same product bought directly from the supplier.

Exceptions to the general rule of free service by a travel agent are the agencies beginning to practice net pricing. In essence, such agencies return their commissions and overrides to their customers and make their income by charging a flat fee per transaction instead (thus adding a charge after a reduction for the commissions has been made). Net fares and fees are a growing practice, though hardly widespread.

Even a conventional travel agent sometimes may charge a fee for special services. These chargeable items may include long-distance telephone or cable costs incurred in making a booking, for reserving a room in a place that does not pay a commission (such as a small, out-of-the-way hotel), or for special attention such as planning a highly personalized itinerary. A fee also may be assessed in instances of deeply discounted airfares.

Choose a travel agent with the same care with which you would choose a doctor or lawyer. You will be spending a good deal of money on the basis of the agent's judgment, so you have a right to expect that judgment to be mature, informed, and interested. At the moment, unfortunately, there aren't many standards within the travel agent industry to help you gauge competence, and the quality of individual agents varies enormously.

At present, only nine states have registration, licensing, or other forms of travel agent–related legislation on their books. Rhode Island licenses travel agents; Florida, Hawaii, Iowa, and Ohio register them; and California, Illinois, Oregon, and Washington have laws governing the sale of transportation or related services. While state licensing of agents cannot absolutely guarantee competence, it can at least ensure that an agent has met some minimum requirements.

Perhaps the best way to find a travel agent is by word of mouth. If the agent (or agency) has done a good job for your friends over a period of time, it probably indicates a certain level of commitment and competence. Always ask for the name of the company *and* for the name of the specific agent with whom your friends dealt, for it is that individual who will serve you, and quality can vary widely within a single agency. There are some superb travel agents in the business, and they can facilitate vacation or business arrangements.

Entry Requirements and Documents

A valid US passport is the only document a US citizen needs to enter Italy, and then to re-enter the US. As a general rule, a US passport entitles the bearer to remain in Italy for up to 3 months as a tourist. A resident alien of the US should inquire at the nearest Italian consulate (see *The Italian Embassy and Consulates in the US,* in this section, for addresses) to find out what documents are needed to enter Italy; similarly, a US citizen intending to work, study, or reside in Italy should also get in touch with the consulate, because a visa will then be required.

Vaccination certificates are required only if the traveler is entering from an area of contagion — which the US is not — as defined by the World Health Organization.

DUTY AND CUSTOMS: As a general rule, the requirements for bringing the majority of items *into Italy* is that they must be in quantities small enough not to imply commercial import. Among the items that may be taken into the country duty-free are 400 cigarettes, 2 bottles of wine, and 1 bottle of liquor. Personal effects and sports equipment appropriate for a pleasure trip also are allowed.

If you are bringing along a computer, camera, or other electronic equipment for your own use that you will be taking back to the US, you should register the item with the US Customs Service in order to avoid paying duty both entering and returning from Italy. (Also see *Customs and Returning to the US,* in this section.) For information on this procedure, as well as for a variety of pamphlets on US customs regulations, contact the local office of the US Customs Service or the central office, PO Box 7407, Washington, DC 20044 (phone: 202-566-8195).

Additional information regarding Italian customs regulations is available from the Italian Government Travel Office and the Italian embassy and consulates. See *Tourist Information Offices* and *The Italian Embassy and Consulates in the US,* in this section, for addresses.

■**One rule to follow:** When passing through customs, it is illegal not to declare dutiable items; penalties range from stiff fines and seizure of the goods to prison terms. So don't try to sneak anything through — it just isn't worth it.

Insurance

 It is unfortunate that most decisions to buy travel insurance are impulsive and usually are made without any real consideration of the traveler's existing policies. Therefore, the first person with whom you should discuss travel insurance is your own insurance broker, not a travel agent or the clerk behind the airport insurance counter.

TYPES OF INSURANCE: To make insurance decisions intelligently, however, you first should understand the basic categories of travel insurance and what they cover. There are seven basic categories of travel insurance:

1. Baggage and personal effects insurance
2. Personal accident and sickness insurance
3. Trip cancellation and interruption insurance
4. Default and/or bankruptcy insurance
5. Flight insurance (to cover injury or death)
6. Automobile insurance (for driving your own or a rented car)
7. Combination policies

Baggage and Personal Effects Insurance – Ask your insurance agent if baggage and personal effects are included in your current homeowner's policy, or if you will need a special floater to cover you for the duration of a trip. The object is to protect your bags and their contents in case of damage or theft anytime during your travels, not just while you're in flight and covered by the airline's policy. Furthermore, only limited protection is provided by the airline and baggage liability varies from carrier to carrier. For most international flights, including domestic portions of international flights, the airline's liability limit is approximately $9.07 per pound or $20 per kilo (which comes to about $360 per 40-pound suitcase) for checked baggage and up to $400 per passenger for unchecked baggage. These limits should be specified on your airline ticket, but to be awarded any amount, you'll have to provide an itemized list of lost property, and if you're including new and/or expensive items, be prepared for a request that you back up your claim with sales receipts or other proof of purchase.

If you are carrying goods worth more than the maximum protection offered by the airline, consider excess value insurance. Additional coverage is available from insurance companies at an average, currently, of $1 to $2 per $100 worth of coverage, up to a maximum of $5,000. This insurance can also be purchased at some airline counters when you check in, though you should arrive early enough to fill out the necessary forms and to avoid holding up other passengers.

Major credit card companies also provide coverage for lost or delayed baggage — and this coverage often is over and above what the airline will pay. The basic coverage usually is automatic for all cardholders who use the credit card to purchase tickets, but to qualify for additional coverage, cardholders generally must enroll.

Additional baggage and personal effects insurance also is included in certain of the combination travel insurance policies discussed below.

■ **A note of warning:** Be sure to read the fine print of any excess value insurance policy; there often are specific exclusions, such as cash, tickets, furs, gold and silver objects, art, and antiques. Insurance companies ordinarily will pay only the depreciated value of the goods rather than their replacement value. The best way to protect your property is to take photos of your valuables, and keep a record of the serial numbers of such items as cameras, typewriters, laptop computers, radios, and so on. If an airline loses your luggage, you will be asked to fill out a Property Irregularity Report before you leave the airport. Also report the loss to the police (since the insurance company will check with the police when processing your claim).

Personal Accident and Sickness Insurance – This covers you in case of illness during your trip or death in an accident. Most policies insure you for hospital and doctor's expenses, lost income, and so on. In most cases, it is a standard part of existing health insurance policies, though you should check with your broker to be sure that your policy will pay for any medical expenses incurred abroad. If not, take out a separate vacation accident policy or an entire vacation insurance policy that includes health and life coverage.

Two examples of such comprehensive health and life insurance coverage are the travel insurance packages offered by *Wallach & Co:*

HealthCare Global: This insurance package, which can be purchased for periods of 10 to 180 days, is offered for two age groups: Men and women up to age 75 receive $25,000 medical insurance and $50,000 accidental injury or death benefit; those from ages 76 to 84 are eligible for $12,500 medical insurance and $25,000 injury or death benefit. For either policy, the cost for a 10-day period is $25.

HealthCare Abroad: This program is available to individuals up to age 75. For $3 per day (minimum 10 days, maximum 90 days), policy holders receive $100,000 medical insurance and $25,000 accidental injury or death benefit.

Both of these basic programs also may be bought in combination with trip cancellation and baggage insurance at extra cost. For further information, write to *Wallach & Co.,* 243 Church St. NW, Suite 100-D, Vienna, VA 22180 (phone: 703-281-9500 in Virginia; 800-237-6615 elsewhere in the US).

Trip Cancellation and Interruption Insurance – Most charter and package tour passengers pay for their travel well before departure. The disappointment of having to miss a vacation because of illness or any other reason pales before the awful prospect that not all (and sometimes none) of the money paid in advance might be returned. So cancellation insurance for any package tour is a must.

Although cancellation penalties vary (they are listed in the fine print of every tour brochure, and before you purchase a package tour you should know exactly what they are), rarely will a passenger get more than 50% of this money back if forced to cancel within a few weeks of scheduled departure. Therefore, if you book a package tour or charter flight, you should have trip cancellation insurance to guarantee full reimbursement or refund should you, a traveling companion, or a member of your immediate family get sick, forcing you to cancel your trip or *return home early.*

The key here is *not* to buy just enough insurance to guarantee full reimbursement for the cost of the package or charter in case of cancellation. The proper amount of coverage should be sufficient to reimburse you for the cost of having to catch up with a tour after its departure or having to travel home at the full economy airfare if you have to forgo the return flight of your charter. There usually is quite a discrepancy between a charter fare and the amount charged to travel the same distance on a regularly scheduled flight at full economy fare.

Trip cancellation insurance is available from travel agents and tour operators in two forms: as part of a short-term, all-purpose travel insurance package (sold by the travel agent); or as specific cancellation insurance designed by the tour operator for a specific charter tour. Generally, tour operators' policies are less expensive, but also less inclusive. Cancellation insurance also is available directly from insurance companies or their agents as part of a short-term, all-inclusive travel insurance policy.

Before you decide on a policy, read each one carefully. (Either type can be purchased from a travel agent when you book the charter or package tour.) Be certain that your policy includes enough coverage to pay your fare from the farthest destination on your itinerary should you have to miss the charter flight. Also, be sure to check the fine print for stipulations concerning "family members" and "pre-existing medical conditions," as well as allowances for living expenses if you must delay your return due to bodily injury or illness.

Default and/or Bankruptcy Insurance – Although trip cancellation insurance usually protects you if *you* are unable to complete — or begin — your trip, a fairly recent innovation is coverage in the event of default and/or bankruptcy on the part of the tour operator, airline, or other travel supplier. In some travel insurance packages, this contingency is included in the trip cancellation portion of the coverage; in others, it is a separate feature. Either way, it is becoming increasingly important. Whereas sophisticated travelers long have known to beware of the possibility of default or bankruptcy when buying a charter flight or tour package, in recent years more than a few respected airlines unexpectedly have revealed their shaky financial condition, sometimes leaving hordes of stranded ticket holders in their wake. Moreover, the value of escrow protection of a charter passenger's funds lately has been unreliable. While default/bankruptcy insurance will not ordinarily result in reimbursement in time to pay for new arrangements, it can ensure that you will get your money back, and even independent travelers buying no more than an airplane ticket may want to consider it.

Flight Insurance – Airlines have carefully established limits of liability for injury to or the death of passengers on international flights. For all international flights to, from, or with a stopover in the US, all carriers are liable for up to $75,000 per passenger. For all other international flights, the liability is based on where you purchase the ticket: If booked in advance in the US, the maximum liability is $75,000; if arrangements are made abroad, the liability is $10,000. But remember, these liabilities are not the same thing as insurance policies; every penny that an airline eventually pays in the case of injury or death may be subject to a legal battle.

But before you buy last-minute flight insurance from an airport vending machine, consider the purchase in light of your total existing insurance coverage. A careful review of your current policies may reveal that you already are amply covered for accidental death. Be aware that airport insurance, the kind typically bought at a counter or from a vending machine, is among the most expensive forms of life insurance coverage, and that even within a single airport, rates for approximately the same coverage vary widely.

If you buy your plane ticket with a major credit card, you generally receive automatic insurance coverage at no extra cost. Additional coverage usually can be obtained at extremely reasonable prices, but a cardholder must sign up for it in advance.

Automobile Insurance – Public liability and property damage (third-party) insurance is compulsory in Europe, and whether you drive your own or a rental car you must carry insurance. Car rentals in Italy usually include public liability, property damage, fire, and theft coverage and, sometimes (depending on the car rental company), collision damage coverage with a deductible.

In your car rental contract, you'll see that for about $11 to $13 a day, you may buy optional collision damage waiver (CDW) protection. (If partial coverage with a deductible is included in the rental contract, the CDW will cover the deductible in the event of an accident, and can cost as much as $25 per day.) If you do not accept the CDW coverage, you may be liable for as much as the full retail value of the rental car if it is damaged or stolen; by paying for the CDW, you are relieved of all responsibility for any damage to the car. Before agreeing to this coverage, however, check with your own broker about your existing personal auto insurance policy. It very well may cover your entire liability exposure without any additional cost, or you automatically may be covered by the credit card company to which you are charging the cost of your rental. To find out the amount of rental car insurance provided by major credit cards, contact the issuing institutions.

You also should know that an increasing number of the major international car rental companies automatically are including the cost of the CDW in their basic rates. Car rental prices have increased to include this coverage, although rental company ad campaigns may promote this as a new, improved rental package "benefit." The disadvantage of this inclusion is that you may not have the option to turn down the CDW — even if you already are adequately covered by your own insurance policy or through a credit card company.

Your rental contract (with the appropriate insurance box checked off), as well as proof of your personal insurance policy, if applicable, are required as proof of insurance. If you will be driving your own car in Italy, you must carry an International Insurance Certificate (called a Green Card), available through insurance brokers in the US.

Combination Policies – Short-term insurance policies, which may include a combination of any or all of the types of insurance discussed above, are available through retail insurance agencies, automobile clubs, and many travel agents. These combination policies are designed to cover you for the duration of a single trip.

Companies offering policies of this type include the following:

Access America International (600 Third Ave., PO Box 807, New York, NY 10163; phone: 800-284-8300 or 212-490-5345).

Carefree Travel Insurance (Arm Coverage, PO Box 310, Mineola, NY 11501; phone: 800-645-2424 or 516-294-0220).

NEAR Services (450 Prairie Ave., Suite 101, Calumet City, IL 60409; phone: 708-868-6700 in the Chicago area; 800-654-6700 elsewhere in the US and Canada).

Tele-Trip Co. (PO Box 31685, 3201 Farnam St., Omaha, NE 68131; phone: 402-345-2400 in Nebraska; 800-228-9792 elsewhere in the US).

Travel Assistance International (1333 15th St. NW, Suite 400, Washington, DC 20005; phone: 202-331-1609 in Washington, DC; 800-821-2828 elsewhere in the US).

Travel Guard International (1145 Clark St., Stevens Point, WI 54481; phone: 715-345-0505 in Wisconsin; 800-826-1300 elsewhere in the US).

Travel Insurance PAK **c/o** *The Travelers Companies* (One Tower Sq., Hartford, CT 06183-5040; phone: 203-277-2319 in Connecticut; 800-243-3174 elsewhere in the US).

WorldCare Travel Assistance Association (605 Market St., Suite 1300, San Francisco, CA 94105; phone: 800-666-4993 or 415-541-4991).

Hints for Handicapped Travelers

 From 40 to 50 million people in the US have some sort of disability, and over half this number are physically handicapped. Like everyone else today, they — and the uncounted disabled millions around the world — are on the move. More than ever before, they are demanding facilities they can use comfortably, and they are being heard.

The city of Florence has been rather slow to develop facilities for the handicapped. Some of the major hotels are accessible to wheelchairs, but few of the rooms are equipped with special handles and bars. You may be able to find some major churches and museums equipped with ramps for wheelchair-bound visitors. Buses are so crowded during rush hours that it would be very difficult for handicapped passengers even to try to get on them. Generally, to thoroughly enjoy Florence's varied delights, a disabled traveler must be accompanied by an able-bodied companion.

PLANNING: Collect as much information as you can about facilities for travelers with your sort of disability in Florence. Make your travel arrangements well in advance and specify to all services involved the exact nature of your condition or restricted mobility. The best way to find out is to write or call the local tourist authority or hotel and ask specific questions. If you require a corridor of a certain width to maneuver a wheelchair or if you need handles on the bathroom walls for support, ask the hotel manager. A travel agent or the local chapter or national office of the organization that deals with your particular disability will supply the most up-to-date information on the subject. The following organizations offer general information on access:

ACCENT on Living (PO Box 700, Bloomington, IL 61702; phone: 309-378-2961). This information service for persons with disabilities provides a free list of travel agencies specializing in arranging trips for the disabled; for a copy send a self-addressed, stamped envelope. It also offers a wide range of publications, including a quarterly magazine ($8 per year; $14 for 2 years) for persons with disabilities.

Associazione Italiana per l'Assistenza Spastics (Italian Spastics Association; 4/H Via Cipro, Rome 00136; phone: 41-389604). This is a major organization for the handicapped, with branches all over Italy. It not only distributes information about and for those with cerebral palsy, it can help arrange transportation for people with any type of disability. Even though it did not have an office in Florence at press time, it might be able to provide vital information about transportation and other services available to the handicapped traveling in the city.

Mobility International USA (*MIUSA;* PO Box 3551, Eugene, OR 97403; phone: 503-343-1284; both voice and TDD). This US branch of *Mobility International,* a nonprofit British organization with affiliates worldwide, offers members advice and assistance — including information on accommodations and other travel services, and publications applicable to the traveler's disability. It also offers a quarterly newsletter and a comprehensive sourcebook, *A World of Options for the 90s: A Guide to International Education Exchange, Community Service and Travel for Persons with Disabilities* ($14 for members; $16 for non-members). Membership includes the newsletter and is $20 a year; subscription to the newsletter alone is $10 annually.

National Rehabilitation Information Center (8455 Colesville Rd., Suite 935, Silver Spring, MD 20910; phone: 301-588-9284). A general information, resource, research, and referral service.

Paralyzed Veterans of America (*PVA;* PVA/ATTS Program, 801 18th St. NW, Washington, DC 20006; phone: 202-416-7708 in Washington, DC; 800-424-8200 elsewhere in the US). The members of this national service organization all are veterans who have suffered spinal cord injuries, but it offers advocacy services and information to all persons with a disability. *PVA* also sponsors Access to the Skies (ATTS), a program that coordinates the efforts of the national and international air travel industry in providing airport and airplane access for the disabled. Members receive several helpful publications, as well as regular notification of conferences on subjects of interest to the disabled traveler.

Royal Association for Disability and Rehabilitation (*RADAR;* 25 Mortimer St., London W1N 8AB, England; phone: 44-71-637-5400). Offers a number of publications for the handicapped. Their comprehensive guide, *Holidays and Travel Abroad 1991/92 — A Guide for Disabled People,* focuses on international travel.

This publication can be ordered by sending payment in British pounds to *RADAR*. As we went to press, it cost just over £6; call for current pricing before ordering.

Society for the Advancement of Travel for the Handicapped (*SATH;* 26 Court St., Penthouse, Brooklyn, NY 11242; phone: 718-858-5483). To keep abreast of developments in travel for the handicapped as they occur, you may want to join *SATH,* a nonprofit organization whose members include consumers, as well as travel service professionals who have experience (or an interest) in travel for the handicapped. For an annual fee of $45 ($25 for students and travelers who are 65 and older), members receive a quarterly newsletter and have access to extensive information and referral services. *SATH* also offers a useful publication, *Travel Tips for the Handicapped* (a series of informative fact sheets); to order, send a self-addressed, #10 envelope and $1.

Travel Information Service (Moss Rehabilitation Hospital, 1200 W. Tabor Rd., Philadelphia, PA 19141-3099; phone: 215-456-9600 for voice; 215-456-9602 for TDD). This service assists physically handicapped people in planning trips and supplies detailed information on accessibility for a nominal fee.

Blind travelers should contact the *American Foundation for the Blind* (15 W. 16th St., New York, NY 10011; phone: 212-620-2147 in New York State; 800-232-5463 elsewhere in the US) and *The Seeing Eye* (Box 375, Morristown, NJ 07963-0375; phone: 201-539-4425); both provide useful information on resources for the visually impaired. *Note:* In Italy, Seeing Eye dogs must be accompanied by a certificate of inoculation against rabies, issued within the previous year and certified by the attending veterinarian. *The American Society for the Prevention of Cruelty to Animals* (*ASPCA,* Education Dept., 441 E. 92 St., New York, NY 10128; phone: 212-876-7700) offers a useful booklet, *Traveling With Your Pet,* which lists inoculation and other requirements by country. It is available for $5 (including postage and handling).

In addition, there are a number of publications — from travel guides to magazines — of interest to handicapped travelers. Among these are the following:

Access to the World, by Louise Weiss, offers sound tips for the disabled traveler. Published by Facts on File (460 Park Ave. S., New York, NY 10016; phone: 212-683-2244 in New York State; 800-322-8755 elsewhere in the US; 800-443-8323 in Canada), it costs $16.95. Check with your local bookstore; it also can be ordered by phone with a credit card.

The Diabetic Traveler (PO Box 8223 RW, Stamford, CT 06905; phone: 203-327-5832) is a useful quarterly newsletter. Each issue highlights a single destination or type of travel and includes information on general resources and hints for diabetics. A 1-year subscription costs $15. When subscribing, ask for the free fact sheet including an index of special articles; back issues are available for $4 each.

Guide to Traveling with Arthritis, a free brochure available by writing to the Upjohn Company (PO Box 307-B, Coventry, CT 06238), provides lots of good, commonsense tips on planning your trip and how to be as comfortable as possible when traveling by car, bus, train, cruise ship, or plane.

Handicapped Travel Newsletter is regarded as one of the best sources of information for the disabled traveler. It is edited by wheelchair-bound Vietnam veteran Michael Quigley, who has traveled to 93 countries around the world. Issued every 2 months (plus special issues), a subscription is $10 per year. Write to *Handicapped Travel Newsletter,* PO Box 269, Athens, TX 75751 (phone: 214-677-1260).

Handi-Travel: A Resource Book for Disabled and Elderly Travellers, by Cinnie Noble, is a comprehensive travel guide full of practical tips for those with disabilities affecting mobility, hearing, or sight. To order this book, send $12.95, plus shipping and handling, to the *Canadian Rehabilitation Council for the Disabled,* 45 Sheppard Ave. E., Suite 801, Toronto, Ontario M2N 5W9, Canada (phone: 416-250-7490; both voice and TDD).

The Itinerary (PO Box 2012, Bayonne, NJ 07002-2012; phone: 201-858-3400). This bimonthly travel magazine for people with disabilities includes information on accessibility, listings of tours, news of adaptive devices, travel aids, and special services, as well as numerous general travel hints. A subscription costs $10 a year.

The Physically Disabled Traveler's Guide, by Rod W. Durgin and Norene Lindsay, rates accessibility of a number of travel services and includes a list of organizations specializing in travel for the disabled. It is available for $9.95, plus shipping and handling, from Resource Directories, 3361 Executive Pkwy., Suite 302, Toledo, OH 43606 (phone: 419-536-5353 in the Toledo area; 800-274-8515 elsewhere in the US).

Ticket to Safe Travel offers useful information for travelers with diabetes. A reprint of this article is available free from local chapters of the *American Diabetes Association.* For the nearest branch, contact the central office at 505 Eighth Ave., 21st Floor, New York, NY 10018 (phone: 212-947-9707 in New York State; 800-232-3472 elsewhere in the US).

Travel for the Patient with Chronic Obstructive Pulmonary Disease, a publication of the George Washington University Medical Center, provides some sound practical suggestions for those with emphysema, chronic bronchitis, asthma, or other lung ailments. To order, send $2 to Dr. Harold Silver, 1601 18th St. NW, Washington, DC 20009 (phone: 202-667-0134).

Traveling Like Everybody Else: A Practical Guide for Disabled Travelers, by Jacqueline Freedman and Susan Gersten, offers the disabled tips on traveling by car, cruise ship, and plane, as well as lists of accessible accommodations, tour operators specializing in tours for disabled travelers, and other resources. It is available for $11.95, plus postage and handling, from Modan Publishing, PO Box 1202, Bellmore, NY 11710 (phone: 516-679-1380).

Travel Tips for Hearing-Impaired People, a free pamphlet for deaf and hearing-impaired travelers, is available from the *American Academy of Otolaryngology* (One Prince St., Alexandria, VA 22314; phone: 703-836-4444). For a copy, send a self-addressed, stamped, business-size envelope to the academy.

Travel Tips for People with Arthritis, a free 31-page booklet published by the *Arthritis Foundation,* provides helpful information regarding travel by car, bus, train, cruise ship, or plane, planning your trip, and medical considerations, and includes listings of helpful resources, such as associations and travel agencies that operate tours for disabled travelers. For a copy, contact your local *Arthritis Foundation* chapter, or write to the national office, PO Box 19000, Atlanta, GA 30326 (phone: 404-872-7100).

A few more basic resources to look for are *Travel for the Disabled,* by Helen Hecker ($9.95), and by the same author, *Directory of Travel Agencies for the Disabled* ($19.95). *Wheelchair Vagabond,* by John G. Nelson, is another useful guide for travelers confined to a wheelchair (hardcover, $14.95; paperback, $9.95). All three are published by Twin Peaks Press, PO Box 129, Vancouver, WA 98666 (phone: 800-637-CALM or 206-694-2462).

The Italian Government Travel Office may also provide brochures for the handicapped, although they may not be in English. (For the addresses of this agency's US branches, see *Tourist Information Offices,* in this section.)

Two organizations based in Great Britain offer information for handicapped persons traveling throughout Europe, including Italy. *Tripscope* (63 Esmond Rd., London W4 1JE, UK; phone: 44-81-994-9294) is a telephone-based information and referral service (not a booking agent) that can help with transportation options for journeys throughout Europe. It may, for instance, be able to recommend outlets leasing small family vehicles adapted to accommodate wheelchairs. *Tripscope* also provides information on cassettes for blind or visually impaired travelers, and accepts written requests for information from those with speech impediments. And for general information, there's *Holiday Care Service* (2 Old Bank Chambers, Station Rd., Horley, Surrey RH6 9HW, UK; phone: 44-293-774535), a first-rate, free advisory service on accommodations, transportation, and holiday packages throughout Europe for disabled visitors.

Regularly revised hotel and restaurant guides use the symbol of access (a person in a wheelchair; see the symbol at the beginning of this section) to point out accommodations suitable for wheelchair-bound guests. The red *Michelin Guide to Italy* (Michelin; $19.95), found in general and travel bookstores, is one such publication.

PLANE: The US Department of Transportation (DOT) has ruled that US airlines must accept all passengers with disabilities. As a matter of course, US airlines were pretty good about accommodating handicapped passengers even before the ruling, although each airline has somewhat different procedures. Foreign airlines also generally are good about accommodating the disabled traveler, but again, policies vary from carrier to carrier. Ask for specifics when you book your flight.

Disabled passengers always should make reservations well in advance and should provide the airline with all relevant details of their conditions. These details include information on mobility and equipment that you will need the airline to supply — such as a wheelchair for boarding or portable oxygen for in-flight use. Be sure that the person to whom you speak fully understands the degree of your disability — the more details provided, the more effective help the airline can give you.

On the day before the flight, call back to make sure that all arrangements have been prepared, and arrive early on the day of the flight so that you can board before the rest of the passengers. It's a good idea to bring a medical certificate with you, stating your specific disability or the need to carry particular medicine.

Because most airports have jetways (corridors connecting the terminal with the door of the plane), a disabled passenger usually can be taken as far as the plane, and sometimes right onto it, in a wheelchair. If not, a narrow boarding chair may be used to take you to your seat. Your own wheelchair, which will be folded and put in the baggage compartment, should be tagged as escort luggage to assure that it's available at planeside upon landing rather than in the baggage claim area. Travel is not quite as simple if your wheelchair is battery-operated: Unless it has non-spillable batteries, it might not be accepted on board, and you will have to check with the airline ahead of time to find out how the batteries and the chair should be packaged for the flight. Usually people in wheelchairs are asked to wait until other passengers have disembarked. If you are making a tight connection, be sure to tell the attendant.

Passengers who use oxygen may not use their personal supply in the cabin, though it may be carried on the plane as cargo when properly packed and labeled. If you will need oxygen during the flight, the airline will supply it to you (there is a charge) provided you have given advance notice — 24 hours to a few days, depending on the carrier.

Useful information on every stage of air travel, from planning to arrival, is provided in the booklet *Incapacitated Passengers Air Travel Guide.* To receive a free copy, write to the *International Air Transport Association* (Publications Sales Department, 2000 Peel St., Montreal, Quebec H3A 2R4, Canada; phone: 514-844-6311). Another helpful publication is *Air Transportation of Handicapped Persons,* which explains the general guidelines that govern air carrier policies. For a copy of this free booklet, write to the

US Department of Transportation (Distribution Unit, Publications Section, M-443-2, Washington, DC 20590) and ask for "Free Advisory Circular #AC-120-32." *Access Travel: A Guide to the Accessibility of Airport Terminals,* a free publication of the *Airport Operators Council International,* provides information on more than 500 airports worldwide — including major airports in Italy — and offers ratings of 70 features, such as accessibility to bathrooms, corridor width, and parking spaces. For a copy, contact the Consumer Information Center, Dept. 563W, Pueblo, CO 81009 (phone: 719-948-3334).

Among the major carriers serving Italy, the following airlines have TDD toll-free lines in the US for the hearing-impaired:

Delta: 800-831-4488.
TWA: 800-252-0622 in California; 800-421-8480 elsewhere in the US.

GROUND TRANSPORTATION: Perhaps the simplest solution to getting around is to travel with an able-bodied companion who can drive. Another alternative in Italy is to hire a driver/translator with a car. The organizations listed above may be able to help you make arrangements — another source is your hotel concierge.

If you are accustomed to driving your own hand-controlled car and are determined to rent one, you may have to do some extensive research, as in Italy it is difficult to find rental cars fitted with hand controls. If agencies do provide hand-controlled cars, they are apt to be offered only on a limited basis in major metropolitan areas, such as Florence, and usually are very much in demand. The best course is to contact the major car rental agencies listed in "Car Rental" in *On Arrival,* in this section, well before your departure (at least 7 days, much earlier preferably); but be forewarned, you still may be out of luck. Other sources for information on vehicles adapted for the handicapped are the organizations discussed above.

The *American Automobile Association (AAA)* publishes a useful booklet, *The Handicapped Driver's Mobility Guide.* Contact the central office of your local *AAA* club for availability and pricing, which may vary at different branch offices.

Although taxis and public transportation also are available in Florence, accessibility for the disabled varies and may be limited in rural areas, as well as in some cities. Check with a travel agent or the Italian Government Travel Office for information.

TOURS: Programs designed for the physically impaired are run by specialists, and the following travel agencies and tour operators specialize in making group and individual arrangements for travelers with physical or other disabilities:

Access: The Foundation for Accessibility by the Disabled (PO Box 356, Malverne, NY 11565; phone: 516-887-5798). A travelers' referral service that acts as an intermediary with tour operators and agents worldwide, and provides information on accessibility at various locations.

Accessible Journeys (412 S. 45th St., Philadelphia, PA 19104; phone: 215-747-0171). Arranges for medical professional traveling companions — registered or licensed practical nurses, therapists, or doctors (all are experienced travelers). Several prospective companions' profiles and photos are sent to the client for perusal, and if one is acceptable, the "match" is made. The client usually pays all travel expenses for the companion, plus a certain amount in "earnings" to replace wages the companion would be making at his or her usual job.

Accessible Tours/Directions Unlimited (720 N. Bedford Rd., Bedford Hills, NY 10507; phone: 914-241-1700 in New York State; 800-533-5343 elsewhere in the continental US). Arranges group or individual tours for disabled persons traveling in the company of able-bodied friends or family members. Accepts the unaccompanied traveler if completely self-sufficient.

C.I.T. (Marco Polo House, 325 Lansdowne Rd., Croydon, Surrey CR9 1LL, Great Britain; phone: 81-686-0677). This tour operator can arrange transportation between airport and hotels for wheelchair-bound travelers anywhere in Italy. It also can recommend hotels with special facilities for the handicapped.

Evergreen Travel Service (4114 198th St. SW, Suite 13, Lynnwood, WA 98036-6742; phone: 206-776-1184 or 800-435-2288 throughout the continental US and Canada). It offers worldwide programs for the disabled (Wings on Wheels Tours) and the sight-impaired/blind (White Cane Tours).

Flying Wheels Travel (143 W. Bridge St., Box 382, Owatonna, MN 55060; phone: 507-451-5005 or 800-535-6790). Handles both tours and individual arrangements.

Guided Tour (613 W. Cheltenham Ave., Suite 200, Melrose Park, PA 19126-2414; phone: 215-782-1370). Arranges tours for people with developmental and learning disabilities and sponsors separate tours for members of the same population who also are physically disabled or who simply need a slower pace.

Handi-Travel (First National Travel Ltd., Thornhill Sq., 300 John St., Suite 405, Thornhill, Ontario L3T 5W4, Canada; phone: 416-731-4714). Handles individual arrangements.

USTS Travel (11 E. 44th St., New York, NY 10017; phone: 800-487-8787 or 212-687-5121). Travel agent and registered nurse Mary Ann Hamm designs trips for individual travelers requiring kidney dialysis and handles arrangements for the dialysis.

Whole Person Tours (PO Box 1084, Bayonne, NJ 07002-1084; phone: 201-858-3400). Handicapped owner Bob Zywicki travels the world with his wheelchair and offers a lineup of escorted tours (many conducted by him) for the disabled. Call for current itinerary at the time you plan to travel. *Whole Person Tours* also publishes *The Itinerary,* a bimonthly newsletter for disabled travelers (see the publication source list above).

Travelers who would benefit from being accompanied by a nurse or physical therapist also can hire a companion through *Traveling Nurses' Network,* a service provided by Twin Peaks Press (PO Box 129, Vancouver, WA 98666; phone: 800-637-CALM or 206-694-2462). For a $10 fee, clients receive the names of three nurses, whom they can then contact directly; for a $125 fee, the agency will make all the hiring arrangements for the client. Travel arrangements also may be made in some cases — the fee for this further service is determined on an individual basis.

A similar service is offered by *MedEscort International* (ABE International Airport, PO Box 8766, Allentown, PA 18105; phone: 800-255-7182 in the continental US; elsewhere, call 215-791-3111). The service arranges for clients to be accompanied by a nurse, paramedic, respiratory therapist, or physician. The fees are based on the disabled traveler's needs. *MedEscort* also can assist in making travel arrangements.

Hints for Single Travelers

Just about the last trip in human history on which the participants were neatly paired was the voyage of Noah's Ark. Ever since, passenger lists and tour groups have reflected the same kind of asymmetry that occurs in real life, as countless individuals set forth to see the world unaccompanied (or unencumbered, depending on your outlook) by spouse, lover, friend, companion, or relative.

The truth is that the travel industry is not very fair to people who vacation by themselves. People traveling alone almost invariably end up paying more than individuals traveling in pairs. Most travel bargains, including package tours, accommodations, resort packages, and cruises, are based on *double-occupancy* rates. The single traveler will have to pay a surcharge, called a single supplement, for exactly the same package. In extreme cases, this can add as much as 30% to 55% to the basic per-person rate.

The obvious, most effective alternative is to find a traveling companion. Even special "singles' tours" that promise no supplements usually are based on people sharing double rooms. Perhaps the most recent innovation along these lines is the creation of organizations that "introduce" the single traveler to other single travelers. Some charge fees, while others are free, but the basic service offered is the same: to match an unattached person with a compatible travel mate, often as part of the company's own package tours. Among such organizations are the following:

Jane's International (2603 Bath Ave., Brooklyn, NY 11214; phone: 718-266-2045). This service puts potential traveling companions in touch with one another. No age limit, no fee.

Odyssey Network (118 Cedar St., Wellesley, MA 02181; phone: 617-237-2400). Originally founded to match single women travelers, this company now includes men in its enrollment. *Odyssey* offers a quarterly newsletter for members who are seeking a travel companion, and occasionally organizes small group tours. A newsletter subscription is $50.

Partners-in-Travel (PO Box 491145, Los Angeles, CA 90049; phone: 213-476-4869). Members receive a list of singles seeking traveling companions; prospective companions make contact through the agency. The membership fee is $40 per year and includes a chatty newsletter (6 issues per year).

Travel Companion Exchange (PO Box 833, Amityville, NY 11701; phone: 516-454-0880). This group publishes a newsletter for singles and a directory of individuals looking for travel companions. On joining, members fill out a lengthy questionnaire and write a small listing (much like an ad in a personal column). Based on these listings, members can request copies of profiles and contact prospective traveling companions. It is wise to join well in advance of your planned vacation so that there's enough time to determine compatibility and plan a joint trip. Membership fees, including the newsletter, are $36 for 6 months or $60 a year for a single-sex listing; $66 and $120, respectively, for a complete listing. Subscription to the newsletter alone costs $24 for 6 months or $36 per year.

In addition, a number of tour packagers cater to single travelers. These companies offer packages designed for individuals interested in vacationing with a group of single travelers or in being matched with a traveling companion. Among these agencies are the following:

Singles in Motion (545 W. 236th St., Suite 1D, Riverdale, NY 10463; phone: 212-884-4464). Recent itineraries include a 12- or 17-day program in Italy that includes Florence, as well as Milan, Rome, and Venice.

Singleworld (401 Theodore Fremd Ave., Rye, NY 10580; phone: 914-967-3334 or 800-223-6490 in the continental US). It offers its own package tours for singles, with departures categorized by age group — 35 or younger — or for all ages. Recent offerings that visit Florence include a 13-day Mediterranean cruise and a 14-day escorted tour of England, France, Italy, and Switzerland.

Student Travel Information (*STI*; 8619 Reseda Blvd., Suite 103, Northridge, CA

91324; phone: 800-525-0525). Specializes in travel for 18 to 30 year olds. Itineraries include 14- to 63-day European escorted tours, with excursions in Florence.

A good book for single travelers is *Traveling On Your Own,* by Eleanor Berman, which offers tips on traveling solo and includes information on trips for singles, ranging from outdoor adventures to educational programs. Available in bookstores, it also can be ordered by sending $12.95, plus postage and handling, to Random House, Order Dept., 400 Hahn Rd., Westminster, MD 21157 (phone: 800-733-3000).

Single travelers also may want to subscribe to *Going Solo,* a newsletter that offers helpful information on going on your own. Issued eight times a year, a subscription costs $36. Contact Doerfer Communications, PO Box 1035, Cambridge, MA 02238 (phone: 617-876-2764).

WOMEN AND STUDENTS: Two specific groups of single travelers deserve special mention: women and students. Countless women travel by themselves in Italy, and such an adventure need not be feared. One lingering inhibition many female travelers still harbor is that of eating alone in public places. The trick here is to relax and enjoy your meal and surroundings; while you may run across the occasional unenlightened waiter, a woman dining solo is no longer uncommon.

Studying Abroad – A large number of single travelers are students. Travel *is* education. Travel broadens a person's knowledge and deepens his or her perception of the world in a way no media or "armchair" experience ever could. In addition, to study a country's language, art, culture, or history in one of its own schools is to enjoy the most productive method of learning.

By "student" we do not necessarily mean a person who wishes to matriculate at a foreign university to earn a degree. Nor do we necessarily mean a younger person. A student is anyone who wishes to include some sort of educational program in a trip to Florence.

There are many benefits for students abroad, and the way to begin to discover them is to consult the *Council on International Educational Exchange (CIEE),* the US sponsor of the International Student Identity Card (ISIC), which permits reductions on airfare, other transportation, and entry fees to most museums and other exhibitions. The organization also is the source of the Federation of International Youth Travel Organizations (FIYTO) card, which provides many of the same benefits. For further information and applications, write to *CIEE* at one of the following addresses: 205 E. 42nd St., New York, NY 10017 (phone: 212-661-1414); 312 Sutter St., Suite 407, San Francisco, CA 94108 (phone: 415-421-3473); and 919 Irving St., Suite 102, San Francisco, CA 94122 (phone: 415-566-6222). Mark the letter "Attn. Student ID."

CIEE also offers a free, informative, annual, 64-page *Student Travel Catalog,* which covers all aspects of youth travel abroad for vacation trips, jobs, or study programs, and also includes a list of other helpful publications. It also sells *Work, Study, Travel Abroad: The Whole World Handbook,* an informative, chatty guide on study programs, work opportunities, and travel hints, with a good section on Italy. It is available for $10.95, plus shipping and handling. The publications are available from the Information and Student Services Department at the New York address given above.

CIEE also sponsors charter flights to Europe that are open to students and non-students of any age. For example, flights between New York and Rome (with budget-priced add-ons available from Chicago, Cleveland, Miami, Minneapolis, Phoenix, Portland, Salt Lake City, San Diego, Seattle, and Spokane) arrive and depart at least three times a week from Kennedy (JFK) Airport during the high season.

Students and singles in general should keep in mind that youth hostels exist throughout Italy, including several in Florence. They always are inexpensive, generally clean and well situated, and they are a sure place to meet other people traveling alone. Hostels are run by the hosteling associations of 68 countries that make up the *International Youth Hostel Federation (IYHF);* membership in one of the national associations affords access to the hostels of the rest. To join the American affiliate, *American Youth Hostels (AYH),* contact the national office (PO Box 37613, Washington, DC 20013-7613; phone: 202-783-6161), or the local *AYH* council nearest you.

Those who go abroad without an *AYH* card may purchase a youth hostel International Guest Card (for the equivalent of about $18), and obtain information on local youth hostels by contacting the *Associazione Italiana Alberghi per la Gioventù (AIG;* 44 Via Cavour, Rome 00184; phone: 6-462342).

Opportunities for study range from summer or academic-year courses in the language and civilization of Italy, designed specifically for foreigners (including those whose school days are well behind them), to long-term university attendance by those intending to take a degree.

Complete details on more than 3,000 courses available abroad (including at Italian universities) and suggestions on how to apply are contained in two books published by the *Institute of International Education* (IIE Books, 809 UN Plaza, New York, NY 10017; phone 212-883-8200): *Vacation Study Abroad* ($24.95, plus shipping and handling) and *Academic Year Abroad* ($31.95, plus shipping and handling). IIE Books also offers a free pamphlet called *Basic Facts on Study Abroad.*

The *National Registration Center for Study Abroad (NRCSA;* PO Box 1393, Milwaukee, WI 53201; phone: 414-278-0631) also offers a publication called *Worldwide Classroom: Study Abroad and Learning Vacations in 40 Countries: 1991-1992* available for $8, which includes information on over 160 schools and cultural centers, including in Florence, that offer courses for Americans, with the primary focus on foreign language and culture. Programs range from 3 to 13 weeks.

Those who are interested in a "learning vacation" abroad also may be interested in *Travel and Learn* by Evelyn Kaye. This guide to educational travel discusses a wide range of opportunities — everything from archaeology to whale watching — and provides information on organizations that offer programs in these areas of interest. The book is available in bookstores for $23.95; or you can send $26 (which includes shipping charges) to Blue Penguin Publications (147 Sylvan Ave., Leonia, NJ 07605; phone: 800-800-8147 or 201-461-6918). *Learning Vacations* by Gerson G. Eisenberg also provides extensive information on seminars, workshops, courses, and so on — in a wide variety of subjects. Available in bookstores, it also can be ordered from Peterson's Guides (PO Box 2123, Princeton, NJ 08543-2123; phone: 609-243-9111) for $11.95, plus shipping and handling.

If you are interested in a home stay travel program, in which you learn about European culture by living with a family, contact the *Experiment in International Living* (PO Box 676, Brattleboro, VT 05302-0676; phone: 802-257-7751 in Vermont; 800-345-2929 elsewhere in the continental US), which sponsors home stay educational travel in more than 40 countries, including locations throughout Italy. The organization aims its programs at high school or college students.

Another organization specializing in travel as an educational experience is the *American Institute for Foreign Study (AIFS;* 102 Greenwich Ave., Greenwich, CT 06830; phone: 800-727-AIFS, 203-869-9090, or 203-863-6087). It offers a college program in Florence, sponsored by Richmond College in London. The program lasts for four months and the participants must take a language course among other courses. Students can enroll in either the spring or fall semesters. *AIFS* caters primarily to bona fide high school or college students, but its non-credit international learning programs are open to independent travelers of all ages (approximately 20% of *AIFS* students are over 25).

Hints for Older Travelers

Special discounts and more free time are just two factors that have given Americans over age 65 a chance to see the world at affordable prices. Senior citizens make up an ever-growing segment of the travel population, and the trend among them is to travel more frequently and for longer periods of time.

PLANNING: When planning a vacation, prepare your itinerary with one eye on your own physical condition and the other on your interests. One important factor to keep in mind is not to overdo anything and to be aware of the effects that the weather may have on your capabilities.

Older travelers may find the following publications of interest:

Discount Guide for Travelers Over 55, by Caroline and Walter Weintz, is an excellent book for budget-conscious older travelers. It is available by sending $7.95, plus shipping and handling, to Penguin USA (Att. Cash Sales, 120 Woodbine St., Bergenfield, NJ 07621); when ordering, specify the ISBN number: 0-525-48358-6.

Going Abroad: 101 Tips for the Mature Traveler offers tips on preparing for your trip, commonsense precautions en route, and some basic travel terminology. This concise, free booklet is available from *Grand Circle Travel,* 347 Congress St., Boston, MA 02210 (phone: 800-221-2610 or 617-350-7500).

International Health Guide for Senior Citizen Travelers, by Dr. W. Robert Lange, covers such topics as trip preparations, food and water precautions, adjusting to weather and climate conditions, finding a doctor, motion sickness, jet lag, and so on. Also includes a list of resource organizations that provide medical assistance for travelers. It is available for $4.95 postpaid from Pilot Books, 103 Cooper St., Babylon, NY 11702 (phone: 516-422-2225).

Mature Traveler is a monthly newsletter that provides information on travel discounts, places of interest, useful tips, and other topics of interest for travelers 49 and up. To subscribe, send $21.95 to GEM Publishing Group, PO Box 50820, Reno, NV 89513 (phone: 702-786-7419).

Travel Easy: The Practical Guide for People Over 50, by Rosalind Massow, discusses a wide range of subjects — from trip planning, transportation options, and preparing for departure to avoiding and handling medical problems en route. It's available for $6.50 to members of the *American Association of Retired Persons (AARP),* and for $8.95 to non-members; call about current charges for postage and handling. Order from *AARP* Books, c/o Customer Service, Scott, Foresman & Company, 1900 E. Lake Ave., Glenview, IL 60025 (phone: 708-729-3000).

Travel Tips for Older Americans is a useful booklet that provides good, basic advice. This US State Department publication (stock number: 044-000-02270-2) can be ordered by sending a check or money order for $1 to the Superintendent of Documents (US Government Printing Office, Washington, DC 20402) or by calling 202-783-3238 and charging the order to a credit card.

Unbelievably Good Deals & Great Adventures That You Absolutely Can't Get Unless You're Over 50, by Joan Rattner Heilman, offers travel tips for older travelers, including discounts on accommodations and transportation, as well as a list of organizations for seniors. It is available for $7.95, plus shipping and handling, from Contemporary Books, 180 N. Michigan Ave., Chicago, IL 60601 (phone: 312-782-9181).

DISCOUNTS AND PACKAGES: Many hotel chains, airlines, cruise lines, bus companies, car rental companies, and other travel suppliers offer discounts to older travelers. For instance, *TWA* offers those age 62 and over (and one traveling companion per qualifying senior citizen) 10% discounts on flights from the US to Rome (where connections can be made to Florence). Other airlines also offer discounts for passengers age 60 (or 62) and over, which also may apply to one traveling companion. For information on current prices and applicable restrictions, contact the individual carriers.

Some discounts, however, are extended only to bona fide members of certain senior citizens organizations. Because the same organizations frequently offer package tours to both domestic and international destinations, the benefits of membership are twofold: Those who join can take advantage of discounts as individual travelers and also reap the savings that group travel affords. In addition, because the age requirements for some of these organizations are quite low (or nonexistent), the benefits can begin to accrue early. In order to take advantage of these discounts, you should carry proof of your age (or eligibility). A driver's license, membership card in a recognized senior citizens organization, or a Medicare card should be adequate. Among the organizations dedicated to helping older travelers see the world are the following:

American Association of Retired Persons (AARP; 1909 K St. NW, Washington, DC 20049; phone: 202-872-4700). The largest and best known of these organizations. Membership is open to anyone 50 or over, whether retired or not; dues are $5 a year, $12.50 for 3 years, or $35 for 10 years, and include spouse. The *AARP* Travel Experience Worldwide program, available through *American Express Travel Related Services,* offers members travel programs worldwide designed exclusively for older travelers. Members can book these services by calling *American Express* at 800-927-0111 for land and air travel.

Mature Outlook (Customer Service Center, 6001 N. Clark St., Chicago, IL 60660; phone: 800-336-6330). Through its *TravelAlert,* vacation packages are available to members at special savings. Hotel and car rental discounts and travel accident insurance also are available. Membership is open to anyone 50 years of age or older, costs $9.95 a year, and includes a bimonthly newsletter and magazine, as well as information on package tours.

National Council of Senior Citizens (1331 F St., Washington, DC 20005; phone: 202-347-8800). Here, too, the emphasis is on keeping costs low. This nonprofit organization offers members a different roster of package tours each year, as well as individual arrangements through its affiliated travel agency *(Vantage Travel Service).* Although most members are over 50, membership is open to anyone (regardless of age) for an annual fee of $12 per person or couple. Lifetime membership costs $150.

Certain travel agencies and tour operators offer special trips geared to older travelers. Among them is *Sun Holidays* (26 Sixth St., Suite 603, Stamford, CT 06905; phone: 800-243-2057 or 203-323-1166), which specializes in year-round travel, including trips to Florence, as well as Rome and Venice, for senior citizens and offers extended-stay packages in winter.

Many travel agencies, particularly the larger ones, are delighted to make presentations to help a group of senior citizens select destinations. A local chamber of commerce should be able to provide the names of such agencies. Once a time and place are determined, an organization member or travel agent can obtain group quotations for transportation, accommodations, meal plans, and sightseeing. Larger groups usually get the best breaks.

Another choice open to older travelers is a trip that includes an educational element.

Elderhostel, a nonprofit organization, offers programs at educational institutions world-wide, including Italy. The foreign programs generally last about 2 weeks, and include double occupancy accommodations in hotels or student residence halls and all meals. Travel to the programs usually is by designated scheduled flights, and participants can arrange to extend their stay at the end of the program. At press time, *Elderhostel* had programs in Florence, as well as Palermo, Rome, and Sorrento. Elderhostelers must be at least 60 years old (younger if a spouse or companion qualifies), in good health, and not in need of a special diet. For a free catalogue describing the program and current offerings, write to *Elderhostel* (75 Federal St., Boston, MA 02110; phone: 617-426-7788). Those interested in the program also can borrow slides at no charge or purchase an informational videotape for $5.

Hints for Traveling with Children

 What better way to encounter the world's variety than in the company of the young, wide-eyed members of your family? Their presence does not have to be a burden or an excessive expense. The current generation of discounts for children and family package deals can make a trip together quite reasonable.

PLANNING: Here are several hints for making a trip with children easy and fun:

1. Children, like everyone else, will derive more pleasure from a trip if they know something about their destination before they arrive. Begin their education about a month before you leave. Using maps, travel magazines, and books, give children a clear idea of where you are going and how far away it is.
2. Children should help to plan the itinerary, and where you go and what you do should reflect some of their ideas. If they already know something about the sites they'll visit, they will have the excitement of recognition when they arrive.
3. Children also will enjoy learning some Italian phrases — a few basics like *"ciao!"* ("hello" and "good-bye") and *"grazie"* ("thank you").
4. Familiarize your children with lire. Give them an allowance for the trip, and be sure they understand just how far it will or won't go.
5. Give children specific responsibilities: The job of carrying their own flight bags and looking after their personal things, along with some other light chores, will give them a stake in the journey.
6. Give each child a diary or scrapbook to take along.

One resource which might be useful to both your children and yourself is the *Berlitz Italian 90-minute Cassette Pak,* an instructional language tape together with a book specifically designed for travelers' use. The book/cassette package is available for $15.95, plus shipping and handling, from Macmillan Publishing Company, Front and Brown Sts., Riverside, NJ 08075 (phone: 800-257-5755).

And for parents, *Travel With Your Children* (*TWYCH;* 80 Eighth Ave., New York, NY 10011; phone: 212-206-0688) publishes a newsletter, *Family Travel Times,* that focuses on families with young travelers and offers helpful hints. An annual subscription (10 issues) is $35 and includes a copy of the "Airline Guide" issue (updated every other year), which focuses on the subject of flying with children. This special issue is available separately for $10.

Another newsletter devoted to family travel is *Getaways.* This quarterly publication provides reviews of family-oriented literature, activities, and useful travel tips. To subscribe, send $25 to *Getaways,* Att. Ms. Brooke Kane, PO Box 11511, Washington, DC 20008 (phone: 703-534-8747).

Also of interest to parents traveling with their children is *How to Take Great Trips With Your Kids,* by psychologist Sanford Portnoy and his wife, Joan Flynn Portnoy. The book includes helpful tips from fellow family travelers, tips on economical accommodations and touring by car, recreational vehicle, and train, as well as over 50 games to play with your children en route. It is available for $8.95, plus shipping and handling, from Harvard Common Press, 535 Albany St., Boston, MA 02118 (phone: 617-423-5803).

Another book on family travel, *Travel with Children* by Maureen Wheeler, offers a wide range of practical tips on traveling with children, and includes accounts of the author's family travel experiences. It is available for $10.95, plus shipping and handling, from Lonely Planet Publications, Embarcadero West, 112 Linden St., Oakland, CA 94607 (phone: 415-893-8555).

Finally, parents arranging a trip with their children may want to deal with an agency specializing in family travel such as *Let's Take the Kids* (1268 Devon Ave., Los Angeles, CA 90024; phone: 213-274-7088 or 800-726-4349). In addition to arranging and booking trips for individual families, this group occasionally organizes trips for single-parent families traveling together. They also offer a parent travel network, whereby parents who have been to a particular destination can evaluate it for others.

PLANE: Begin early to investigate all available family discounts and charter flights, as well as any package deals and special rates offered by the major airlines. When you make your reservations, tell the airline that you are traveling with a child. Children ages 2 through 11 generally travel at about a 20% to 30% discount off regular full-fare adult ticket prices on domestic flights. This children's fare, however, usually is much higher than the excursion fare, which may be used by any traveler, regardless of age. An infant under 2 years of age usually can travel free if it sits on an adult's lap. A second infant without a second adult would pay the fare applicable to children ages 2 through 11.

Although some airlines will, on request, supply bassinets for infants, most carriers encourage parents to bring their own safety seat on board, which then is strapped into the airline seat with a regular seat belt. This is much safer — and certainly more comfortable — than holding the child in your lap. If you do not purchase a seat for your baby, you have the option of bringing the infant restraint along on the off-chance that there might be an empty seat next to yours — in which case some airlines will let you use that seat at no charge for your baby and infant seat. However, if there is no empty seat available, the infant seat no doubt will have to be checked as baggage (and you may have to pay an additional charge), since it generally does not fit under the seat or in the overhead racks. The safest bet is to pay for a seat.

Be forewarned: Some safety seats designed primarily for use in cars do not fit into plane seats properly. Although nearly all seats manufactured since 1985 carry labels indicating whether they meet federal standards for use aboard planes, actual seat sizes may vary from carrier to carrier. At the time of this writing, the FAA was in the process of reviewing and revising the federal regulations regarding infant travel and safety devices — it was still to be determined if children should be *required* to sit in safety seats and whether the airlines will have to provide them.

If using one of these infant restraints, you should try to get bulkhead seats, which will provide extra room to care for your child during the flight. You also should request a bulkhead seat when using a bassinet — again, this is not as safe as strapping the child in. On some planes bassinets hook into a bulkhead wall; on others it is placed on the floor in front of you. (Note that bulkhead seats often are reserved for families traveling with small children.) As a general rule, babies should be held during takeoff and landing.

Request seats on the aisle if you have a toddler or if you think you will need to use the bathroom frequently. Carry onto the plane all you will need to care for and occupy your children during the flight — formula, diapers, a sweater, books, favorite stuffed animals, and so on. Dress your baby simply, with a minimum of buttons and snaps, because the only place you may have to change a diaper is at your seat or in a small lavatory.

On US carriers, you also can ask for a hot dog or hamburger instead of the airline's regular dinner if you give at least 24 hours' notice. Some, but not all, airlines have baby food aboard, and the flight attendant can warm a bottle for you. While you should bring along toys from home, also ask about children's diversions. Some carriers have terrific free packages of games, coloring books, and puzzles.

When the plane takes off and lands, make sure your baby is nursing or has a bottle, pacifier, or thumb in its mouth. This sucking will make the child swallow and help to clear stopped ears. A piece of hard candy will do the same thing for an older child.

Parents traveling by plane with toddlers, children, or teenagers may want to consult *When Kids Fly,* a free booklet published by Massport (Public Affairs Department, 10 Park Plaza, Boston, MA 02116-3971; phone: 617-973-5600), which includes helpful information on airfares for children, infant seats, what to do in the event of overbooked or canceled flights, and so on.

■**Note:** Newborn babies, whose lungs may not be able to adjust to the altitude, should not be taken aboard an airplane. And some airlines may refuse to allow a pregnant woman in her 8th or 9th month to fly. Check with the airline ahead of time, and carry a letter from your doctor stating that you are fit to travel — and indicating the estimated date of birth.

ACCOMMODATIONS AND MEALS: Often a cot for a child will be placed in a hotel room at little or no extra charge. If you wish to sleep in separate rooms, special rates sometimes are available for families; some places do not charge for children under a certain age. In many of the larger chain hotels, the staffs are more used to children. These hotels also are likely to have swimming pools or gamerooms — both popular with most youngsters. Apartments, condominiums, and other rental options offer families privacy, flexibility, some kitchen facilities, and often lower costs.

Most better hotels will try to arrange for a sitter for the times you will want to be without the children — for an evening's entertainment or a particularly rigorous stint of sightseeing.

At mealtime, don't deny yourself or your children the delights of a new style of cooking. Children like to know what kind of food to expect, so the family can have the pleasure of looking up Italian dishes before leaving. Encourage your children to try new things, although sometimes you can find American-style food in Florence.

Things to Remember
1. Pace the days with children in mind. Break the touring time into half-day segments, with running around or "doing" time built in.
2. Don't forget that a child's attention span is far shorter than an adult's. Children don't have to see every sight or all of any sight to learn something from their trip; watching, playing with, and talking to other children can be equally enlightening.
3. Let your children lead the way sometimes; their perspective is different from yours, and they may lead you to things you would never have noticed on your own.
4. Remember the places that children love to visit: aquariums, zoos, amusement parks, beaches, and so on. Among the activities that may pique their interest are bicycling, snorkeling, boat trips, horseback riding, visiting children's museums, and viewing natural habitat exhibits. The Cascine Park, along the Arno in the eastern part of the city, is a favorite playground for children. There is bike rental

and a good spot for a family picnic. On *Ascension Day* (in May), children buy crickets and set them free to celebrate the *Festa del Grillo.*

Staying Healthy

The surest way to return home in good health is to be prepared for medical problems that might occur while on vacation. Below, we've outlined some things about which you need to think before you go.

Older travelers or anyone suffering from a chronic medical condition, such as diabetes, high blood pressure, cardiopulmonary disease, asthma, or ear, eye, or sinus trouble, should consult a physician before leaving home. Those with conditions requiring special consideration when traveling should think about seeing, in addition to their regular physician, a specialist in travel medicine. For a referral in a particular community, contact the nearest medical school or ask a local doctor to recommend such a specialist. Dr. Leonard Marcus, a member of the *American Committee on Clinical Tropical Medicine and Travelers' Health,* provides a directory of more than 100 travel doctors across the country. For a copy, send a 9-by-12-inch self-addressed, stamped envelope to Dr. Marcus at 148 Highland Ave., Newton, MA 02165 (phone: 617-527-4003).

FIRST AID: Put together a compact, personal medical kit including Band-Aids, first-aid cream, antiseptic, nose drops, insect repellent, aspirin, an extra pair of prescription glasses or contact lenses (and a copy of your prescription for glasses or contact lenses), sunglasses, over-the-counter remedies for diarrhea, indigestion, and motion sickness, a thermometer, and a supply of those prescription medicines you take regularly.

In a corner of your kit, keep a list of all the drugs you have brought and their purpose, as well as duplicate copies of your doctor's prescriptions (or a note from your doctor). As brand names may vary in different countries, it's a good idea to ask your doctor for the generic name of any drugs you use so that you can ask for their equivalent should you need a refill.

It also is a good idea to ask your doctor to prepare a medical identification card that includes such information as your blood type, your social security number, any allergies or chronic health problems you have, and your medical insurance information. Considering the essential contents of your medical kit, keep it with you, rather than in your checked luggage.

HELPFUL PUBLICATIONS: Practically every phase of health care — before, during, and after a trip — is covered in *The New Traveler's Health Guide,* by Drs. Patrick J. Doyle and James E. Banta. It is available for $4.95, plus postage and handling, from Acropolis Books Ltd., 13950 Park Center Rd., Herndon, VA 22071 (phone: 800-451-7771 or 703-709-0006).

The *Traveling Healthy Newsletter,* which is published six times a year, also is brimming with health-related travel tips. For a year's subscription, which costs $24, contact Dr. Karl Neumann (108-48 70th Rd., Forest Hills, NY 11375; phone: 718-268-7290). Dr. Neumann also is the editor of the useful free booklet *Traveling Healthy,* which is available by writing to the *Travel Healthy Program* (PO Box 10208, New Brunswick, NJ 08906-9910; phone: 215-732-4100).

For more information regarding preventive health care for travelers, contact the *International Association for Medical Assistance to Travelers (IAMAT;* 417 Center St., Lewiston, NY 14092; phone: 716-754-4883). The Centers for Disease Control also publishes an interesting booklet, *Health Information for International Travel.* To order send a check or money order for $5 to the Superintendent of Documents (US Government Printing Office, Washington, DC 20402), or charge it to your credit card by calling 202-783-3238. For information on vaccination requirements, disease outbreaks, and other health information pertaining to traveling abroad, you also can call the Centers for Disease Control's 24-hour International Health Requirements and Recommendations Information Hotline: 404-332-4559.

On the Road

Credit and Currency

 It may seem hard to believe, but one of the greatest (and least understood) costs of travel is money itself. So your one single objective in relation to the care and retention of travel funds is to make them stretch as far as possible. Herewith, a primer on making money go as far as possible overseas.

CURRENCY: The basic unit of Italian currency is the *lira*. This is distributed in coin denominations of 50, 100, 200, and 500 lire. Paper money is issued in bills of 1,000, 2,000, 5,000, 10,000, 50,000, and 100,000 lire. The value of Italian currency in relation to the US dollar fluctuates daily, affected by a wide variety of phenomena.

To avoid problems anywhere along the line, it's advisable to fill out any customs forms provided when leaving the US on which you can declare all money you are taking with you — cash, traveler's checks, and so on. US law requires that anyone taking more than $10,000 into or out of the US must report this fact on customs form No. 4790, which is available from US Customs. If taking over $10,000 out of the US, you must report this *before* leaving the US; if returning with such an amount, you should include this information on your customs declaration. Although travelers usually are not questioned by customs officials about currency when entering or leaving, the sensible course is to observe all regulations just to be on the safe side.

In Florence, as in the rest of Italy, you will find the official rate of exchange posted in banks, airports, money exchange houses, and some shops. As a general rule, expect to get more local currency for your US dollar at banks than at any other commercial establishment. Exchange rates do change from day to day, and most banks offer the same (or very similar) exchange rates. (In a pinch, the convenience of cashing money in your hotel — sometimes on a 24-hour basis — *may* make up for the difference in the exchange rate.) Don't try to bargain in banks or hotels — no one will alter the rates for you.

A money exchange house *(ufficio di cambio)* is a financial institution that charges a fee for the service of exchanging dollars into local currency. When considering alternatives, be aware that although the rate varies among these establishments, the rates of exchange offered are bound to be slightly less favorable than the terms offered at nearby banks — again, don't be surprised if you get fewer lire for your dollar than the rate published in the papers.

That said, however, the following rules of thumb are worth remembering:

Rule number one: Never (repeat: *never*) exchange dollars for foreign currency at hotels, restaurants, or retail shops. If you do, you are sure to lose a significant amount of your US dollar's buying power. If you do come across a storefront exchange counter offering what appears to be an incredible bargain, there's too much counterfeit specie in circulation to take the chance. (see Rule number three, below.)

Rule number two: Estimate your needs carefully; if you overbuy you lose twice — buying and selling back. Every time you exchange money, someone is making a profit, and rest assured it isn't you. Use up foreign notes before leaving, saving just enough for last-minute incidentals, and tips.

Rule number three: Don't buy money on the black market. The exchange rate may be better, but it is a common practice to pass off counterfeit bills to unsuspecting foreigners who aren't familiar with the local currency. It's usually a sucker's game, and you almost always are the sucker; it also can land you in jail.

Rule number four: Learn the local currency quickly and keep abreast of daily fluctuations in the exchange rate. These are listed in the English-language *International Herald Tribune* daily for the preceding day, as well as in every major newspaper in Europe. Rates change to some degree every day. For rough calculations, it is quick and safe to use round figures, but for purchases and actual currency exchanges, carry a small pocket calculator to help you compute the exact rate. Inexpensive calculators specifically designed to convert currency amounts quickly for travelers are widely available.

When changing money, don't be afraid to ask how much commission you're being charged, and the exact amount of the prevailing exchange rate. In fact, in any exchange of money for goods or services, you should work out the rate before making any payment.

TRAVELER'S CHECKS: It's wise to carry traveler's checks instead of (or in addition to) cash, since it's possible to replace them if they are stolen or lost. Issued in various denominations and available in both US dollars and Italian lire, with adequate proof of identification (credit cards, driver's license, passport), traveler's checks are as good as cash in most hotels, restaurants, stores, and banks. Don't assume, however, that restaurants, small shops, and other establishments are going to be able to change checks of large denominations.

Although traveler's checks are available in foreign currencies such as Italian lire, the exchange rates offered by the issuing companies in the US generally are far less favorable than those available from banks both in the US and abroad. Therefore, it usually is better to carry the bulk of your travel funds abroad in US dollar–denomination traveler's checks.

Every type of traveler's check is legal tender in banks around the world, and each company guarantees full replacement if checks are lost or stolen. After that the similarity ends. Some charge a fee for purchase, while others are free; you can buy traveler's checks at almost any bank, and some are available by mail. Most important, each traveler's check issuer differs slightly in its refund policy — the amount refunded immediately, the accessibility of refund locations, the availability of a 24-hour refund service, and the time it will take for you to receive replacement checks. For instance, *American Express* guarantees replacement of lost or stolen traveler's checks in under 3 hours at any *American Express* office — other companies may not be as prompt. Travelers should keep in mind that *American Express*'s 3-hour policy is based on the traveler being able to provide the serial numbers of the lost checks. Without these numbers, refunds can take much longer.

We cannot overemphasize the importance of knowing how to replace lost or stolen checks. All of the traveler's check companies have agents around the world, both in their own name and at associated agencies (usually, but not necessarily, banks), where refunds can be obtained during business hours. Most of them also have 24-hour toll-free telephone lines, and some will even provide emergency funds to tide you over on a Sunday.

Be sure to make a photocopy of the refund instructions that will be given you at the time of purchase. To avoid complications should you need to replace lost checks (and to speed up the process), keep the purchase receipt and an accurate list, by serial number, of the checks that have been spent or cashed. Always keep these records separate from the checks and the original records themselves (you may want to give them to a traveling companion to hold).

Following is a list of the major companies issuing traveler's checks and the numbers to call in the event that loss or theft makes replacement necessary:

American Express: The company advises travelers in Europe to call 44-273-571600 (in Brighton, England), collect. Another (slower) option is to call 801-968-8300 (in the US), collect, or contact the nearest *American Express* office (see above for the Florence address).

Bank of America: In Florence and elsewhere worldwide, call 415-624-5400 or 415-622-3800, collect.

Citicorp: In Florence and elsewhere worldwide, call 813-623-1709 or 813-626-4444, collect.

MasterCard: In Florence, call the New York office at 212-974-5696, collect.

Thomas Cook MasterCard: In Florence, call 609-987-7300 (in the US) or 44-733-502995 (in England), collect, and they will direct you to the nearest branch of *Thomas Cook* or *Wagons-Lits,* their European agent.

Visa: In Florence, call 415-574-7111, collect. In Europe, you also can call this London number collect: 44-71-937-8091.

CREDIT CARDS: Some establishments you encounter during the course of your travels may not honor any credit cards and some may not honor all cards, so there is a practical reason to carry more than one. Most US credit cards, including the principal bank cards, are honored in Florence; however, keep in mind that some cards may be issued under different names in Europe. For example, *MasterCard* may go under the name *Access* or *Eurocard,* and *Visa* often is called *Carte Bleue* — wherever these equivalents are accepted, *MasterCard* and *Visa* may be used. The following is a list of credit cards that enjoy wide international acceptance:

American Express: For information call 800-528-4800 in the US; to report a lost or stolen *American Express* card in Florence, contact the local *American Express* office (see address above) or call 212-477-5700, collect.

Carte Blanche: For medical, legal, and travel assistance in Florence, call 214-680-6480, collect. For information call 800-525-9135 in the US; to report a lost or stolen *Carte Blanche* card in Florence, call 303-790-2433, collect.

Diners Club: For medical, legal, and travel assistance in Florence, call 214-680-6480, collect. For information call 800-525-9135 in the US; to report a lost or stolen *Diners Club* card in Florence, call 303-790-2433, collect.

Discover Card: For information call 800-DISCOVER in the US; to report a lost or stolen *Discover* card, in Florence call 302-323-7652, collect.

MasterCard: For 24-hour emergency lost card service, call 314-275-6690, collect, from abroad.

Visa: For 24-hour emergency lost card service in Florence, call 415-574-7700, collect.

SENDING MONEY ABROAD: If you have used up your traveler's checks, cashed as many emergency personal checks as your credit card allows, drawn on your cash advance line to the fullest extent, and still need money, have it sent to you via one of the following services:

American Express (phone: 800-543-4080). Offers a service called "Moneygram," completing money transfers in anywhere from 15 minutes to 5 days. The sender can go to any *American Express* office in the US and transfer money by presenting cash, a personal check, money order, or credit card — *Discover, MasterCard, Visa,* or *American Express Optima Card* (no other *American Express* or other credit cards are accepted). *American Express Optima* cardholders also can arrange for this transfer over the phone. To collect at the other end, the receiver must show identification (passport, driver's license, or other picture ID) at the *American Express* office in Florence (49r Via Guicciardini; phone: 288751) and present a passport as identification.

Western Union Telegraph Company (phone: 800-325-4176 throughout the US). A friend or relative can go, cash in hand, to any *Western Union* office in the US, where, for a *minimum* charge of $13 (it rises with the amount of the transaction) and a $25 surcharge, the funds will be transferred to a branch of *Western Union*'s Italian correspondent bank, *Credito Italiano,* in Florence. When the money arrives, you will not be notified — you must go to the bank to inquire. Transfers generally take about 2 days. The funds will be turned over in local currency, based on the rate of exchange in effect on the day of receipt. For a higher fee, the US party to this transaction may call *Western Union* with a *MasterCard* or *Visa* number to send up to $2,000.

If you are literally down to your last lira, the nearest US consulate (see *Medical and Legal Aid and Consular Services,* in this section) will let you call home to set these matters in motion.

CASH MACHINES: Automatic teller machines (ATMs) are increasingly common worldwide. If your bank participates in one of the international ATM networks (most do), the bank will issue you a "cash card" along with a personal identification code or number (also called a PIC or PIN). You can use this card at any ATM in the same electronic network to check your account balances, transfer monies between checking and savings accounts, and — most important for a traveler — withdraw cash instantly. Network ATMs generally are located in banks, commercial and transportation centers, and near major tourist attractions.

Some financial institutions offer exclusive automatic teller machines for their own customers only at bank branches. At the time of this writing, ATMs which *are* connected generally belong to one of the following two international networks: *Cirrus,* which has over 55,000 ATMs in more than 22 countries and *Plus System,* which has over 30,000 automatic teller machines worldwide. However, at the time of this writing, neither one of them has installed ATMs in Florence.

Accommodations

Those watching their wallets will be pleased to find that compared with most of the rest of Europe, hotel prices in Florence can be quite reasonable. Although it is still relatively affordable, Italy has experienced inflation, and the recent decline in the strength of the US dollar has not helped. At the lower end of the price scale, you will not necessarily have to forgo charm. While a fair number of inexpensive establishments are simply no-frills, "generic" places to spend the night, even the sparest room may have the cachet of once having been the nightly retreat of a monk or nun. And some of the most delightful places to stay are the smaller, less expensive, often family-run small inns. For more information, see *Best in Town* in THE CITY..

Time Zones, Business Hours, and Public Holidays

TIME ZONES: The countries of Europe fall into three time zones. Greenwich Mean Time — the time in Greenwich, England, at longitude 0°0′ — is the base from which all other time zones are measured. Areas in zones west of Greenwich have earlier times and are called Greenwich Minus; those to the east have later times and are called Greenwich Plus. For example, New York City — which falls into the Greenwich Minus 5 time zone — is 5 hours earlier than Greenwich, England.

Italy is in the Greenwich Plus 1 time zone — which means that the time is 1 hour later than it is in Greenwich, England, and when it is noon in Florence, it is 6 AM in New York.

As do most Western European nations, Italy moves its clocks ahead an hour in late spring and an hour back in the fall, although the date of the change tends to be about a week earlier (in spring) and a week later (in fall) than the dates we have adopted in the US. For about 2 weeks a year, then, the time difference between the US and Italy is 1 hour more or less than usual.

Italian and other European timetables use a 24-hour clock to denote arrival and departure times, which means that hours are expressed sequentially from 1 AM. By this method, 9 AM is recorded as 0900, noon as 1200, 1 PM as 1300, 6 PM as 1800, midnight as 2400, and so on. For example, the departure of a train at 7 AM will be announced as "0700"; one leaving at 7 PM will be noted as "1900."

BUSINESS HOURS: In Florence, as throughout Italy, most businesses and shops are open Mondays through Saturdays from 9 AM to 1 PM, then from 3:30 or 4 PM until 7:30 or 8 PM, although some businesses now are open through midday and close at 5 PM. During summer (June through September), most shops close on Saturday afternoons. Some major department stores and shopping centers stay open through midday and are open Mondays through Saturdays from 9:30 AM to 6:30 PM.

Weekday banking hours in Florence are from 8:20 AM to 1:20 PM and from 2:45 to 3:45 PM. Banks are closed on Saturdays and Sundays.

Restaurant hours are similar to those in the US. Most restaurants are open all week during the high season and closed 1 day each week during the off-season — the day varies from restaurant to restaurant.

PUBLIC HOLIDAYS: In Florence, as in the rest of Italy, the public holidays (and their dates this year) are as follows:

New Year's Day (January 1)
Epiphany (January 6)
Good Friday (April 17)
Easter Monday (April 20)
Liberation Day (April 25)
Labor Day (May 1)
Feast of St. John the Baptist (June 24)
Assumption of the Virgin (August 15)
All Saints' Day (November 1)
Day of Immaculate Conception (December 8)
Christmas Day (December 25)
Santo Stefano (December 26)

Mail and Electricity

MAIL: The main post office is located at Palazzo delle Poste, Via Pellicceria (phone: 211147). It's open from 8:15 AM to 7 PM Mondays through Fridays, and 8·15 AM to noon on Saturdays. Most other post offices are open Mondays through Fridays from 8:15 AM to 1:40 PM; Saturdays till noon. Postal rates change frequently; stamps *(francobolli)* can be bought at the post office, at authorized tobacconists *(tobaccheria),* and at some hotels.

Be advised that delivery from Italy can be erratic (postcards often are given lowest priority, so don't use them for important messages). Airmail letters from Italy to the US usually take about 1 week.

If your correspondence is important, you may want to send it via a special courier service: *DHL International* has an office at 245 Via della Cupola (phone: 316907) and *Federal Express* has an office in Calencano, at 21 Via di Pratignone (phone: 882-5741). The cost is considerably higher than sending something via the postal services — but the assurance of its timely arrival may be worth it.

If you're mailing to an address within Italy, a good way to ensure or speed delivery is to use the postal code. And since small towns in Italy may have similar names, the postal code always should be specified — delivery of a letter may depend on it. If you do not know the correct postal code, call the Italian Government Travel Office (see *Tourist Information Offices,* in this section, for telephone numbers) — they might be able to look it up for you.

There are several places that will receive and hold mail for travelers in Italy. Mail sent to you at a hotel and clearly marked *fermo in posta* (literally, "hold mail") is one safe approach. Italian post offices, including the main Florence office, also will extend this service to you if the mail is addressed to the equivalent of US general delivery — called *fermo posta* or *Posta Restante.* Address the mail to Fermo Posta, Palazzo delle Poste, 3 Via Pelliceria, Florence 50123; call 215364 to inquire about mail. Also, don't forget to take your passport with you when you go to collect it. Most Italian post offices require formal identification before they will release anything; there also may be a small charge for picking up your mail.

If you are an *American Express* customer (a cardholder, a carrier of *American Express* traveler's checks, or traveling on an *American Express Travel Service* tour) you can have mail sent to its office in Florence. Letters are held free of charge — registered mail and packages are not accepted. You must be able to show an *American Express* card, traveler's checks, or a voucher proving you are on one of the company's tours to avoid paying for mail privileges. Those who aren't clients must pay a nominal charge each time they inquire if they have received mail, whether or not they actually have a letter. Mail should be addressed to you, care of *American Express,* and should be marked "Client Mail Service."

While US embassies and consulates abroad will not under ordinary circumstances accept mail for tourists, they *may* hold mail for US citizens in an emergency situation, especially if the papers sent are important. It is best to inform them either by separate letter or cable, or by phone (particularly if you are in the country already), that you will be using their address for this purpose.

ELECTRICITY: The US runs on 110-volt, 60-cycle alternating current; Florence runs on 220-volt, 50-cycle alternating current. Different parts of Italy may have different voltage. (Some large tourist hotels may offer 110-volt currency for your convenience; if not, they may have convertors available.) The difference between US and Italian voltage means that, without a converter, at 220 volts the motor of a US appliance used overseas would run at twice the speed at which it's meant to operate and would quickly burn out.

Medical and Legal Aid and Consular Services

MEDICAL AID ABROAD: Nothing ruins a vacation or business trip more effectively than sudden injury or illness. Medical institutes in Italy, especially in the larger cities, generally provide the same basic specialties and services that are available in the US.

Before you go, be sure to check with your insurance company about the applicability of your hospitalization and major medical policies while you're abroad; many policies do not apply, and others are not accepted in Italy. Older travelers should know that Medicare does not make payments outside the US.

There are two types of hospitals in Italy — public and private. The non-public ones are called *case di cura* (houses of care or cure), villas, or clinics — to distinguish them from public hospitals. There also are some private clinics *(cliniche),* which are like small hospitals and can provide medial aid for less serious cases. Foreign travelers will have to pay full fees for medical service, which, depending on your coverage, may or may not be reimbursed by your insurance compay.

Italian law specifies that seriously injured, ill, or unconscious persons be taken directly to one of the public hospitals. (After treatment in the emergency room, *pronto soccorso,* a patient in stable condition may transfer to the hospital of his or her choice.) The efficiency and speed of the service will be variable. If you require an ambulance, be aware that, in some cases, it may provide only transportation to the nearest public hospital. At the time of this writing, advanced EMS technology (similar to that provided in the US) was only just being added in Italy.

If a bona fide emergency occurs, the fastest way to get attention may be to take a taxi to the emergency room of the nearest hospital. A centrally located hospital in Florence is the *Ospedale Santa Maria Nuova* (Piazza Santa Maria Nuova; phone: 27581). It is a major hospital with advanced equipment and technology to deal with acute medical situations; also, all of the staff speak English. An alternative is to dial the free national "emergency" number used to summon the police and ambulances — 113 in Italy.

If a doctor is needed for something less than an emergency, there are several ways to find one. If you are staying in a hotel or at a resort, ask for help in reaching a doctor or other emergency services, or for the house physician, who may visit you in your room or ask you to visit an office. Travelers staying at a hotel of any size probably will find that the doctor on call speaks at least a modicum of English — if not, request one who does.

Dialing the nationwide emergency number (113) also may be of help in locating a physician. It also usually is possible to obtain a referral through a US consulate (see addresses and phone numbers below) or directly through a hospital, especially if it is an emergency.

If you have a minor medical problem, a pharmacist might offer some help. There are a number of 24-hour drugstores *(le farmacie)* in Florence: *Comunale No. 13* (Santa Maria Novella railway station; phone: 289435); *Molteni* (7r Via Calzaiuoli; phone: 289490); and *Taverna* (20r Piazza San Giovanni; phone: 284013).

Bring along a copy of any prescription you may have from your doctor in case you should need a refill. In the case of minor complaints, Italian pharmacists may do some prescribing and *may* fill a foreign prescription; however, do not count on this. In most cases, you will need a local doctor to rewrite the prescription. Even in an emergency, a traveler will more than likely be given only enough of a drug to last until a local prescription can be obtained.

Emergency assistance also is available from the various medical programs designed for travelers who have chronic ailments or whose illness requires them to return home:

International Association for Medical Assistance to Travelers (IAMAT; 417 Center St., Lewiston, NY 14092; phone: 716-754-4883). Entitles members to the services of participating doctors around the world, as well as clinics and hospitals in various locations. Participating physicians agree to adhere to a basic charge of around $40 to see a patient referred by *IAMAT.* To join, simply write to *IAMAT;* in about 3 weeks you will receive a membership card, the booklet of members, and an inoculation chart. A nonprofit organization, *IAMAT* appreciates donations; with a donation of $25 or more, you will receive a set of worldwide climate charts detailing weather and sanitary conditions. (Delivery can take up to 5 weeks, so plan ahead.)

International SOS Assistance (PO Box 11568, Philadelphia, PA 19116; phone: 800-523-8930 or 215-244-1500). Subscribers are provided with telephone access — 24 hours a day, 365 days a year — to a worldwide, monitored, multilingual network of medical centers. A phone call brings assistance ranging from a telephone consultation to transportation home by ambulance or aircraft, or, in some cases, transportation of a family member to wherever you are hospitalized. Individual rates are $35 for 2 weeks of coverage ($3.50 for each additional day), $70 for 1 month, or $240 for 1 year; couple and family rates also are available.

Medic Alert Foundation (2323 N. Colorado, Turlock, CA 95380; phone: 800-ID-ALERT or 209-668-3333). If you have a health condition that may not be readily perceptible to the casual observer — one that might result in a tragic error in an emergency situation — this organization offers identification emblems specifying such conditions. The foundation also maintains a computerized central file from which your complete medical history is available 24 hours a day by phone (the telephone number is clearly inscribed on the emblem). The onetime membership fee (between $25 and $45) is based on the type of metal from which the emblem is made — the choices range from stainless steel to 10K gold-filled.

TravMed (PO Box 10623, Baltimore, MD 21204; phone: 800-732-5309 or 301-296-5225). For $3 per day, subscribers receive comprehensive medical assistance while abroad. Major medical expenses are covered up to $100,000, and special transportation home or of a family member to wherever you are hospitalized is provided at no additional cost.

■**Note:** Those who are unable to take a reserved flight due to personal illness or who must fly home unexpectedly due to a family emergency should be aware that airlines may offer a discounted airfare (or arrange a partial refund) if the traveler can demonstrate that his or her situation is indeed a legitimate emergency. Your inability to fly or the illness or death of an immediate family member usually must be substantiated by a doctor's note or the name, relationship, and funeral home from which the deceased will be buried. In such cases, airlines often will waive certain advance purchase restrictions or you may receive a refund check or voucher for future travel at a later date. Be aware, however, that this bereavement fare may not necessarily be the least expensive fare available and, if possible, it is best to have a travel agent check all possible flights through a computer reservations system (CRS).

LEGAL AID AND CONSULAR SERVICES: There is one crucial place to keep in mind when outside the US, namely, the US Consulate, which in this city is located at 38 Lungarno Amerigo Vespucci (phone: 298276).

If you are injured or become seriously ill, or if you encounter legal difficulties, the consulate is the first place to turn, although its powers and capabilities are limited. It will direct you to medical assistance and notify your relatives if you are ill; it can advise you of your rights and provide a list of lawyers if you are arrested, but it cannot interfere with the local legal process.

For questions about US citizens arrested abroad, how to get money to them, and other useful information, call the *Citizens' Emergency Center* of the Office of Special

Consular Services in Washington, DC, at 202-647-5225. (For further information about this invaluable hotline, see below.)

A consulate exists to aid US citizens in serious matters, such as illness, destitution, and the above legal difficulties. It is not there to aid in trivial situations, such as canceled reservations or lost baggage, no matter how important these matters may seem to the victimized tourist. If you should get sick, the US consul can provide names of doctors, dentists, local hospitals, and clinics; the consul also will contact family members in the US and help arrange special ambulance service for a flight home. In a situation involving "legitimate and proven poverty" of an US citizen stranded abroad without funds, the consul will contact sources of money (such as family or friends in the US), apply for aid to agencies in foreign countries, and in the last resort — which is *rarely* — arrange for repatriation at government expense, although this is a loan that must be repaid. And in case of natural disasters or civil unrest, consulates around the world handle the evacuation of US citizens if it becomes necessary.

As mentioned above, the US State Department operates a *Citizens' Emergency Center,* which offers a number of services to US citizens abroad and their families at home. In addition to giving callers up-to-date information on trouble spots, the center will contact authorities abroad in an attempt to locate a traveler or deliver an urgent message. In case of illness, death, arrest, destitution, or repatriation of an US citizen on foreign soil, it will relay information to relatives at home if the consulate is unable to do so. Travel advisory information is available 24 hours a day to people with touch-tone phones (phone: 202-647-5225). Callers with rotary phones can get information at this number from 8:15 AM to 10 PM (eastern standard time) on weekdays, 9 AM to 3 PM Saturdays. In the event of an emergency, this number also may be called during these hours. For emergency calls only, at all other times, call 202-634-3600 and ask for the duty officer.

Drinking and Drugs

DRINKING: It is more than likely that some of the warmest memories of a trip to Florence will be moments of conviviality shared over a drink in a neighborhood bar or sunlit café. Visitors will find that liquor, wine, and brandies in Italy are distilled to the same proof and often are the same labels as those found at home.

Bars and cafés in Florence open at about 7 AM to serve coffee and breakfast; most remain open until midnight. In Italy, there is no legal drinking age and eateries do not need a license to serve liquor. You may find it strange to see both bars and cafés serving up anything from coffee to cocktails, ice cream, and light meals.

As in the US, national taxes on alcohol affect the prices of liquor in Italy, and as a general rule, mixed drinks — especially imported liquors such as whiskey and gin — are more expensive than at home. If you like a drop before dinner, a good way to save money is to buy a bottle of your favorite brand at the airport before leaving the US and enjoy it in your hotel before setting forth.

Visitors to Italy may bring in 2 bottles of wine and 1 bottle of liquor per person duty-free. If you are buying any quantity of alcohol (such as a case of wine) in Italy and traveling through other European countries on your route back to the US, you will have to pass through customs and pay duty at each border crossing, so you might want to arrange to have it shipped home. Whether bringing it with you or shipping, you will have to pay US import duties on any quantity over the allowed 1 liter (see *Customs and Returning to the US,* in this section).

DRUGS: Illegal narcotics are as prevalent in Italy as in the US, but the moderate legal penalties and vague social acceptance that marijuana has gained in the US have no equivalents in Italy. Due to the international war on drugs, enforcement of drug laws is becoming increasingly strict throughout the world. Local European narcotics officers and customs officials are renowned for their absence of understanding and lack of a sense of humor — especially where foreigners are involved.

Opiates and barbiturates, and other increasingly popular drugs — ""white powder" substances like heroin, cocaine, and "crack" (the cocaine derivative) — continue to be of major concern to narcotics officials. Most European countries — including Italy — have toughened laws regarding illegal drugs and narcotics, and it is important to bear in mind that the type or quantity of drugs involved is of minor importance. Particularly for foreigners, the maximum penalties may be imposed for possessing even *traces* of illegal drugs. There is a high conviction rate in these cases, and bail for foreigners is rare. Persons arrested are subject to the laws of the country they are visiting, and there isn't much that the US consulate can do for drug offenders beyond providing a list of lawyers. The best advice we can offer is this: Don't carry, use, buy, or sell illegal drugs.

Those who carry medicines that contain a controlled drug should be sure to have a current doctor's prescription with them. Ironically, travelers can get into almost as much trouble coming through US customs with over-the-counter drugs picked up abroad that contain substances that are controlled in the US. Cold medicines, pain relievers, and the like often have codeine or codeine derivatives that are illegal, except by prescription, in the US. Throw them out before leaving for home.

■**Be forewarned:** US narcotics agents warn travelers of the increasingly common ploy of drug dealers asking travelers to transport a "gift" or other package back to the US. Don't be fooled into thinking that the protection of US law applies abroad — accused of illegal drug trafficking, you will be considered guilty until you prove your innocence. In other words, do not, under any circumstances, agree to take anything across the border for a stranger.

Tipping

 In Florence, as throughout Italy and most of the rest of Europe, you will find the custom of including some kind of service charge on the bill for a meal more common than in North America. This can confuse Americans unfamiliar with the custom. On the one hand, many a traveler, unaware of this policy, has left many a superfluous tip. On the other hand, travelers aware of this policy may make the mistake of assuming that it takes care of everything. It doesn't. While "service included" in theory eliminates any question about how much and whom to tip, in practice there still are occasions when on-the-spot tips are appropriate. Among these are tips to show appreciation for special services, as well as tips meant to say "thank you" for services rendered. So keep a pocketful of 1000 lire bills ready, and hand these out like dollar bills.

In Italian restaurants, the service charge *(servizio compreso)* is usually calculated in the prices listed, if not, it will be added to the final bill. For the most part, if you see a notation at the bottom of the menu (such as *compreso* or *incluso*), the charge should be included in the prices; otherwise, the service charge has not yet been added. To further confuse the issue, not every restaurant notes what its policy is. If you are at all unsure, ask a waiter.

This service charge generally ranges from 10% to 15%. In the rare instance where it isn't added, a 15% tip to the waiter — just as in the US — usually is a safe figure, although one should never hesitate to penalize poor service or reward excellent and efficient attention by leaving less or more. In Italy, the service charge usually goes to the restaurant, and it is a common practice to leave 5% to 10% (less if you're in a moderate restaurant, more in an expensive one).

Although it's not necessary to tip the maître d' of most restaurants — unless he has been especially helpful in arranging a special party or providing a table (slipping him something in a crowded restaurant *may* get you seated sooner or procure a preferred table) — when tipping is desirable or appropriate, the least amount should be the local equivalent of $5. In the finest restaurants, where a multiplicity of servers are present, plan to tip 5% to the captain. The sommelier (wine waiter) is entitled to a gratuity of approximately 10% of the price of the bottle.

As in restaurants, visitors usually will find a service charge of 15% to 20% included in their final bill at most Florence hotels. No additional gratuities are required — or expected — beyond this billed service charge. It is unlikely, however, that a service charge will be added to bills in small family-run guesthouses or other modest establishments. In these cases, guests should let their instincts be their guide; no tipping is expected by members of the family who own the establishment, but it is a nice gesture to leave something for others — such as a dining room waiter or a maid — who may have been helpful. A gratuity of around $1 per night is adequate in most cases.

If a hotel does not automatically add a service charge, it is perfectly proper for guests to ask to have an extra 10% to 15% added to their bill, to be distributed among those who served them. This may be an especially convenient solution in a large hotel, where it's difficult to determine just who out of a horde of attendants actually performed particular services.

For those who prefer to distribute tips themselves, a chambermaid generally is tipped at the rate of approximately $1 per day. Tip the concierge or hall porter for specific services only, with the amount of such gratuities dependent on the level of service provided. For any special service you receive in a hotel, a tip is expected — the current equivalent of $1 being the minimum for a small service.

Bellhops, doormen, and porters at hotels and transportation centers generally are tipped at the rate of $1 per piece of luggage, along with a small additional amount if a doorman helps with a cab or car. Once upon a time, taxi drivers in Europe would give you a rather odd look if presented with a tip for a fare, but times have changed, and 10% to 15% of the amount on the meter is now a standard gratuity.

Miscellaneous tips: Tipping ushers in a movie house, theater, or concert hall used to be the rule, but is becoming less common — the best policy is to check what other patrons are doing and follow suit. Most of the time, the program is not free, and in lieu of a tip it is common practice to purchase a program from the person who seats you. Sightseeing tour guides also should be tipped. If you are traveling in a group, decide together what you want to give the guide and present it from the group at the end of the tour. If you have been individually escorted, the amount paid should depend on the degree of your satisfaction, but it should not be less than 10% of the total tour price. Museum and monument guides also usually are tipped, and it is a nice touch to tip a caretaker who unlocks a small church or turns on the lights in a chapel.

In barbershops and beauty salons, tip as you would at home, keeping in mind that the percentages vary according to the type of establishment — 10% in the most expensive salons; 15% to 20% in less expensive establishments. (As a general rule, the person who washes your hair should get an additional small tip.) The washroom attendants in these places, or wherever you see one, should get a small tip — they usually set out a little plate with a coin already on it indicating the suggested denomination.

Tipping always is a matter of personal preference. In the situations covered above, as well as in any others that arise where you feel a tip is expected or due, feel free to express your pleasure or displeasure. Again, never hesitate to reward excellent and efficient attention and to penalize poor service. Give an extra gratuity and a word of thanks when someone has gone out of his or her way for you. Either way, the more personal the act of tipping, the more appropriate it seems. And if you didn't like the service — or the attitude — don't tip.

Duty-Free Shopping and Value Added Tax

DUTY-FREE SHOPS: Note that because of the newly integrated European economy, there was some question at the time of this writing as to the fate and number of duty-free shops that would be maintained at international airports in member countries of the European Economic Community (EEC). It appears, however, that those traveling between EEC countries and any country *not* a member of the Common Market will still be entitled to buy duty-free items. Since the United States is not a Common Market member, duty-free purchases by US travelers will, presumably, remain as they have been even after the end of 1992.

If common sense says that it always is less expensive to buy goods in an airport duty-free shop than to buy them at home or in the streets of a foreign city, travelers should be aware of some basic facts. Duty-free, first of all, does not mean that the goods travelers buy will be free of duty when they return to the US. Rather, it means that the shop has paid no import tax in acquiring goods of foreign make, because the goods are not to be used in the country where the shop is located. This is why duty-free goods are available only in the restricted, passengers-only area of international airports or are delivered to departing passengers on the plane. In a duty-free store, travelers save money only on goods of foreign make because they are the only items on which an import tax would be charged in any other store. There usually is no saving on locally made items, although in countries such as Italy that impose value added taxes (see below) that are refundable to foreigners, the prices in airport duty-free shops are minus this tax, sparing travelers the often cumbersome procedures they otherwise have to follow to obtain a VAT refund.

Beyond this, there is little reason to delay buying locally made merchandise and/or souvenirs until reaching the airport. In fact, because airport duty-free shops usually pay high rents, the locally made goods they sell may well be more expensive than they would be in downtown stores. The real bargains are foreign goods, but — let the buyer beware — not all foreign goods automatically are less expensive in an airport duty-free shop. You can get a good deal on even small amounts of perfume, costing less than the usually required minimum purchase, tax-free. Other fairly standard bargains include spirits, smoking materials, cameras, clothing, watches, chocolates, and other food and luxury items — but first be sure to know what these items cost elsewhere. Terrific savings do exist (they are the reason for such shops, after all), but so do overpriced items that an unwary shopper might find equally tempting. In addition, if you wait to do your shopping at airport duty-free shops, you will be taking the chance that the desired item is out of stock or unavailable.

Duty-free shops are located in most major international airports throughout Europe, including Peretola Civic Airport in Florence and the Galileo Galilei Airport in Pisa.

VALUE ADDED TAX: Commonly abbreviated as VAT, this is a tax levied by various European countries, including Italy, and added to the purchase price of most goods and services. The standard VAT (known as IVA in Italy) ranges from 9% on general items to 30% on luxury goods such as watches, jewelry, furs, glass, and cameras. However, the rate will likely be changed in 1992 when the Economic Community comes into effect. At press time, discussions are still being held to decide on one uniform VAT for all EC members.

The tax is intended for residents (and already is included in the price tag), but visitors are also required to pay it unless they have purchases shipped by the store directly to an address abroad. If visitors pay the tax and take purchases with them, however, they generally are entitled to a refund.

In order to qualify for a refund, you must make a single purchase of a minimum value of 625,000 lire (about $480 US at press time) — numerous purchases in one store or from several stores cannot be combined. In most cases, you must ask the store to provide a receipt and describe in full detail the purchased item. This receipt must be stamped by the customs officer when you leave the country. Visitors leaving Italy must have all of their receipts for purchases and refund vouchers stamped by customs; as customs officials may well ask to see the merchandise, it's a good idea not to pack it in the bottom of your suitcase. A copy of that stamped receipt must be sent within 90 days from the date of original issue back to the store, which can then start the procedure for requesting a refund. Also, you can arrange with the store owner whether you wish to have the refund credited to your credit card or have a check sent to you.

Also note that at Leonardo da Vinci Airport (better known as Fiumicino) in Rome you may be able to receive an on-the-spot cash VAT refund at desks near customs and passport control (an Italian customs official can direct you). There will be a small charge for this service, deducted from the refund.

A VAT refund by dollar check or by credit to a credit card account is relatively hassle-free. If it arrives in the form of a foreign currency check and if the refund is less than a significant amount, charges imposed by US banks for converting foreign currency refund checks — which can run as high as $15 or more — could make the whole exercise hardly worth your while.

Far less costly is sending your foreign currency check (after endorsing it) to *Ruesch International,* which will covert it to a check in US dollars for a $2 fee (deducted from the dollar check). Other services include commission-free traveler's checks and foreign currency, which can be ordered by mail. Contact *Ruesch International* at one of the following address: 191 Peachtree St., Atlanta, GA 30303 (phone: 404-222-9300); 3 First National Plaza, Suite 2020, Chicago, IL 60602 (phone: 312-332-5900); 1925 Century Park E., Suite 240, Los Angeles, CA 90067 (phone: 213-277-7800); 608 Fifth Ave., "Swiss Center," New York, NY 10020 (phone: 212-977-2700); and 1350 Eye St. NW, 10th Floor and street level, Washington, DC 20005 (phone: 800-424-2923 or 202-408-1200).

■**Buyer Beware:** You may come across shops *not* at airports that call themselves duty-free shops. These require shoppers to show a foreign passport but are subject to the same rules as other stores, including paying import duty on foreign items. What "tax-free" means in the case of these establishments is something of an advertising strategy: They are announcing loud and clear that they do, indeed, offer the VAT refund service — sometimes on the spot (minus a fee for higher overhead). Prices may be no better at these stores, and could be even higher due to this service.

Customs and Returning to the US

Whether you return to the United States by air or sea, you must declare to the US Customs official at the point of entry everything you have bought or acquired while in Europe. The customs check can go smoothly, lasting only a few minutes, or can take hours, depending on the officer's instinct. To speed up the process, keep all your receipts handy and try to pack your purchases together in an accessible part of your suitcase. It might save you from unpacking all your belongings.

DUTY-FREE ARTICLES: In general, the duty-free allowance for US citizens returning from abroad is $400. This duty-free limit covers purchases that accompany you and are for personal use. This limit includes items used or worn while abroad, souvenirs for friends, and gifts received during the trip. A flat 10% duty based on the "fair retail value in country of acquisition" is assessed on the next $1,000 worth of merchandise brought in for personal use or gifts. Amounts above those two levels are dutiable at a variety of rates. The average rate for typical tourist purchases is about 12%, but you can find out about specific items by consulting *Tariff Schedules of the United States* in a library or at any US Customs Service office.

Families traveling together may make a joint declaration to customs, which permits one member to exceed his or her duty-free exemption to the extent that another falls short. Families also may pool purchases dutiable under the flat rate. A family of three, for example, would be eligible for up to a total of $3,000 at the 10% flat duty rate (after each member had used up his or her $400 duty-free exemption) rather than three separate $1,000 allowances. This grouping of purchases is extremely useful when considering the duty on a high-tariff item, such as jewelry or a fur coat.

Personal exemptions can be used once every 30 days; in order to be eligible, an individual must have been out of the country for more than 48 hours. If any portion of the exemption has been used once within any 30-day period or if your trip is less than 48 hours long, the duty-free allowance is cut to $25.

There are certain articles, however, that are duty-free only up to certain limits. The $25 allowance includes the following: 10 cigars (not Cuban), 60 cigarettes, and 4 ounces of perfume. Individuals eligible for the full $400 duty-free limit are allowed 1 carton of cigarettes (200), 100 cigars, and 1 liter of liquor or wine if the traveler is over 21. Alcohol above this allowance is liable for both duty and an Internal Revenue tax. Antiques, if they are 100 or more years old and you have proof from the seller of that fact, are duty-free, as are paintings and drawings if done entirely by hand.

To avoid paying duty twice, register the serial numbers of foreign-made watches and electronic equipment with the nearest US Customs bureau before departure; receipts of insurance policies also should be carried for other foreign-made items. (Also see the note at the end of *Entry Requirements and Documents,* in this section.)

Gold, gold medals, bullion, and up to $10,000 in currency or negotiable instruments may be brought into the US without being declared. Sums over $10,000 must be declared in writing.

The allotment for individual "unsolicited" gifts mailed from abroad (no more than one per day per recipient) is $50 retail value per gift. These gifts do not have to be declared and are not included in your duty-free exemption (see below). Although you should include a receipt for the purchases with each package, the examiner is empowered to impose a duty based on his or her assessment of the value of the goods. The duty owed is collected by the US Postal Service when the package is delivered (also see below). More information on mailing packages home from abroad is contained in the US Customs Service pamphlet *Buyer Beware, International Mail Imports* (see below for where to write for this and other useful brochures).

CLEARING CUSTOMS: This is a simple procedure. Forms are distributed by airline or ship personnel before arrival. (Note that a $5-per-person service charge — called a user fee — is collected by airlines to help cover the cost of customs checks, but this is included in the ticket price.) If your purchases total no more than the $400 duty-free limit, you need only fill out the identification part of the form and make an oral declaration to the customs inspector. If entering with more than $400 worth of goods, you must submit a written declaration.

Customs agents are businesslike, efficient, and not unkind. During the peak season, clearance can take time, generally because of the strain imposed by a number of jumbo jets simultaneously discharging their passengers, not because of unwarranted zealousness on the part of the customs people.

Efforts to streamline procedures used to include the so-called Citizens' Bypass Program, which allowed US citizens whose purchases were within their duty-free allowance to go to the "green line," where they simply showed their passports to the customs inspector. Although at the time of this writing this procedure still is being followed at some international airports in the US, most airports have returned to an earlier system. US citizens arriving from overseas now have to go through a passport check by the Immigration & Naturalization Service (INS) before recovering their baggage and proceeding to customs. (This additional wait will delay clearance on re-entry into the US, although citizens will not be on the same line as foreign visitors.) Although all passengers have to go through this passport inspection, those entering with purchases within the duty-free limit may be spared a thorough customs inspection. Inspectors still retain the right to search any luggage they choose, however, so don't do anything foolish.

It is illegal not to declare dutiable items; not to do so, in fact, constitutes smuggling, and the penalty can be anything from stiff fines and seizure of the goods to prison sentences. It simply isn't worth doing. Nor should you go along with the suggestions of foreign merchants who offer to help you secure a bargain by deceiving customs officials in any way. Such transactions frequently are a setup, using the foreign merchant as an agent of US customs. Another agent of US customs is TECS, the Treasury Enforcement Communications System, a computer that stores all kinds of pertinent information on returning citizens. There is a basic rule to buying goods abroad, and it should never be broken: *If you can't afford the duty on something, don't buy it.* Your list or verbal declaration should include all items purchased abroad, as well as gifts received abroad, purchases made at the behest of others, the value of repairs, and anything brought in for resale in the US.

Do not include in the list items that do not accompany you, i.e., purchases that you have mailed or had shipped home. These are dutiable in any case, even if for your own use and even if the items that accompany your return from the same trip do not exhaust your duty-free exemption. It is a good idea, if you have accumulated too much while abroad, to mail home any personal effects (made and bought in the US) that you no longer need rather than your foreign purchases. These personal effects pass through US Customs as "American goods returned" and are not subject to duty.

If you cannot avoid shipping home your foreign purchases, however, the US Customs Service suggests that the package be clearly marked "Not for Sale," and that a copy of the bill of sale be included. The US Customs examiner usually will accept this as indicative of the article's fair retail value, but if he or she believes it to be falsified or feels the goods have been seriously undervalued, a higher retail value may be assigned.

FORBIDDEN ITEMS: Narcotics, plants, and many types of food are not allowed into the US. Drugs are totally illegal, with the exception of medication prescribed by a physician. It's a good idea not to travel with too large a quantity of any given prescription drug (although, in the event that a pharmacy is not open when you need it, bring along several extra doses) and to have the prescription on hand in case any question arises either abroad or when re-entering the US.

Any sculpture that is part of an architectural structure, any authentic archaeological find, or other artifacts may not be exported from Italy without the permission of Beni Culturali e Ambientali (Ministry of Culture; 27 Via del Collegio Romano, Rome 00187; phone: 6 6723) If you do not obtain prior permission of the proper regulatory agencies, such items will be confiscated at the border, and you will run the risk of being fined or imprisoned.

Tourists have long been forbidden to bring into the US foreign-made, US-trade-marked articles purchased abroad (if the trademark is recorded with customs) without written permission. It's now permissible to enter with one such item in your possession as long as it's for personal use.

The US Customs Service implements the rigorous Department of Agriculture regulations concerning the importation of vegetable matter, seeds, bulbs, and the like. Living vegetable matter may not be imported without a permit, and everything must be inspected, permit or not. Approved items (which do not require a permit) include dried bamboo and woven items made of straw; beads made of most seeds (but not jequirity beans — the poisonous scarlet and black seed of the rosary pea); cones of pine and other trees; roasted coffee beans; most flower bulbs; flowers (without roots); dried or canned fruits, jellies, or jams; polished rice, dried beans and teas; herb plants (not witchweed); nuts (but not acorns, chestnuts, or nuts with outer husks); dried lichens, mushrooms, truffles, shamrocks, and seaweed; and most dried spices.

Other processed foods and baked goods usually are okay. Regulations on meat products generally depend on the country of origin and manner of processing. As a rule, commercially canned meat, hermetically sealed and cooked in the can so that it can be stored without refrigeration, is permitted, but not all canned meat fulfills this requirement. Be careful when buying European-made pâté, for instance. Goose liver pâté in itself is acceptable, but the pork fat that often is part of it, either as an ingredient or a rind, may not be. Even canned pâtés may not be admitted for this reason. (The imported ones you see in US stores have been prepared and packaged according to US regulations.) So before stocking up on a newfound favorite, it pays to check in advance — otherwise you might have to leave it behind.

The US Customs Service also enforces federal laws that prohibit the entry of articles made from the furs or hides of animals on the endangered species list. Beware of shoes, bags, and belts made of crocodile and certain kinds of lizard, and anything made from tortoiseshell; this also applies to preserved crocodiles, lizards, and turtles sometimes sold in gift shops. And if you're shopping for big-ticket items, beware of fur coats made from the skins of spotted cats. They are sold in Europe, but they will be confiscated upon your return to the US, and there will be no refund. For information about other animals on the endangered species list, contact the Department of the Interior, US Fish and Wildlife Service (Publications Unit, 4401 N. Fairfax Dr., Room 130, Arlington, VA 22203; phone: 703-358-1711), and ask for the free publication *Facts About Federal Wildlife Laws.*

Also note that some foreign governments prohibit the export of items made from certain species of wildlife, and the US honors any such restrictions. Before you go shopping in any foreign country, check with the US Department of Agriculture (G110 Federal Bldg., Hyattsville, MD 20782; phone: 301-436-8413) and find out what items are prohibited by the country you will be visiting.

The US Customs Service publishes a series of free pamphlets with customs information. It includes *Know Before You Go,* a basic discussion of customs requirements pertaining to all travelers; *Buyer Beware, International Mail Imports; Travelers' Tips on Bringing Food, Plant, and Animal Products into the United States; Importing a Car; GSP and the Traveler; Pocket Hints; Currency Reporting; Pets, Wildlife, US Customs; Customs Hints for Visitors (Nonresidents);* and *Trademark Information for Travelers.* For the entire series or individual pamphlets, write to the US Customs Service (PO Box 7407, Washington, DC 20044) or contact any of the seven regional offices — in Boston, Chicago, Houston, Long Beach (California), Miami, New Orleans, and New York. The US Customs Service has a tape-recorded message whereby callers using touch-tone phones can get more information on various topics; the number is 202-566-8195. These pamphlets provide great briefing material, but if you still have questions when you're in Europe, contact the nearest US consulate.

Sources and Resources

Tourist Information Offices

North American branches of the Italian Government Tourist Office generally are the best sources of travel information, and most of their many, varied publications are free for the asking. For the best results, request general information on specific provinces or cities, as well as publications relating to your particular areas of interest: accommodations, restaurants, special events, sports, guided tours, and facilities for specific sports. There is no need to send a self-addressed, stamped envelope with your request, unless specified. Following are the tourist information offices located in the US:

Chicago: 500 N. Michigan Ave., Chicago, IL 60611 (phone: 312-644-0990).
New York: 630 Fifth Ave., Suite 1565, New York, NY 10111 (phone: 212-245-4822).
San Francisco: 360 Post St., Suite 801, San Francisco, CA 94108 (phone: 415-392-6206).

The Italian Embassy and Consulates in the US

The Italian government maintains an embassy and a number of consulates in the US. One of their primary functions is to provide visas for certain resident aliens (depending on their country of origin) and for Americans planning to visit for longer than 6 months, or to study, reside, or work in Italy. Consulates also are empowered to sign official documents and to notarize copies or translations of US documents, which may be necessary for those papers to be considered legal abroad.

The Italian Embassy is located at 1601 Fuller St. NW, Washington, DC 20009 (phone: 202-328-5500). Listed below are the Italian consulates in the US. In general, these offices are open 9 AM to 1 PM, Mondays through Fridays — call ahead to be sure.

Italian Consulates in the US
Boston: Italian Consulate-General, 100 Boylston St., Suite 900, Boston, MA 02116 (phone: 617-542-0483).
Chicago: Italian Consulate-General, 500 N. Michigan Ave., Chicago, IL 60611 (phone: 312-467-1550).
Detroit: Italian Consulate, Buhl Bldg., 535 Griswold, Suite 1840, Detroit, MI 48226 (phone: 313-963-8560).
Houston: Italian Consulate, 1300 Post Oak Rd., Suite 660, Houston, TX 77056 (phone: 713-850-7520).

Los Angeles: Italian Consulate-General, 12400 Wilshire Blvd., Suite 300, Los Angeles, CA 90025 (phone: 213-820-0622).

New Orleans: Italian Consulate, 630 Camp St., New Orleans, LA 70130 (phone: 504-524-2271).

New York: Italian Consulate, 690 Park Ave., New York, NY 10021 (phone: 212-737-9100).

Philadelphia: Italian Consulate-General, 421 Chestnut St., Philadelphia, PA 19106 (phone: 215-592-7329).

San Francisco: Italian Consulate-General, 2590 Webster St., San Francisco, CA 94115 (phone: 415-931-4924).

The Italian Cultural Institute (Istituto Italiano di Cultura) is the Italian Embassy's cultural arm abroad. It serves as a liaison between the American and Italian people and is an especially good source of information. There are five branches in the US:

Chicago: 500 N. Michigan Ave., Suite 530, Chicago, IL 60611 (phone: 312-822-9545).

Los Angeles: 12400 Wilshire Blvd., Suite 310, Los Angeles, CA 90025 (phone: 213-207-4737).

New York: 686 Park Ave., New York, NY 10021 (phone: 212-879-4242).

San Francisco: 425 Bush St., Suite 305, San Francisco, CA 94108 (phone: 415-788-7142).

Washington, DC: 1601 Fuller St. NW, Washington, DC 20009 (phone: 202-328-5526).

The New York branch maintains a library of books, periodicals, and newspapers that is open to the public; San Francisco, too, has a small library, open to the public by appointment. A free booklet published three times a year lists cultural events in Italy — theater, folklore, cinema, and exhibitions. Copies are available on request from any of the offices listed above.

Theater and Special Event Tickets

As you read this book, you will learn about events that spark your interest — everything from music festivals and special theater seasons to sporting championships — along with telephone numbers and addresses to which to write for descriptive brochures, reservations, or tickets. The Italian Government Tourist Office can supply information on these and other special events and festivals that take place in Florence and the rest of Italy, though they cannot in all cases provide the actual program or detailed information on ticket prices.

Since many of these occasions often are fully booked well in advance, think about having your reservation in hand before you go. In some cases, tickets may be reserved over the phone and charged to a credit card, or you can send an international money order or foreign draft. If you do write, remember that any request from the US should be accompanied by an International Reply Coupon to ensure a response (send two of them for an airmail response). These international coupons, money orders, and drafts are available at US post offices.

For further information, write for the *European Travel Commission*'s extensive list of events scheduled for the entire year for its 24 member countries (including Italy). For a free copy, send a self-addressed, stamped, business-size (4 x 9½) envelope to "European Events," *European Travel Commission,* PO Box 1754, New York, NY 10185.

Books, Newspapers, Magazines, and Newsletters

BOOKS: Throughout GETTING READY TO GO, numerous books and brochures have been recommended as good sources of further information on a variety of topics.

Suggested Reading – The list below is made up of books we have seen and think worthwhile; it is by no means complete — but meant merely to start you on your way. These titles include some informative guides to special interests, solid fictional tales, and books that call your attention to things you might not notice otherwise.

Travel

Florence Explored, by Rupert Scott (New Amsterdam Books; $14.95).

Italian Country Inns and Villas, by Karen Brain (Warner; $12.95).

Italian Days, by Barbara Grizutti Harrison (Houghton-Mifflin; $12.95).

Italian Gardens, by Alex Ramsey and Helena Attlee (Seven Hills Books; $19.95).

Italy: The Places in Between, by Kate Simon (HarperCollins; $12.95, paperback).

The Stones of Florence, by Mary McCarthy (Harcourt Brace Jovanovich; $7.95).

History, Biography, and Culture

The Agony and the Ecstasy, by Irving Stone (Doubleday hardcover, $19.95; NAL paperback, $5.95).

The Architecture of the Italian Renaissance, by Peter Murray (Schocken; $10.95).

The Art of the Renaissance, by Linda and Peter Murray (World of Art Series, Thames and Hudson; $11.95).

Christopher Columbus, by Gianni Granzotto (University of Oklahoma Press; $11.95).

The Civilization of the Renaissance in Italy, by Jacob Burckhardt (HarperCollins; Vol. 1: $6.95; Vol. 2: $7.95).

A Concise Encyclopedia of the Italian Renaissance, edited by J. R. Hale (World of Art Series, Thames and Hudson; $11.95).

The Decline and Fall of the Roman Empire, by Edward Gibbon (Penguin; $6.95).

The Diary of the First Voyage of Christopher Columbus, edited by Oliver Dunn and James E. Kelly, Jr. (University of Oklahoma Press; $65 hardcover, $24.95 paperback).

Four Voyages of Christopher Columbus, by Cecil Jane (Dover ; $12.95).

History of Italian Renaissance Art: Painting, Sculpture, Architecture, by Frederick Hartt (Abrams; $55).

The Italians, by Luigi Barzini (Atheneum; $9.95).

The Last Italian: Portrait of a People, by William Murray (Prentice Hall; $21.95).

Lives of the Artists, by Giorgio Vasari (Penguin Classics; published in two volumes, $5.95 each).

The Romans, by R. H. Barrow (Penguin; $5.95).

Roman Art and Architecture, by Mortimer Wheeler (World of Art Series, Thames and Hudson; $11.95).

The Story of Art, by E. H. Gombrich (Prentice Hall; $36.67).

Literature

Crown of Columbus, by Michael Dorris and Louise Erdrich (HarperCollins; $22).

The Name of the Rose, by Umberto Eco (Warner; $5.95).

A Room with a View, by E. M. Forster (Penguin; $4.50).

Summer's Lease, by John Mortimer (Penguin; $7.95).

Food, Wine, and Shopping

Celebrating Italy, by Carol Field (Morrow; $24.95).

The Classic Italian Cook Book and More Classic Italian Cooking, by Marcella Hazan (Knopf hardcover, $25; Ballantine paperback; $5.95).

Eating in Italy: A Traveler's Guide to the Gastronomic Pleasures of Northern Italy, by Faith Heller Willinger (Morrow; $12.45).

The Food of Italy, by Waverley Root (Vintage; $10.95).

Honey from a Weed, by Patience Gray (North Point Press; $15.95).

Italian Wine, by Victor Hazan (Knopf; $18.95).

Italy the Beautiful Cookbook, by Lorenza de' Medici (Knapp Press; $39.95).

Made in Italy: A Shopper's Guide to Rome, Florence, Venice, and Milan, by Annie Brody and Patricia Schultz (Workman; $14.95).

Marling Menu-Master for Italy, by Clare F. and William E. Marling (Altarinda Books; $5.95).

Pasta Classica, by Julia Della Croce (Penguin; $25).

Simon & Schuster's Guide to Italian Wines (Simon & Schuster; $8.95, paperback).

The Wine Atlas of Italy, by Burton Anderson (Simon & Schuster; $40).

Wines of Italy, by David Gleave (Price Stearn; $12.95).

In addition, *Culturgrams* is a handy series of pamphlets that provides a good sampling of information on the people, cultures, sights, and bargains to be found in over 90 countries around the world. Each four-page, newsletter-size leaflet covers one country, and Italy is included in the series. The topics included range from customs and courtesies to lifestyles and demographics. These fact-filled pamphlets are published by the David M. Kennedy Center for International Studies at Brigham Young University; for an order form, contact the group c/o Publication Services (280 HRCB, Provo, UT 84602; phone: 801-378-6528). When ordering from 1 to 5 *Culturgrams,* the price is $1 each; 6 to 49 pamphlets cost 50¢ each; and for larger quantities, the price per copy goes down proportionately.

Another source of cultural information is *Do's and Taboos Around the World,* compiled by the Parker Pen Company and edited by Roger E. Axtell. It focuses on protocol, customs, etiquette, hand gestures and body language, gift giving, the dangers of using US jargon, and so on, and can be fun to read even if you're not going anyplace. It's available for $10.95 in bookstores or through John Wiley & Sons, 1 Wiley Dr., Somerset, NJ 08875 (phone: 212-850-6418).

NEWSPAPERS AND MAGAZINES: A subscription to the *International Herald Tribune* is a good idea for dedicated travelers. This English-language newspaper is written and edited mostly in Paris and is *the* newspaper read most regularly and avidly by Americans abroad to keep up with world news, US news, sports, the stock market (US and foreign), fluctuations in the exchange rate, and an assortment of help-wanted ads, real estate listings, and personals, global in scope. Published 6 days a week (no Sunday paper), it is available at newsstands throughout the US and in cities worldwide. It can be found on some newsstands in Florence, and larger hotels usually have copies in the lobby for guests — if you don't see a copy, ask the hotel concierge if it is available.

A 1-year subscription in the US costs $349. To subscribe, write or call the Subscription Manager, *International Herald Tribune,* 850 Third Ave., 10th Floor, New York, NY 10022 (phone: 800-882-2884 or 212-752-3890).

Among the major US publications that can be bought (generally a day or two after distribution in the US) in many of the larger cities, such as Florence, at hotels, airports, and newsstands, are the *The New York Times, USA Today,* the *Wall Street Journal,* and the *Washington Post.* As with other imports, expect these and other US publications to cost considerably more in Italy than in the US.

Before or after your trip, you may want to subscribe to a publication that specializes in information about Italy. A very interesting magazine for Italophiles is *Italy Italy,* which comes out 6 times a year, full of beautifully illustrated travel articles bound to whet your appetite for a visit or to provoke nostalgia for a return. Subscriptions are available for $30 a year from *Speedimpex,* 45-45 39th St., Long Island City, NY 11104 (phone: 718-392-7477).

Italians are well known for their fine food, and sampling the regional fare is likely to be one of the highlights of any visit. You will find reading about local edibles worthwhile before you go or after you return. *Gourmet,* a magazine specializing in food, frequently features mouth-watering articles on Italian *cucina,* although its scope is much broader. It is available at newsstands throughout the US for $2.50 an issue or for $18 a year from *Gourmet* (PO Box 53780, Boulder, CO 80322; phone: 800-365-2454). There are numerous additional magazines for every special interest available; check at your library information desk for a directory of such publications, or look over the selection offered by a well-stocked newsstand.

NEWSLETTERS: Throughout GETTING READY TO GO we have mentioned specific newsletters that our readers may be interested in consulting for further information. One of the very best sources of detailed travel information is *Consumer Reports Travel Letter.* Published monthly by Consumers Union (PO Box 53629, Boulder, CO 80322-3629; phone: 800-999-7959), it offers comprehensive coverage of the travel scene on a wide variety of fronts. A year's subscription costs $37; 2 years, $57.

In addition, the following travel newsletters provide useful up-to-date information on travel services and bargains:

Entree (PO Box 5148, Santa Barbara, CA 93150; phone: 805-969-5848). This newsletter caters to a sophisticated, discriminating traveler with the means to explore the places mentioned. Subscribers have access to a 24-hour hotline providing information on restaurants and accommodations around the world. Monthly; a year's subscription costs $59.

Travel Smart (Communications House, 40 Beechdale Rd., Dobbs Ferry, NY 10522; phone: 914-693-8300 in New York; 800-327-3633 elsewhere in the US). This monthly covers a wide variety of trips and travel discounts. A year's subscription costs $37.

■**Computer Services:** Anyone who owns a personal computer and a modem can subscribe to a database service providing everything from airline schedules and fares to restaurant listings. Two such services of particular use to travelers are *CompuServe* (5000 Arlington Center Blvd., Columbus, OH 43220; phone: 800-848-8199 or 614-457-8600; $39.95 to join, plus usage fees of $6 to $12.50 per hour) and *Prodigy Services* (445 Hamilton Ave., White Plains, NY 10601; phone: 800-822-6922 or 914-993-8000; $12.95 per month's subscription, plus variable usage fees). Before using any computer bulletin-board services, be sure to take precautions to prevent downloading of a computer "virus." First install one of the programs designed to screen out such nuisances.

Weights and Measures

When traveling in Italy, you'll find that just about every quantity, whether it is length, weight, or capacity, will be expressed in unfamiliar terms. In fact, this is true for travel almost everywhere in the world, since the US is one of the last countries to make its way to the metric system. Your trip to Florence may serve to familiarize you with what one day may be the weights and measures at your grocery store.

There are some specific things to keep in mind during your trip. Fruits and vegetables at a market are recorded in kilos (kilograms), as is your luggage at the airport and your body weight. (This latter is particularly pleasing to people of significant size, who instead of weighing 220 pounds hit the scales at a mere 100 kilos.) A kilo equals 2.2 pounds and 1 pound is .45 kilo. Body temperature is measured in degrees centigrade or Celsius rather than on the Fahrenheit scale, so that a normal body temperature is 37C, not 98.6F, and freezing is 0 degrees C rather than 32F.

Gasoline is sold by the liter (approximately 3.8 liters to 1 gallon). Tire pressure gauges and other equipment measure in kilograms per square centimeter rather than pounds per square inch. Highway signs are written in kilometers rather than miles (1 mile equals 1.6 kilometers; 1 kilometer equals .62 mile). And speed limits are in kilometers per hour, so think twice before hitting the gas when you see a speed limit of 100. That means 62 miles per hour.

The tables and conversion factors listed below should give you all the information you will need to understand any transaction, road sign, or map you encounter during your travels.

APPROXIMATE EQUIVALENTS		
Metric Unit	**Abbreviation**	**US Equivalent**
LENGTH		
meter	m	39.37 inches
kilometer	km	.62 mile
millimeter	mm	.04 inch
CAPACITY		
liter	l	1.057 quarts
WEIGHT		
gram	g	.035 ounce
kilogram	kg	2.2 pounds
metric ton	MT	1.1 tons
ENERGY		
kilowatt	kw	1.34 horsepower

CONVERSION TABLES
METRIC TO US MEASUREMENTS

Multiply:	by:	to convert to:
LENGTH		
millimeters	.04	inches
meters	3.3	feet
meters	1.1	yards
kilometers	.6	miles
CAPACITY		
liters	2.11	pints (liquid)
liters	1.06	quarts (liquid)
liters	.26	gallons (liquid)
WEIGHT		
grams	.04	ounces (avoir.)
kilograms	2.2	pounds (avoir.)

US TO METRIC MEASUREMENTS

LENGTH		
inches	25.0	millimeters
feet	.3	meters
yards	.9	meters
miles	1.6	kilometers
CAPACITY		
pints	.47	liters
quarts	.95	liters
gallons	3.8	liters
WEIGHT		
ounces	28.0	grams
pounds	.45	kilograms

TEMPERATURE

$$°F = (°C \times 9/5) + 32 \qquad °C = (°F - 32) \times 5/9$$

USEFUL WORDS
AND PHRASES

Useful Words and Phrases

QUI?
WHO?
CHI?
QUIEN? Unlike the French, who have a reputation for being snobbish and brusque if you don't speak their language perfectly, the Italians do not expect you to speak Italian — but are very flattered when you try.

In many circumstances, you won't have to, because staffs at most of the larger hotels and popular attractions — as well as at a fair number of restaurants — speak serviceable English, or at least a modicum of it, which they usually are eager to improve — and that means practicing on you. If you find yourself in a situation where your limited Italian is the only means of communication, take the plunge. Don't be afraid of misplaced accents or misconjugated verbs. (Italians themselves often lapse into the all-purpose infinitive form of a verb when speaking with a novice.) In most cases you will be understood, and then will be advised on the menu or pointed in the right direction. The list on the following pages is a selection of commonly used words and phrases to speed you on your way.

Note that in Italian, nouns are either masculine or feminine, as well as singular or plural, and the adjectives that modify them must correspond. Most nouns ending in *o* are masculine; the *o* becomes an *i* in the plural. The masculine articles are *un* (indefinite), *il* (definite singular), and *i* (definite plural), except before words beginning with the *s* sound (however spelled) and with *i* + vowel, where they are *uno, lo,* and *gli.*

Most nouns ending in *a* are feminine; the *a* becomes *e* in the plural. The feminine articles are *una* (indefinite), *la* (definite singular), and *le* (definite plural). Final vowels or articles usually are contracted to an apostrophe (') before words beginning with vowels, as in *l'acqua* (the water). Singular nouns ending in *e* can be either masculine or feminine; *e* becomes *i* in the plural. Adjectives follow the nouns they modify.

Italy has several markedly different regional dialects, each with its own vocabulary and pronunciation rules. There is, however, a generally accepted standard used on national radio and television and understood, if not used, by almost everybody. Traditional spelling reflects standard pronunciation fairly well. These suggestions should help you pronounce most words intelligibly.

- *i* is pronounced as in *machine.*
- *e* is pronounced with a sound somewhere between the vowels of *let* and *late.* It is never diphthongized, as in *lay.* Final *e* is never silent.
- *a* is pronounced as in *father.*
- *o* is pronounced with a sound somewhere between the vowels of *ought* and *boat.* It is never diphthongized, as in *know.*
- *u* is pronounced as in *rude.*

In vowel letter sequences, both vowels are pronounced; *i* and *u* before vowels usually are pronounced *y* and *w,* respectively.

Italian consonants are pronounced as in English with these exceptions:

Consonants spelled double are pronounced double. Compare the *k* sounds of blacker (single consonant) and black cur (double consonant), and the *d* sounds of the Italian *cade* (he falls) and *cadde* (he fell).

p and *t* are unaspirated; that is, they are pronounced as in *spit* and *stop*, not as in *pit* and *top*.

t and *d* are dental; the tongue tip touches the upper teeth, not the gums.

s before a vowel or between a vowel and a voiced consonant (*b, d, g, v, m, n, l, r*) is pronounced *z*.

ci stands for *ch* (as in English *chip*), as does *c* before *e* or *i: ciao!* is pronounced *chow.*

gh always stands for *g,* as in English *ghost.*

gi stands for *j,* as does *g* before *e* or *i: buon giorno* is pronounced *bwon jorno.*

gn stands for the medial consonant of English *canyon: bagno* (bath) is pronounced *banyo.*

gl stands for the medial consonant of English *billion: gli* (pronoun and article) is pronounced *lyee.*

h is never pronounced.

q is pronounced as *k; qu* is pronounced *kw: cinque* (five) is pronounced *chinkweh.*

r is "rolled," as it is in Spanish or Scots.

z is pronounced *dz* in a word initially; within words it is pronounced either *dz* or *ts,* depending on the word.

More often than not, the vowel preceding the last consonant in the word is accented. Final vowels marked with an accent are stressed.

These are only the most basic rules, and even they may seem daunting at first, but they shouldn't remain so for long. Nevertheless, if you can't get your mouth to speak Italian, try your hands at it: With a little observation, you'll pick it up quickly and be surprised at how often your message will get across.

Greetings and Everyday Expressions

Good morning!	
(also, Good day!)	*Buon giorno!*
Good evening!	*Buona sera!*
Hello!	
(familiar)	*Ciao!*
(on the telephone)	*Pronto!*
How are you?	*Come sta?*
Pleased to meet you!	*Piacere!* or *Molto lieto/a!*
Good-bye!	*Arrivederci!*
(final)	*Addio!*
So long! (familiar)	*Ciao!*
Good night!	*Buona notte!*
Yes!	*Sì!*
No!	*No!*
Please!	*Per favore* or *per piacere!*
Thank you!	*Grazie!*
You're welcome!	*Prego!*
Excuse me!	
(I beg your pardon.)	*Mi scusi!*
(May I get by?; on a bus or in a crowd)	*Permesso!*
I don't speak Italian.	*Non parlo italiano.*
Do you speak English?	*Parla inglese?*

Is there someone there who speaks English?	*C'è qualcuno che parla inglese?*
I don't understand.	*Non capisco.*
Do you understand?	*Capisce?*
My name is . . .	*Mi chiamo . . .*
What is your name?	*Come si chiama?*
miss	*signorina*
madame	*signora*
mister	*signor(e)*
open	*aperto*
closed	*chiuso*
. . . for annual vacation	*chiuso per ferie*
. . . for weekly day of rest	*chiuso per riposo settimanale*
. . . for restoration	*chiuso per restauro*
Is there a strike?	*C'è uno sciopero?*
Until when?	*Fino a quando?*
entrance	*entrata*
exit	*uscita*
push	*spingere*
pull	*tirare*
today	*oggi*
tomorrow	*domani*
yesterday	*ieri*

Checking In

I would like . . .	*Vorrei . . .*
I have reserved . . .	*Ho prenotato . . .*
a single room	*una camera singola*
a double room	*una camera doppia*
a quiet room	*una camera tranquilla*
with private bath	*con bagno privato*
with private shower	*con doccia privata*
with a sea view	*con vista sul mare*
with air conditioning	*con aria condizionata*
with balcony	*con balcone/terrazza*
for one night	*per una notte*
for a few days	*per qualche giorno*
for a week	*per una settimana*
with full board	*con pensione completa*
with half board	*con mezza pensione*
Does the price include . . .	*Il prezzo comprende . . .*
breakfast	*la prima colazione*
service charge	*servizio*
taxes	*tasse*
What time is breakfast served?	*A che ora si serve la prima colazione?*

It doesn't work.	*Non funziona.*
May I pay with traveler's checks?	*Posso pagare con traveler's checks?*
Do you accept this credit card?	*Accettate questa carta di credito?*

Shopping

bakery	*il panificio*
bookstore	*la libreria*
butcher shop	*la macelleria*
camera shop	*il negozio d'apparecchi fotografici*
delicatessen	*la salumeria/la pizzicheria*
department store	*il grande magazzino*
drugstore (for medicine)	*la farmacia*
grocery	*la drogheria/la pizzicheria*
jewelry store	*la gioielleria*
newsstand	*l'edicola/il giornalaio*
pastry shop	*la pasticceria*
perfume (and cosmetics) store	*la profumeria*
shoestore	*il negozio di scarpe*
supermarket	*il supermercato*
tobacconist	*il tabaccaio*

cheap	*a buon mercato*
expensive	*caro/a*
large	*grande*
larger	*più grande*
too large	*troppo grande*
small	*piccolo/a*
smaller	*più piccolo*
too small	*troppo piccolo*
long	*lungo/a*
short	*corto/a*
antique	*antico/a*
old	*vecchio/a*
new	*nuovo/a*
used	*usato/a*
handmade	*fatto/a a mano*
washable	*lavabile*

How much does it cost?	*Quanto costa?*
What is it made of?	*Di che cosa è fatto/a?*
camel's hair	*pelo di cammello*
cotton	*cotone*
corduroy	*velluto a coste*
lace	*pizzo*
leather	*pelle/cuoio*
linen	*lino*
silk	*seta*
suede	*pelle scamosciata*
synthetic material	*materiale sintetico*
wool	*lana*

brass	*ottone*
bronze	*bronzo*
copper	*rame*
gold	*oro*
gold plate	*placcato d'oro*
silver	*argento*
silver plate	*placcato d'argento*
stainless steel	*acciaio inossidabile*
wood	*legno*

Colors

beige	*beige*
black	*nero/a*
blue	*celeste* or *azzurro/a*
(navy)	*blu*
brown	*marrone*
gray	*grigio/a*
green	*verde*
orange	*arancio*
pink	*rosa*
purple	*viola*
red	*rosso/a*
white	*bianco/a*
yellow	*giallo/a*
dark	*scuro/a*
light	*chiaro/a*

Getting Around

north	*nord*
south	*sud*
east	*est*
west	*ovest*
right	*destra*
left	*sinistra*
straight ahead	*sempre diritto*
far	*lontano/a*
near	*vicino/a*
gas station	*la stazione di rifornimento/stazione per benzina*
train station	*la stazione ferroviaria*
bus stop	*la fermata dell'autobus*
subway	*la metropolitana*
airport	*l'aeroporto*
travel agency	*l'agenzia di viaggio*
map	*una carta geografica*
one-way ticket	*un biglietto di sola andata*
round-trip ticket	*un biglietto di andata e ritorno*
track	*il binario*
first class	*prima classe*
second class	*seconda classe*
no smoking	*non fumare/divieto di fumare*

tires	*le gomme/i pneumatici*
oil	*l'olio*
gasoline	
generic reference or regular (leaded) gas	*la benzina*
unleaded gas	*benzina verde* or *benzina senza piombo*
diesel gas	*diesel* or *gasolio*
Fill it up, please.	*Faccia il pieno, per favore.*
Where is . . . ?	*Dov'è . . . ?*
Where are . . . ?	*Dove sono . . . ?*
How many kilometers are we from . . . ?	*Quanti chilometri siamo da . . . ?*
Does this bus go to . . . ?	*Quest'autobus va a . . . ?*
What time does it leave?	*A che ora parte?*
Danger	*Pericolo*
Dead End	*Strada Senza Uscita*
Detour	*Deviazione*
Do Not Enter	*Vietato l'Accesso*
Falling Rocks	*Caduta Massi*
Men Working	*Lavori in Corso*
No Parking	*Divieto di Sosta*
No Passing	*Divieto di Sorpasso*
One Way	*Senso Unico*
Pay Toll	*Pagamento Pedaggio*
Pedestrian Zone	*Zona Pedonale*
Reduce Speed	*Rallentare*
Ring Road	*Raccordo Anulare*
Stop	*Alt*
Use Headlights in Tunnel	*Accendere i Fari in Galleria*
Yield	*Dare la Precedenza*

Personal Items and Services

aspirin	*l'aspirina*
Band-Aids	*i cerotti*
barbershop	*il barbiere*
beauty shop	*l'istituto di bellezza*
condom	*il profilattico/il preservativo*
dry cleaner	*la tintoria*
hairdresser	*il parucchiere per donna*
laundromat	*la lavanderia automatica*
laundry	*la lavanderia*
post office	*l'ufficio postale*
sanitary pads	*gli assorbenti igienici*
shampoo	*lo shampoo*
shaving cream	*la crema da barba*
shoemaker	*il calzolaio*
soap	*il sapone*
soap powder	*il sapone in polvere*
stamps	*i francobolli*
tampons	*i tamponi*

tissues	*i fazzoletti di carta*
toilet	*il gabinetto/la toletta/il bagno*
toilet paper	*la carta igienica*
toothbrush	*lo spazzolino da denti*
toothpaste	*il dentifricio*

Where is the men's/ladies' room?	*Dov'è la toletta?*
The door will say:	
for men	*Uomini* or *Signori*
for women	*Donne* or *Signore*
Is it occupied/free?	*E occupato/libero?*

Days of the Week

Monday	*lunedì*
Tuesday	*martedì*
Wednesday	*mercoledì*
Thursday	*giovedì*
Friday	*venerdì*
Saturday	*sabato*
Sunday	*domenica*

Months

January	*gennaio*
February	*febbraio*
March	*marzo*
April	*aprile*
May	*maggio*
June	*giugno*
July	*luglio*
August	*agosto*
September	*settembre*
October	*ottobre*
November	*novembre*
December	*dicembre*

Numbers

zero	*zero*
one	*uno*
two	*due*
three	*tre*
four	*quattro*
five	*cinque*
six	*sei*
seven	*sette*
eight	*otto*
nine	*nove*
ten	*dieci*
eleven	*undici*
twelve	*dodici*
thirteen	*tredici*
fourteen	*quattordici*
fifteen	*quindici*
sixteen	*sedici*

seventeen	*diciassette*
eighteen	*diciotto*
nineteen	*diciannove*
twenty	*venti*
thirty	*trenta*
forty	*quaranta*
fifty	*cinquanta*
sixty	*sessanta*
seventy	*settanta*
eighty	*ottanta*
ninety	*novanta*
one hundred	*cento*
one thousand	*mille*

Eating Out

ashtray	*un portacenere*
bottle	*una bottiglia*
chair	*una sedia*
cup	*una tazza*
fork	*una forchetta*
knife	*un coltello*
napkin	*un tovagliolo*
plate	*un piatto*
spoon	*un cucchiaio*
table	*una tavola*
beer	*una birra*
cocoa	*una cioccolata*
coffee	*un caffè* or *un espresso*
coffee with milk (served in a bar with steamed milk)	*un cappuccino*
(usually served at breakfast or at a bar, with warm milk — more than is in a cappuccino)	*un caffè latte*
fruit juice	*un succo di frutta*
lemonade	*una limonata*
mineral water	*acqua minerale*
carbonated	*gassata*
not carbonated	*non gassata*
orangeade	*un'aranciata*
tea	*un tè*
water	*acqua*
red wine	*vino rosso*
rosé wine	*vino rosato*
white wine	*vino bianco*
cold	*freddo/a*
hot	*caldo/a*
sweet	*dolce*
(very) dry	*(molto) secco*

bacon	*la pancetta*
bread/rolls	*il pane/i panini*
butter	*il burro*
eggs	*le uova*
hard-boiled	*un uovo sodo*
poached	*uova affogate/in camicia*
soft-boiled	*uova à la coque*
scrambled	*uova strapazzate*
sunny-side up	*uova fritte all'occhio di bue*
honey	*il miele*
jam/marmalade	*la confettura/la marmellata*
omelette	*la frittata*
orange juice	*la spremuta d'arancia*
pepper	*il pepe*
salt	*il sale*
sugar	*lo zucchero*
Waiter!	*Cameriere!*
I would like . . .	*Vorrei . . .*
a glass of	*un bicchiere di*
a bottle of	*una bottiglia di*
a half bottle of	*una mezza bottiglia di*
a carafe of	*una caraffa di*
a liter of	*un litro di*
a half liter of	*un mezzo litro di*
a quarter liter of	*un quarto di*
The check, please.	*Il conto, per favore.*
Is the service charge included?	*Il servizio è incluso?*

Pasta Shapes

round or semicircular ravioli	*agnolotti*
small rings used in soup	*anellini*
small pockets, usually stuffed	*anolini*
large stuffed tubes	*cannelloni*
angel's hair — extra-thin spaghetti	*capelli d'angelo*
little hats	*cappelletti*
short curly noodles	*cavatelli*
ridged shells	*conchiglie*
crêpes	*crespelle*
bows	*farfalle*
flat, straight noodles	*fettuccine*
spirals	*fusilli*
potato dumplings	*gnocchi*
very wide, flat pasta, used in layers	*lasagna*
narrow, flat spaghetti	*linguine*

general term for hollow pasta	*maccheroni*
little ears	*orecchiette*
barley shape; looks like rice	*orzo*
broad noodles	*pappardelle*
green pasta made with spinach	*pasta verde*
quills	*penne*
stuffed squares	*ravioli*
large grooved tubes	*rigatoni*
corkscrews	*rotini*
stars	*stelline*
flat noodles	*tagliatelle*
stuffed rings	*tortellini*
large stuffed rings	*tortelloni*
little tubes	*tubetti*
squiggly thin spaghetti	*vermicelli*
large grooved macaroni	*ziti*

THE CITY

FLORENCE

Florence, city of the arts, jewel of the Renaissance, symbol of the Tuscan pride in grace and refinement, is an acquired taste for many. Rome has romance, Venice intrigue, and Naples a poignant gaiety; Florence may seem too austere, too serious, too severe. The elegance that is Florence does not seize you immediately — not like the splashing fountains of Rome, the noisy laughter and song of Naples, the pastel chandeliers peeking out of patrician palaces along Venice's Grand Canal.

Next to the mellow tangerine hues of Rome, the pinks of Venice, and the orgy of color that is Naples, Florence is a study in neutral shades: blacks and whites, beiges and browns, a splattering of dark green. Its people seem less spontaneous and exuberant than Romans or Neapolitans, more hardworking and reserved, with a sort of innate sense of dignity and pride.

Florentine palaces are more like fortresses, at first glance rather forbidding and uninviting to the visitor; the city's somber streets are lined with solid, direct architecture; its civic sculpture is noble and restrained. But this is only a superficial view of Florence. Step into the palaces and you will be awed by the beauty of fine details, as well as by some of the world's greatest art treasures. Look at the fine Florentine crafts in gold and leather and exquisite fabrics in the elegant but classically serious shops. It won't take long before you will understand why the culture and art of Florence have attracted people from around the world through the centuries, and why it is as much a favorite of artists, students, and expatriates today as it was at its apogee under the Medicis in the 15th century.

Florence was the home of Cimabue and Giotto, the fathers of Italian painting; of Brunelleschi, Donatello, and Masaccio, who paved the way for the Renaissance; of the Della Robbias, Botticelli, Leonardo da Vinci, and Michelangelo; of Dante Alighieri, Petrarch, and Boccaccio; of Machiavelli and Galileo. Art, science, and life found their finest, most powerful expression in Florence, and records of this splendid past fill the city's many galleries, museums, churches, and palaces, demanding attention.

Florence — *Firenze* in Italian — probably originated as an Etruscan center, but it was only under the Romans in the 1st century BC that it became a true city. Like so many other cities of its time, Roman Florence grew up along the fertile banks of a river, in this case the Arno, amid the rolling green hills of Tuscany. Its Latin name, *Florentia* ("flowering"), probably referred to the city's florid growth, although some ancient historians attributed it to Florinus, the Roman general who besieged the nearby Etruscan hilltown of Fiesole in 63 BC.

During the Roman rule, Florence became a thriving military and trading center, with its share of temples, baths, a town hall, and an amphitheater, but few architectural monuments of that epoch have survived.

After the fall of the Roman Empire, Florence sank into the decadence of the Dark Ages, and despite a temporary reprieve during Charlemagne's 8th- and 9th-century European empire, it did not really flourish again until the late 11th century. It was then that the great guilds developed and the florin-based currency began to appear, and Florence became a powerful, self-governing republic.

In the 12th century, interfamily feuds were widespread, and over 150 square stone towers — built for defense by influential families right next to their houses — dominated the city's skyline. Even so, during that and the next century, the Florentine population of about 60,000 (twice that of London at the time) was busily engaged in trade with the rest of the Mediterranean. The amazing building boom that followed, bringing about the demolition of the fortified houses in favor of more gracious public and private palazzi and magnificent churches, reflected the great prosperity of the city's trading and banking families, its wool and silk industries, and the enormous strength of the florin.

As a free city-state or *comune*, Florence managed to maintain a balance between the authority of the Germanic emperors and that of the popes, overcoming the difficulties of internal struggles between the burgher Guelphs (who supported the pope) and the aristocratic Ghibellines (who were behind the Holy Roman Emperor). Eventually, by the late 13th century, the Guelphs won power and a democratic government was inaugurated by the famous Ordinances of Justice. So began Florence's ascent, which spanned 3 centuries and reached its height and greatest splendor under the Medici family.

Owing in large measure to the patronage of the Medicis, Florence became the liveliest and most creative city in Europe. While this certainly pertained during the time of Giovanni di Bicci de' Medici (1360–1429) and his illustrious dynasty of merchants, bankers, and art patrons, as well as that of his son Cosimo the Elder (1389–1464), who continued to gather artists around him, it was Cosimo's grandson Lorenzo the Magnificent (1449–1492) who put Florence in the forefront of the Italian Renaissance. An elaborate celebration will take place this year to mark the 500th anniversary of Lorenzo's death (see *Special Events*).

Today, the Medici might be thought of as something of a political machine, since they controlled — through their wealth and personal power alone — a city that was, in theory at least, still a democratic republic governed by members of the trade guilds. Their de facto rule was not uncontested, however. They suffered reversals, such as the Pazzi Conspiracy in 1478, and twice they were expelled — from 1494 to 1512, when a revolution brought the religious reformer Savonarola briefly to power (and an attempt was made to reestablish democracy), and again from 1527 to 1530, when another republic was set up, only to fall to the troops of Emperor Charles V and lead to the Medici restoration.

Finally, in the late 16th century, their glory days behind them, the Medici gained an official title. They became grand dukes (Cosimo I was the first), and Florence became the capital of the grand duchy of Tuscany. In the 18th century, the grand duchy of the Medici was succeeded by that of the house of Lorraine, until Tuscany became part of the kingdom of Italy in 1860. From 1865 to 1871, Florence reigned as temporary capital of the kingdom, but with the capital's transfer to Rome, the history of Florence merges with that of the rest of Italy.

Two catastrophes in this century have caused inestimable damage to Florence's art treasures. In 1944, all the beloved bridges crossing the Arno — except for the Ponte Vecchio — were blown up by the retreating Nazis. Reconstruction began as soon as the Germans were gone. Then, 2 decades later, in November 1966, the Arno burst its banks, covering the historic center with a muddy slime. Over 1,400 works of art, 2 million valuable books, and countless homes were damaged by floodwaters that reached depths of 23 feet. The people of Florence, with help from all over the world, rose to the challenge. Even before the floodwaters had receded, they began the painstaking chore of rescuing their treasures from 600,000 tons of mud, oil, and debris.

Today, the city of Florence — with a population of slightly less than half a million — still is a vital force in the arts, in culture, and in science, as well as an industrial, commercial, and university center and a leader in the fields of handicrafts and fashion. Note, indeed, how the Florentines dress, their fine attention to detail and the remarkable sense of style that turns an ordinary outfit into something personal and very special. And note the almost arrogant local swagger. Then realize that these are people who wake up every morning to the marvels of Michelangelo, who literally live in a 15th-century Renaissance textbook. Their artistic and cultural heritage is unsurpassed, truly unique in the world. No doubt you'll agree that they have every reason to be proud.

FLORENCE AT-A-GLANCE

 SEEING THE CITY: The picture-postcard view of Florence is the one from Piazzale Michelangelo, on the far side of the Arno. From here, more than 300 feet above sea level, the eye embraces the entire city and neighboring hilltowns as far as Pistoia, but it is the foreground that rivets the attention. The Arno, with all its bridges, from Ponte San Niccolò to Ponte della Vittoria, the Palazzo Vecchio, with its tower and crenelations, the *Uffizi,* the flank of Santa Croce, numerous spires and domes — all are in the picture. And looming over the whole, like a whale washed ashore in the land of Lilliput, is the massive Duomo, with its bell tower and giant red cupola. The piazzale is reached by a splendid tree-lined avenue, called the Viale dei Colli, which begins at Ponte San Niccolò and winds up to the enormous square under the name of Viale Michelangelo. It then proceeds beyond the square as far as the Porta Romana under the names of Viale Galileo and Viale Machiavelli. From the bridge to the Roman Gate is a scenic 4-mile walk, but it's also possible to trace the same route aboard bus No. 13 from the station. Another extraordinary view, of Florence and the entire Arno Valley, can be enjoyed from the lookout terrace just before the Church of St. Francis, perched on a hill studded with cypress trees and sumptuous villas in neighboring Fiesole (see *Special Places*).

 SPECIAL PLACES: The Arno is a good orientation point for first-time visitors to Florence. Most of the city sits on the north, or right, bank of the river, including its principal squares: Piazza del Duomo, the religious heart of Florence; Piazza della Repubblica, its bustling commercial center; and

Piazza della Signoria, the ancient political center and today a favorite meeting place because of its outdoor cafés. The most elegant shopping street, Via Tornabuoni, runs from the Arno to Piazza Antinori. The other side of the river is known as the Oltrarno, literally "beyond the Arno." Sights here include the Pitti Palace and Boboli Gardens, the churches of Santo Spirito and Santa Maria del Carmine, and Piazzale Michelangelo. For more information about this area, see *Walk 4: Oltrarno* in DIRECTIONS.

THE CATHEDRAL (DUOMO) COMPLEX

Il Duomo (The Cathedral) – The Cathedral of Santa Maria del Fiore was begun in 1296 by the Sienese architect Arnolfo di Cambio, and took 173 years to complete. Dominating a large double square, it is the fourth-longest church in the world (after St. Peter's in Rome, St. Paul's in London, and the Duomo of Milan) and is said to be capable of holding over 20,000 people. The gigantic project was financed by the Florentine republic and the Clothmakers Guild, in an age of faith when every city-state aspired to claim the biggest and most important cathedral as its own.

Besides religious services, the Duomo has served as the site of major civic ceremonies and many noteworthy historical events, such as the Pazzi Conspiracy, when Giuliano de' Medici was assassinated in 1478. The original façade, never completed, was destroyed in the 16th century and replaced in the late 19th century. Whereas the exterior walls are encased in colorful marble (white from Carrara, green from Prato, and pink from Siena), the interior seems plain and cold by comparison, a brownish-gray sandstone called *pietra forte* and soberly decorated in keeping with the Florentine character. Most of the original statuary that adorned the Duomo, including Michelangelo's unfinished *Pietà*, has been moved to the *Museo dell'Opera del Duomo* (see below). The remains of the ancient Church of Santa Reparata, the original cathedral of Florence, which came to light under the Duomo during the extensive excavation after the 1966 flood, are very interesting (take the staircase near the entrance on the right side of the nave). The crypt is particularly haunting. Closed Sunday and holiday afternoons; admission charge.

The public competition for the design of the dome was won by a Florentine, Filippo Brunelleschi, who had marveled at the great engineering feat of ancient Rome, the dome of the Pantheon. The Renaissance architect's mighty cupola, built between 1420 and 1436, the first since antiquity, subsequently inspired Michelangelo as he faced the important task of designing the dome of St. Peter's in Rome.

Brunelleschi's dome surpasses both the Pantheon and St. Peter's, although today it is seriously cracked and monitored by computer. Over 371 feet high and 148 feet across, it has double walls between which a 463-step staircase leads to a lantern at the top (also a Brunelleschi design). Restorations have been under way for more than a decade and, due to the necessity of scaffolding — not to mention the huge green canvas drape — there is little available light for viewing the dome's immense fresco (begun by Vasari). Still, the 40-minute climb up and down is well worth the effort for the breathtaking panorama from the top and for a true sense of the awesome size of this artistic and technical masterpiece. No, Virginia, there is no elevator. Closed Sundays and holidays. Admission charge.

Il Campanile (Bell Tower) – The graceful freestanding belfry of the Duomo, one of the most unusual in Italy, was begun by Giotto in 1334 (when he was 67) and eventually completed by Francesco Talenti. The bas-reliefs adorning the base are copies of originals by Giotto and Luca della Robbia that have been removed to the *Duomo Museum*, as have the statues of the Prophets (done by various artists, including Donatello) that stood in the niches. The 414-step climb to the top leads to a terrace with another bird's-eye view of Florence. There's no elevator. Closed Sunday and holiday afternoons; admission charge.

Il Battistero (The Baptistry) – Dedicated to St. John the Baptist, the patron saint of Florence, the Baptistry is a unique treasure, the origins of which are lost in time.

The octagonal building may date to the 4th century, contemporary with the Church of Santa Reparata, while the exterior of green-and-white marble dates to the 12th century and is typical of the Tuscan Romanesque style, with an Oriental influence. To this day, the Baptistry still is used for baptisms, and many a famous Florentine (such as Dante Alighieri) has been baptized here. On the *Feast of St. John* (June 24), the relics of the saint are displayed in the building and candles are lit in his honor (see *Special Events*).

The interior is covered with magnificent Byzantine mosaics by 13th- and 14th-century Florentine and Venetian masters, but it is the three gilded bronze doorways that are the main tourist attraction. The South Door, by Andrea Pisano, is the oldest, dating from the early 14th century. In the Gothic style, it has 28 panels with reliefs of the life of St. John the Baptist and the cardinal and theological virtues. The North Door (1403–1424), in late Gothic style, was the result of a competition in which the unanimous winner was Lorenzo Ghiberti (Brunelleschi was among the competitors). It, too, is divided into 28 panels depicting scenes from the life of Christ, the Evangelists, and the Doctors of the Church. Ghiberti's East Door, however, facing the cathedral, is his masterpiece. In full Renaissance style, it was defined by Michelangelo as worthy of being the "gate of paradise." Begun in 1425 and completed in 1452, when Ghiberti was 74 years old, it consists of 10 panels illustrating Old Testament stories and medallions containing self-portraits of Ghiberti and his adopted son, Vittorio (who designed the frame), as well as portraits of their principal contemporaries.

Museo dell'Opera del Duomo (Duomo Museum) – Masterpieces from the Duomo, the Baptistry, and the Campanile are here, especially sculpture: Michelangelo's unfinished *Pietà* (third of his four), Donatello's *Mary Magdalene,* the famous choir lofts (*cantorie*) by Luca della Robbia and Donatello, the precious silver altar frontal from the Baptistry, fragments from the original cathedral façade, even the original wooden scale model of Brunelleschi's dome. Closed Sunday afternoons; admission charge. 9 Piazza del Duomo (no phone).

ELSEWHERE DOWNTOWN

Galleria degli Uffizi (Uffizi Museum and Gallery) – Italy's most important art museum is in a Renaissance palace built on the site of an 11th-century church (San Piero Scheraggio), the remains of which are incorporated in the palazzo and may still be seen. The splendor of this museum derives not only from the great works it contains but also from the 16th-century building itself, which was commissioned by Cosimo I and designed by Vasari (completed by Buontalenti) to house the Medicis' administrative offices, or *uffizi*. In 1581, Francesco I began converting the top floor into an art museum destined to become one of the world's greatest. The three corridors, with light streaming through their great windows, are a spectacle in themselves, and the collection they contain is so vast — the most important Italian and European paintings of the 13th through the 18th century — that we suggest taking along a good guide or guidebook (Luciano Berti's is excellent) and comfortable shoes. Remember also to allow more time for a visit here than you think you'll need. At the top of the monumental staircase (there also is an elevator) on the second floor is the Prints and Drawings Collection; the museum proper (painting and sculpture) is on the third floor. Fifteen rooms are devoted to Florentine and Tuscan masterpieces, including the work of Cimabue, Giotto, Fra Filippo Lippi, Paolo Uccello, Fra Angelico, Da Vinci, and Michelangelo, not to mention such other non-Florentine masters as Raphael, Titian, Tintoretto, Caravaggio, Rubens, Van Dyck, and Rembrandt. The Botticelli Room contains the master's *Birth of Venus* and his restored *Allegoria della Primavera* (Allegory of Spring), as well as other allegorical and mythological works that make this the most important Botticelli collection in the world. Open Tuesdays through Saturdays from 9 AM to 7 PM, Sundays to 1 PM. Admission charge. Piazza della Signoria (phone: 218341).

For diehards, there is an important collection of self-portraits lining the Corridoio

Vasariano (Vasari Corridor) that may be visited by special arrangement. The portraits include those of Raphael, Rubens, Van Dyck, Velázquez, Bernini, Canova, Corot, Fattori, and Chagall. Even without the portraits, the half-mile walk would be fascinating. The corridor actually is a raised passageway built in the 1560s to allow members of the Medici court to move from their old palace and offices (Palazzo Vecchio and Uffizi) to their new palace (Palazzo Pitti) without having to resort to the streets. It crosses the river on the tops of shops on the Ponte Vecchio, and affords splendid views of the Arno, the Church of Santa Felicità, and the Boboli Gardens. Closed Mondays and Sundays and holiday afternoons; admission charge. The rooms are decorated with frescoes that span the 17th, 18th, and 19th centuries. To visit the Vasari Corridor, write to the *Uffizi* well in advance of your arrival (there's no extra fee). 6 Loggiato degli Uffizi (phone: 218341).

Palazzo della Signoria or Palazzo Vecchio (Old Palace) – This fortress-like palace, built by Arnolfo di Cambio between 1298 and 1314 as the seat of Florence's new democratic government of *priori,* or guild leaders, began as Florence's town hall and is still just that. From 1540 to 1550, it was temporarily the residence of the Medicis as they progressed from their ancestral home, the Medici-Riccardi Palace, to their new home in the Palazzo Pitti. Although in a rather severe Gothic style, it is at once powerful and graceful, with a lofty tower 308 feet high. Beyond its rusticated façade is an elaborately ornate courtyard highlighted by Verrocchio's delightful fountain of a bronze cherub holding a dolphin (1476).

The medieval austerity of the exterior also contrasts with the sumptuous apartments inside. The massive Salone dei Cinquecento (Salon of the Five Hundred) on the first floor, built in 1496 for Savonarola's short-lived republican Council of Five Hundred, is decorated with frescoes by Vasari. Also, don't miss Vasari's *studiolo,* Francesco de' Medici's gem of a study, with magnificent *armadio* doors painted by artists of the schools of Bronzino and Vasari. On the third floor is an exhibition of 140 works of art removed from Italy by the Nazis and recovered by Rodolfo Siviero, the famed Italian art sleuth. Open Mondays through Fridays from 9 AM to 7 PM, Sundays and holidays from 8 AM to 1 PM. Piazza della Signoria (phone: 2768465).

Loggia dei Lanzi or Loggia della Signoria – Built between 1376 and 1382 for the election and proclamation of public officials and other ceremonies, it took its name in the 16th century from Cosimo I's Germano-Swiss mercenary soldiers (known in Italian as *lanzichenecchi*), who were stationed here. Today the loggia is a delightful open-air museum with masterpieces of sculpture from various periods under its arches. Particularly noteworthy are Cellini's *Perseus* and Giambologna's *Rape of the Sabines.* Piazza della Signoria.

Ponte Vecchio – The "old bridge" is indeed Florence's oldest (and the only one to survive the Nazi destruction in 1944), although the houses at either end were blown up by the Germans. Built on the site of a Roman crossing, the first stone version was swept away in a flood in 1333 and rebuilt in 1345 as it is now, with rows of shops lining both sides (the backs of which, supported on brackets, overhang the Arno). They were occupied by butchers until Cosimo I assigned them to gold- and silversmiths in the late 16th century. See also *Quintessential Florence,* DIVERSIONS.

Palazzo Pitti e Galleria Palatina (Pitti Palace and Palatine Gallery) – Across the Arno from the *Uffizi,* and a few blocks from the riverbank, is a rugged, austere, 15th-century palace built for Lucia Pitti by Brunelleschi. It was bought by Cosimo I and his wife, Eleonora of Toledo, in 1550, and expanded by Ammannati, becoming the seat of the Medici grand dukes and later of the Savoy royal family until 1871. Three dynasties — Medici, Lorraine, and Savoy — resided in this palace, which now houses several museums. The *Galleria Palatina,* upstairs on the first floor and one of the must-sees, is devoted to 16th- and 17th-century art — works by Raphael, Rubens, Murillo, Andrea del Sarto, Fra Filippo Lippi, Titian, Veronese, and Tintoretto, to name a few (there are over 650) — arranged in no apparent order. The gallery, in fact, still resembles a sumptuous apartment in a palace more than it does a museum. Priceless masterpieces seem to hang at random in elaborately decorated rooms filled with tapestries, frescoes, and gilded stuccoes. The *Appartamenti Monumentali* (Royal Apartments), in another wing of the same floor and once inhabited in turn by the Medici, Lorraine, and Savoy families, reopened in 1989 after 2 years of restoration work.

The *Museo degli Argenti* (Silver Museum), occupying 16 rooms on the ground floor and another must-see, is filled not only with silverware but also with gold, jewels, cameos, Oriental tapestries, furniture, crystal, and ivory of the Medicis. Still another museum, the *Galleria d'Arte Moderna,* on the second floor, houses mainly 19th-century Tuscan works, including a lovely selection from the Macchiaioli School. There is also a *Coach and Carriage Museum* (temporarily closed). An entrance on the left side of the palace leads to the Boboli Gardens, which extend for acres and are open until dusk. A delightful example of a 16th-century Italian garden, they were laid out for Eleonora of Toledo and are studded with cypress trees, unusual statuary, grottoes, and fountains — as well as two museums. The *Galleria del Costume* (Costume Gallery) in the Palazzina della Meridiana, contains an impressive collection of 18th- to 20th-century costumes. Attention is paid to every detail, with careful documentation and an exceptional sense of display and lighting. The *Museo delle Porcellane* (Porcelain Museum), at the top of the Boboli Gardens, consists of three rooms filled with Austrian, French, German, and Italian porcelain objects.

The *Palatine Gallery* (phone: 210323), the *Gallery of Modern Art* (phone: 287096), the *Silver Museum* (phone: 212557), and the *Costume Gallery* (phone: 287096) are open Mondays through Saturdays from 9 AM to 2 PM; Sundays from 9 AM to 1 PM. One admission charge covers the *Palatine Gallery,* the *Silver Museum,* and the Royal Apartments. The *Gallery of Modern Art* charges a separate admission. No admission charge to the Boboli Gardens (phone: 213440), *Porcelain Museum,* and *Costume Gallery.* Piazza Pitti (phone: 213440).

Giardini di Boboli (Boboli Gardens) – Designed in 1550 by Il Tribolo (Niccolò Pericolo) for the Medicis when they moved into the Pitti Palace, these exquisite gardens encompass lanes, fountains, statuary, an amphitheater, a pond with enormous goldfish, a tiny garden with lemon trees, and even a grotto with a statue of Venus by Giambologna for cool summer rendezvous. In the afternoon, the field near the Porta Romana entrance is full of children at play. Piazza Pitti (phone: 213440).

Chiesa di Santo Spirito (Church of the Holy Spirit) – This is one of Brunelleschi's last works, and a gem, though you'll notice the church's stark façade is very different from its interior. Brunelleschi died before he could complete what is generally acknowledged as one of the finest examples of a Renaissance church, so a team of architects finished it. There are 2 dozen chapels inside, with masterpieces by Donatello, Ghirlandaio, Filippino Lippi, Sansovino, and others. Piazza Santo Spirito itself is a charming quiet spot, surrounded by 16th-century buildings — the perfect place to escape from the bustle on the other side of the Arno. Open daily from 8:30 AM to noon and 3:30 to 6:30 PM. Piazza Santo Spirito (phone: 210030).

Palazzo del Bargello e Museo Nazionale (Bargello Palace and National Museum) – The *Bargello* is to sculpture what the *Uffizi* is to painting, yet for some reason it is visited far less frequently by tourists. Its most noteworthy piece just might be Florence's second-most famous *David* — the bronze by Donatello — sculpted in 1530. The building, the Palazzo del Podestà, is one of the finest and best-preserved examples of Florence's 13th- and 14th-century medieval architecture. Inside, all of the schools of Florentine and Tuscan sculpture are represented: Donatello, Verrocchio, Cellini, Michelangelo, the Della Robbias, and others. Open Tuesdays through Saturdays from 9 AM to 12:30 PM; Sundays from 9 AM to 1:30 PM. Admission charge. 4 Via del Proconsolo (phone: 210801).

Santa Croce (Church of the Holy Cross) – Italy's largest and best-known Franciscan church, Santa Croce was begun late in the 13th century and was enriched over the centuries with numerous works of art, as well as tombs of many famous Italians, including Michelangelo, Machiavelli, Rossini, and Galileo (there is a funeral monument to Dante here, but he is buried in Ravenna). Under Santa Croce are the remains of an earlier chapel founded by St. Francis of Assisi in 1228. The church is particularly noteworthy for a wooden crucifix by Donatello, for chapels with frescoes by Taddeo and Agnolo Gaddi, and above all for the fresco cycles by Giotto in the Bardi and Peruzzi chapels.

Go outside the church and turn left to visit the 14th-century cloister and the 15th-century Pazzi Chapel, a Renaissance gem by Brunelleschi, designed at the height of his career. During the 1966 flood, the waters reached the top of the cloister's arches and damage here was particularly severe. Piazza Santa Croce (phone: 244619). For more information about the church and the surrounding area, see *Walk 3: Santa Croce* in DIRECTIONS.

Galleria dell'Accademia (Academy of Fine Arts Gallery) – Michelangelo's original *David* was brought here from the Piazza della Signoria (where one of many first-rate copies has taken its place) in 1873. Since then, millions of visitors have come just to see this monumental sculpture (about a million a year now — one of whom smashed a toe on *David*'s left foot, last fall) carved from a single block of Carrara marble and, in the same room, the four unfinished *Slaves* that Michelangelo meant to adorn Pope Julius II's unrealized tomb for St. Peter's in Rome. In the summer, lines form down the street and the doors often close when it gets too crowded.

Unfortunately, many visitors ignore the rich collection of Florentine paintings — from 13th-century primitives to 16th-century Mannerists — and the five rooms opened in 1985 to display works that had never before been shown to the public. These include 14th- and 15th-century paintings and an extraordinary collection of Russian icons brought to Florence by the Lorraines when they succeeded the Medicis during the first half of the 18th century. Open Tuesdays through Saturdays from 9 AM to 2 PM; Sundays and holidays to 1 PM. Admission charge. 60 Via Ricasoli (phone: 214375).

Museo di San Marco (Museum of St. Mark) – Vasari described this monastery as a perfect example of monastic architecture. It was built in the 15th century by the Medici architect Michelozzo (who actually rebuilt a more ancient Dominican monastery) and its walls — as well as more than 40 monks' cells — were frescoed by Fra Angelico (and his assistants), who lived here as a monk from 1438 to 1445. Now a Fra Angelico museum, it contains panel paintings brought from various churches and galleries, in addition to the painter's wonderful *Crucifixion* (in the chapter house across the cloister) and his exquisite *Annunciation* (at the top of the stairs leading to the dormitory). In addition to the cells decorated by Fra Angelico, see the one used by the reforming martyr Savonarola. There also are paintings by Fra Bartolomeo (see his portrait of Savonarola), Ghirlandaio, Paolo Uccello, and others. Open Tuesdays through Saturdays from 9 AM to 2 PM; Sundays to 1 PM. Admission charge. 1 Piazza San Marco (phone: 210741).

Piazza della Santissima Annunziata (Square of the Most Holy Annunciation) – This square best preserves the essence of the Florentine Renaissance spirit. It has porticoes on three sides, a 16th-century palace (by Ammannati) on the fourth, plus an early-17th-century equestrian statue of Ferdinando I de' Medici by Giambologna in the middle. Most interesting is the portico on the east side, that of the Ospedale degli Innocenti (Hospital of the Innocents), built in the early 15th century by Brunelleschi as a home for orphans and abandoned children, one of Florence's oldest charity institutions and the world's first foundling hospital. Except for the two imitations at either end, the ceramic tondos of swaddled babies are by Andrea della Robbia. Inside, the *Galleria dello Spedale degli Innocenti* (closed Wednesdays; admission charge) contains works by Ghirlandaio and others.

Chiesa della Santissima Annunziata (Church of the Most Holy Annunciation), on the north side of the square, is much loved by Florentine brides, who traditionally leave their bouquets at one of its altars after the wedding ceremony. The church was founded in the 13th century, but rebuilt in the 15th century by Michelozzo. The left door of the church portico leads into the Chiostro dei Morti (Cloister of the Dead), which contains the *Madonna del Sacco,* a famous fresco by Andrea del Sarto. The middle door leads into the church via the Chiostrino dei Voti (Little Cloister of the Vows), with frescoes by several famous artists of the 16th century, including Del Sarto, Pontormo, and Rosso Fiorentino. Of the numerous artworks in the church itself, Andrea del Castagno's fresco of the Trinity, over the altar of the second chapel on the left, is one of the most prized.

Chiesa di San Lorenzo (Church of St. Lawrence) – This 15th-century Renaissance building was designed by Brunelleschi as the Medici parish church. A later façade, by Michelangelo, was never completed. Make your way to the Sagrestia Vecchia (Old Sacristy), the earliest part of the church and one of Brunelleschi's most notable early creations, remarkable for the purity and harmony of the overall conception. It contains, besides decorations by Donatello, the tombs of several Medicis, including Giovanni di Bicci. Be sure to go outside and through a doorway to the left of the façade to the Chiostro di San Lorenzo and to the Biblioteca Laurenziana (Laurentian Library; closed Sundays and holidays), a Michelangelo masterpiece designed to hold the Medici collection of manuscripts — 10,000 precious volumes. Piazza San Lorenzo (phone: 216634).

Mercato di San Lorenzo – This colorful open-air market has stalls where everything — from a special wooden rolling pin for making ravioli to a handmade mohair sweater — is sold. And because this is Florence, the leather goods can be a good buy, especially belts, jackets, and handbags. There also is a 2-story covered building with a lovely glass dome, where all kinds of food products are on sale, including local meat, cheese, and produce, and fresh eggs and homemade wine brought in by peasant farmers from the Tuscan countryside. The indoor market is closed Sundays. Piazza San Lorenzo.

Cappelle Medicee (Medici Chapels) – Once part of San Lorenzo, these famous Medici funerary chapels now have a separate entrance. The first of the chapels, the Cappella dei Principi (Chapel of the Princes), where Cosimo I and the other grand dukes of Tuscany lie, is the later of the two, and it is a family burial vault supreme: The elaborate baroque interior took all of the 17th and 18th centuries to complete. Note the fine examples of Florentine mosaic, fine inlay done with semi-precious stones. But the real attraction here is the other chapel, the Sagrestia Nuova (New Sacristy), a companion piece to the Sagrestia Vecchia (see above). This magnificent show is by Michelangelo, who was commissioned by Cardinal Giulio de' Medici (later Pope Clement VII) and Pope Leo X (another Medici) to design both the interior — Michelangelo's first architectural job — and the statuary as a fitting resting place for members of their family. Michelangelo worked on it from 1521 to 1533 and left two of the projected tombs incomplete, but those he finished — the tomb of Lorenzo II, Duke of Urbino, with the figures of Dawn and Dusk, and the tomb of Giuliano, Duke of Nemours, with the figures of Night and Day, are extraordinary. (Lorenzo il Magnifico and his brother Giuliano, the latter murdered in the Duomo, are buried in the tomb opposite the altar, which bears a splendid *Madonna with Child* by Michelangelo.)

The Sagrestia Nuova was being restored at press time as part of the 500th anniversary celebration of Il Magnifico's death. Don't miss the feeling of this room as a whole; with its square plan and imposing dome (especially its unusual trapezoidal windows), one almost has a sensation of soaring upward! Open Tuesdays through Saturdays from 9

AM to 2 PM; Sundays to 1 PM. Admission charge. Piazza Madonna degli Aldobrandini (phone: 213206).

Palazzo Medici-Riccardi (Medici-Riccardi Palace) – Not far from San Lorenzo is the palace where the Medici family lived until 1540, when they moved to the Palazzo Vecchio. When Cosimo the Elder decided to build a mansion for the family, he first asked Brunelleschi to design it, but rejected the architect's plans as too luxurious and likely to create excessive envy. So Michelozzo was the master responsible for what was to be the first authentic Renaissance mansion — as well as a barometer of the proper lifestyle for a Florentine banker. Be sure to visit the tiny chapel to see Benozzo Gozzoli's wonderful fresco of the Three Kings on their way to Bethlehem. At press time, the palazzo was being restored for the Medici anniversary celebration. Open daily except Wednesdays from 9 AM to noon and from 3 to 5 PM; Sundays from 9 AM to noon. Admission charge. 1 Via Cavour (phone: 217601).

Santa Maria Novella – Designed by two Dominican monks in the late 13th century and largely completed by the mid-14th century (except for the façade, which was designed by Leon Battista Alberti and finished in the late 15th century), this church figures in Boccaccio's *Decameron* as the place where his protagonists discuss the plague of 1348, the Black Death. Michelangelo, at the age of 13, was sent here to study painting under Ghirlandaio, whose frescoes adorn the otherwise gloomy interior, as do others by Masaccio, Filippino Lippi, and followers of Giotto. See the Gondi and Strozzi chapels and the great Chiostro Verde (Green Cloister), so called for the predominance of green in the decoration by Paolo Uccello and his school. Piazza Santa Maria Novella (phone: 282187). For more information about the church and the piazza, see *Walk 2: Santa Maria Novella* in DIRECTIONS.

Orsanmichele – This solid, square, 14th-century structure once housed wheat for emergency use on its upper floors, while the ground floor was a church. The whole was adopted by the city's artisans and guilds and used as an oratory — an unusual combination. Outside, the 14 statues in the niches representing patron saints of the guilds were sculpted by the best Florentine artists of the 14th to 16th centuries. The interior is dominated by a huge 14th-century tabernacle of colored marble by Andrea Orcagna. On July 26, *St. Anne's Day,* the building is decorated with flags of the guilds to commemorate the expulsion of the tyrannical Duke of Athens from Florence on July 26, 1343. Via dei Calzaiuoli.

Sinagoga (Synagogue) – Built in the late 19th century by the Florentine Jewish community in the Sephardic-Moorish style, this is one of the world's most beautiful temples. It was severely damaged during the 1966 floods, but was lovingly and accurately restored. Visits are permitted from 9 AM until 6 PM. Ring the bell at the smaller of the two gates, and an English-speaking woman will take you around. 4 Via Farini (phone: 284715).

Mercato Nuovo (Straw Market) – This covered market near the Piazza della Signoria dates from the 16th century. It holds an amazing assortment of handbags, sun hats, and placemats in traditional Florentine straw and raffia, wonderful embroidery work, typical gilt-pattern wooden articles, and other souvenirs, although the focus in recent years has been more on goods from African countries. The symbol of the market is the *Porcellino,* an imposing and slightly daunting bronze statue of a wild boar. Rub its shiny nose and toss a coin into the fountain to ensure a return visit. Open daily. Piazza del Mercato Nuovo.

ENVIRONS

San Miniato al Monte – Near Piazzale Michelangelo, this lovely church (beloved by the Florentines) dominates the hill of the same name and looks out over a broad panorama of Florence and the surrounding hills — a romantic setting that makes it a particular favorite for weddings. One of the best examples of Tuscan Romanesque architecture and design in the city, it was built from the 11th to the 13th century on the spot where St. Miniato, martyred in the 3rd century, is reputed to have placed his severed head after carrying it up from Florence. The façade is in the typical green-and-white marble of the Florentine Romanesque style, as is the pulpit inside, and the geometric patterns on the inlaid floor are Oriental. Art treasures include Michelozzo's Crucifix Chapel, with terra cotta decorations by Luca della Robbia; Spinello Aretino's frescoes in the sacristy; and the Chapel of the Cardinal of Portugal, a Renaissance addition that contains works by Baldovinetti, Antonio and Piero del Pollaiolo, and Luca della Robbia. The church was being restored as we went to press, in preparation for the festivities that will mark the 500th anniversary of the death of Lorenzo de' Medici. The monks of San Miniato repeat vespers in Gregorian chants every day from 4:45 to 5:30 PM. Tourists are welcome if they plan to attend the entire mass (before the service, a monk asks visitors to leave if their time is short). By all means stop by the adjoining cemetery, a wonderful collection of Italian funerary art (the English painter Henry Savage Landor and Carlo Lorenzini, a.k.a. Carlo Collodi, author of *Pinocchio,* are buried here). The fortifications surrounding the church were designed by Michelangelo against the imperial troops of Charles V. Viale Galileo (phone: 2342731). For more information about the church and the surrounding area, see *Walk 5: San Miniato and Piazzale Michelangelo* in DIRECTIONS.

Forte Belvedere – A 15-minute walk or a short bus ride from the center of Florence will take you to this imposing 16th-century fort — built by the famous Florentine architect Buontalenti — which forms part of the Old City walls. There are splendid views of the city below and the fortress itself often has exhibitions of painting and sculpture inside. In summer, the grounds become a makeshift open-air movie theater. It's a pleasant walk either up through the Boboli Gardens or up the steep Costa San Giorgio from the Ponte Vecchio. Alternatively, take bus Nos. 12 or 13 from the center. Open daily from 9 AM to 8 PM. Admission charge. Costa San Giorgio (phone: 2342822).

Fiesole – This beautiful village, on a hill overlooking Florence and the Arno, was an ancient Etruscan settlement and, later, a Roman city. The Duomo, begun in the 11th century and radically restored in the 19th, is on the main square, Piazza Mino da Fiesole, and just off the square is the *Teatro Romano,* built about 80 BC, where classical plays are sometimes performed, especially during the summer festival (*L'Estate Fiesolana*), which is devoted primarily to music.

Take the picturesque Via San Francesco leading out of the square and walk up to the Church of St. Francis, passing the public gardens along the way and stopping at the terrace to enjoy the splendid view of Florence. The church, built during the 14th and 15th centuries, contains some very charming cloisters, especially the tiny Choistrino di San Bernardino. Nearby is the monastery, with an altarpiece by Fra Angelico, and monks' cells, which are furnished as they were in the 15th century. Badia Fiesolana, a 15th-century abbey, is also located in the vicinity.

Gelato fans can make a pilgrimage to *Villani* (8 Via S. Domenico) for a cup of custard-like *crema Villani.* Fiesole's tourist office is at 37 Piazza Mino (phone: 598720). Fiesole is 5 miles (8 km) north of Florence and can be reached by bus No. 7 from the railway station, Santa Maria Novella, or Piazza San Marco (be careful, as this bus is a notorious venue for pickpockets).

Arcetri and Pian dei Giullari – Just 5 minutes from the city of Florence, these outlying neighborhoods look as if they were centuries old. Ancient olive trees peek out over villa walls, and the entire area resembles a Renaissance painting. Take a cab or bus No. 38 from Porta Romana past elegant villas and gentrified farmhouses, and disembark at the last stop. From here you can walk to the early 14th-century country church of Santa Margherita a Montici, located on the street of the same name. In the center of this tiny village is the Villa Il Gioiello (42 Via Pian dei Guillari), where Galileo spent the last years of his life after he was exiled from Florence. Torre del Gallo (at the intersection of Via Pian dei Guillari and Via Torre del Gallo) is a reconstruction of a medieval castle.

Certosa di Galluzzo – Southwest of downtown is this monastery 7 miles (11 km) away, where the monks have been growing herbs (and making liqueurs from them) for centuries. Visitors can tour this splendid working facility, set in a magnificent countryside of rolling Tuscan hills, and buy some of their products to take home. There also is a small museum with some beautiful frescoes, most notably those by Pontormo, from the 16th century. The No. 37 bus from the center goes directly to the *certosa* (monastery). By car, it is a 15-minute trip. Follow the signs for Galluzzo, and you'll see the monastery loom in front of you. Open daily except Mondays from 9 AM to noon and 3 to 5 PM; admission charge. Galluzzo (phone: 204-9226).

Casa di Machiavelli – In the small village of Sant'Andrea in Percussina, 12 miles (20 km) and a half-hour drive from the city, is this house (known as Albergaccio) where Niccolò Machiavelli lived after being exiled from Florence by the Medicis. He wrote his masterpiece *Il Principe* (The Prince) here. The house is furnished as it was when Machiavelli was in residence. Open daily from 9 AM to 12:30 PM and 3:30 to 6 PM. Admission charge. Across the road (you can't miss it) is a small trattoria where the writer apparently was wont to repair for a jug of wine between chapters. It still serves an excellent dish of Tuscan beans and very good peasant bread. A private bus company, *Sita* (phone: 48365 weekdays, 211487 weekends), runs from Piazza Santa Maria Novella to the village; by car, take SS2 heading toward Siena and turn off at San Casciano Val di Pesa. The village is signposted from there. Sant'Andrea in Percussina (no phone).

■**EXTRA SPECIAL:** Scattered about the Florentine countryside are a number of stately villas of the historic aristocracy of Florence, three of which are associated with the Medici family. For more information see *Drive 1: The Medici Villas* in DIRECTIONS. On the road to Sesto Fiorentino, about 5 miles (8 km) north of the city, are the 16th-century Villa della Petraia (originally a castle of the Brunelleschi family, rebuilt in 1575 for a Medici cardinal by Buontalenti) and, just down the hill, the 15th-century Villa di Castello, which was taken over by the Medicis in 1477. Both have lovely gardens and fountains by Il Tribolo.

The Villa Medici at Poggio a Caiano, at the foot of Monte Albano, about 10 miles (16 km) northwest of Florence, was rebuilt for Lorenzo the Magnificent by Giuliano da Sangallo from 1480 to 1485. The gardens of all three villas usually are open daily except Mondays; the interiors of the Petraia and Poggio a Caiano villas also may be visited (but hours and policies change; call 451208 for information regarding the former, 877012 for the latter). *Agriturist* runs organized excursions to the villas, as well as to country estates in the neighboring wine growing region. For information, contact *Agriturist,* 3 Piazza San Firenze (phone: 287838).

LOCAL SOURCES AND RESOURCES

TOURIST INFORMATION: The Ente Provinciale per il Turismo (16 Via Alessandro Manzoni; phone: 247-8141/2/3/4/5) will provide general information, brochures, and maps of the city and the surrounding area. It is open Mondays through Saturdays from 8:30 AM to 1:30 PM. There's also a tourist information booth just outside the train station as well as an office at 15 Via Tornabuoni (phone: 217459), open Mondays through Saturdays from 9 AM to 1 PM. For information on Tuscany, contact the Regional Tourist Office (26 Via di Novoli; phone: 438-2111). Helpful for younger travelers is the *Student Travel Service (STS;* 18r Via Zannetti; phone: 268396 or 292067).

The US Consulate is at 38 Lungarno Amerigo Vespucci (phone: 298276).

Numerous maps and pocket-size guidebooks to Florence, such as the *Storti Guides,* are published in Italy and are available at newsstands throughout the city. Excellent guides in English available in bookstores are by Luciano Berti and by Rolando and Piero Fusi. Background reading before your trip might include Mary McCarthy's classic *The Stones of Florence* (Harcourt Brace Jovanovich; $7.95), a discussion of the history and character of the city as seen through its art, and Christopher Hibbert's *The House of Medici: Its Rise and Fall* (Morrow; $12.95), a study of the city's most influential family.

Local Coverage – Check the brochure *Florence Concierge Information,* available at most hotels, or pick up a copy of *Florence Today* at the tourist information office. *Vista* and *Q.B.* are two English-language magazines published every 3 months that also list activities of interest to visitors. They are found at major hotels and tourist offices. Florence's daily newspaper is *La Nazione.* A national newspaper, *La Repubblica,* has a section on Florence in which there is a daily calendar of events in English.

 TELEPHONE: The city code for Florence is 55. When calling from within Italy, dial 055 before the local number.

The procedure for calling the US from Italy is as follows: dial 00 (the international access code) + 1 (the US country code) + the area code + the local number. For instance, to call New York from Florence, dial 00 + 1 + 212 + the local number. For calling from one Italian city to another, simply dial 0 + the city code + the local number; and for calls within the same city code coverage area, simply dial the local number.

Italcable, Italy's major international phone company, introduced a new feature, Country Direct Service, in 1989. By dialing 172-1011 from any telephone in Florence, Rome, Naples, or Milan, you can phone the US direct, either by calling collect or by using your credit card. An American operator will answer. (Note that as we went to press, *Italcable* was in the process of extending this service to include other cities throughout Italy.)

Pay telephones in Florence can be found in cafés and restaurants (look for the sign outside — a yellow disk with the outline of a telephone or a receiver in black) and, less commonly, in booths on the street. (All too often, however, these are out of order — if you're lucky, a *guasto* sign will warn you.) There are two kinds of pay phones: The old-fashioned kind works with a *gettone* (token) only, which can be bought for 200 lire from a bar or restaurant cashier and at newsstands; newer phones function with *gettoni,* a 200-lire coin, or two 100-lire coins. To use a *gettone,* place it in the slot at the top of the phone. When your party answers — and *not* before — push the button at the top of the phone, causing the token to drop (otherwise the answering party will not be able to hear you). If your party doesn't answer, hang up and simply lift the unused *gettone* out of the slot. In newer phones using either *gettoni* or coins, the coins or *gettoni* drop automatically when you put them in, as in US phones; if your party doesn't answer, you have to press the return button (sometimes repeatedly) to get them back.

Although the majority of Italian pay phones take tokens or coins, phones that take specially designated phone cards are increasingly common, particularly in metropolitan areas and at major tourist destinations. These telephone cards have been instigated to cut down on vandalism, as well as to free callers from the necessity of carrying around a pocketful of change, and are sold in various lire denominations. The units per card, like message units in US phone parlance, are a combination of time and distance. To use such a card, insert it into a slot in the phone and dial the number you wish to reach. A display gradually will count down the value that remains on your card. When you run out of units on the card, you can insert another. In Italy, these phone cards are available from any SIP telephone center.

Although you can use a telephone company credit card number on any phone, pay phones that take major credit cards are increasingly common worldwide, particularly in transportation and tourism centers. Also now available is the "affinity card," a combined telephone calling card/bank credit card that can be used for domestic and international calls. Cards of this type include the following:

AT&T/Universal (phone: 800-662-7759). Cardholders can charge calls to the US from overseas.

Executive Telecard International (phone: 800-950-3800). Cardholders can charge calls to the US from overseas, as well as between most European countries.

Sprint Visa (phone: 800-446-7625). Cardholders can charge calls to the US from overseas.

Similarly, *MCI VisaPhone* (phone: 800-866-0099) can add phone card privileges to the services available through your existing Visa card. This service allows you to use your Visa account number, plus an additional code, to charge calls on any touch-tone phone in the US and Europe.

 GETTING AROUND: Most visitors find Florence one of the easiest of European cities to navigate. Although it is fairly large, the scale is rather intimate, and it's easy to get just about anywhere on foot. Almost all the major sites are on the north side, or right bank, of the river, but most of those on the Oltrarno side ("beyond the Arno") are within easy walking distance of the center. Part of the city's center is closed to traffic, except for those with permits, making it quite pleasant for pedestrians. Visitors sometimes are confused by the numbers on Florentine buildings, for houses are numbered according to a double system. Black (*nero*) numbers indicate dwellings, while red (*rosso*) numbers — indicated by an "r" after the number in street addresses — are commercial buildings (shops and such). The black and the red have little relationship to each other, so you may find a black 68 next to a red 5.

Bicycles, Mopeds, and Motorbikes – *Ciao & Basta* (33 Via Bardi; phone: 2342726) rents bicycles; *Bici-Città* (phone: 499319 or 296335) will furnish two free bikes for 2 hours upon presentation of a *SCAF* car park coupon, and has three locations: Fortezza da Basso, Piazza Pitti, and Stazione Centrale on Via Alamanni (by the stairway). Motorbikes are available from *Program* (135r Borgo Ognissanti; phone: 282916), *Motorent* (9r Via San Zanobi; phone: 490113), and *Sabra* (8 Via Artisti; phone: 576256 or 579609), which also rents mopeds. Ride carefully!

Buses – *ATAF* is the city bus company, running about 40 city and suburban routes. Bus routes are listed in the yellow pages of the telephone directory. Tickets — which should be purchased before boarding — can be bought at tobacco counters, in bars, and at some newsstands; they cost about $1 and can be used more than once, within a 1½-hour time limit. Children under 1 meter (39 inches) tall ride free. As there are no ticket collectors (only automatic stamping machines), many passengers do not buy tickets, but anybody caught without one by the occasional controller is fined on the spot. The back door of the bus is for boarding, the middle for disembarking; the front door is only for season ticket holders. At rush hour, buses are impossibly crowded and it's sometimes difficult to get off at the desired stop. Walking often is faster and more enjoyable, but pedestrians are cautioned to watch out for buses and taxis in special lanes permitting them to travel the wrong way on many one-way streets.

Car Rental – *Avis* (128r Borgo Ognissanti; phone: 289010 or 213629); *Europcar* (53

determined at press time) will re-create the workshops of some of the major artists who worked during Il Magnifico's lifetime, including Botticelli, Lippi, Ghirlandaio, and Perugino. For a detailed program of the festivities, contact the tourist office.

MUSEUMS: Since museums are possibly the city's top attraction, quite a few have already been described under *Special Places.* A few more of the 70 or so museums in the city are listed here, along with additional churches and palaces whose artwork makes them, in effect, museums, too. As hours may vary, contact the tourist information office (phone: 217459) or the Superintendent of Museums and Galleries (phone: 218341) for information about hours.

Badia Fiorentina – The church of a former Benedictine abbey *(badia)*, with a part-Romanesque, part-Gothic campanile, it was founded in the 10th century, enlarged in the 13th, and rebuilt in the 17th. Opposite the *Bargello.* Via del Proconsolo (no phone).

Biblioteca Laurenziana (Laurentian Library) – Michelangelo designed the building, interiors, bookstands, and chairs for this spectacular library built for Cosimo I. 9 Piazza San Lorenzo (phone: 210760).

Biblioteca Riccardiana (Riccardi Library) – Housed in a wing of the Medici-Riccardi Palace, this library specializes in manuscripts, miniature books, and antique printed editions. 10 Via dei Ginori (phone: 212586).

Casa Buonarroti – The small house Michelangelo bought for his next of kin, containing some of the master's early works, as well as works done in his honor by some of the foremost artists of the 16th and 17th centuries. Open Tuesdays through Saturdays from 9:30 AM to 1:30 PM, Sundays from 9:30 AM to 12:30 PM. Admission charge. 70 Via Ghibellina (phone: 241752).

Casa di Dante – A small museum in what is believed to have been Dante's house, it documents his life, times, and work. Open from 9:30 AM to 12:30 PM and 3:30 to 6:30 PM, Sundays from 9:30 AM to 12:30 PM. Closed Wednesdays. No admission charge. 1 Via Santa Margherita (phone: 283343).

Casa Guidi – Robert and Elizabeth Barrett Browning lived on the first floor of this 15th-century palazzo at the corner of the Pitti Palace from shortly after their secret marriage in 1846 until Elizabeth's death in 1861. Now called the *Browning Institute,* it is an unfinished museum and a memorial to both poets. It's best to ask the tourist office about when the museum is open. Admission charge. 8 Piazza San Felice (no phone).

Cenacolo di Sant'Apollonia – The refectory of a former convent, containing Andrea del Castagno's remarkable fresco of the Last Supper (ca. 1450). Closed Mondays. Admission charge. 1 Via XXVII Aprile (phone: 287074).

Gipsoteca Dell'Instituto Statale d'Arte (Art School Plaster Cast Gallery) – More than 3,000 plaster casts of mostly Florentine works, including busts, bas-reliefs, and statues by artists such as Michelangelo and Della Robbia, are showcased here. 9 Piazzale di Porta Romana (phone: 220521).

Museo di Antropologia ed Etnologia (Museum of Anthropology and Ethnology) – First of its genre in Italy, continually enlarged, now with more than 30 rooms and a vast collection divided by race, continent, and culture. Open Thursdays, Fridays, and Saturdays from 9 AM to 1 PM and the third Sunday of the month (except July through September). Admission charge. 12 Via del Proconsolo (phone: 296449).

Museo Archeologico (Archaeological Museum) – This fascinating museum contains a permanent jewelery exhibit of gold and gems from the Medicis. There also is an outstanding collection of Etruscan, Greek, and Roman art housed in six halls (damaged during the 1966 flood) that were reopened after a lengthy, costly restoration. A topographical section features objects from ancient Etruria; and an Egyptian area has mummies, statues, and a well-preserved chariot found in Thebes. Open Tuesdays through Saturdays from 9 AM to 2 PM, Sundays from 9 AM to 1 PM. Admission charge. 38 Via Colonna (phone: 247-8641).

Museo Archeologico di Fiesole – A fine selection of treasures from both the Etruscan and Roman periods of Fiesolan history, including an especially rich collection of Etruscan pottery. The museum is part of a complex that also has a Roman theater — used for concerts in the summer — and the remains of an Etruscan temple. Open daily from 9 AM to 7 PM. Admission charge. Piazza Mino, Fiesole (phone: 59477).

Museo Bardini – An eclectic collection of sculpture, tapestries, bronzes, furniture, and paintings. Open from 9 AM to 2 PM, Sundays from 9 AM to 1 PM. Closed Wednesdays. Admission charge. 1 Piazza dei Mozzi (phone: 2342427).

Museo Firenze Com'Era (Florence "As It Was" Museum) – Collection of prints, maps, paintings, documents, and photos illustrating aspects of the city from the 15th century to the present. There also is a permanent exhibition of works by the 20th-century artist Ottone Rosai. Open from 9 AM to 2 PM, Sundays from 9 AM to 1 PM. Closed Thursdays. Admission charge. 24 Via dell'Oriuolo (phone: 217305).

Museo della Fondazione Horne (Horne Museum) – A jewel of a museum — paintings, drawings, sculptures, furniture, ceramics, coins, and unusual old household utensils, the collection of an Englishman, Herbert Percy Horne, bequeathed to the city in 1916 and set up in his 15th-century *palazzetto.* Open from 9 AM to 1 PM. Closed Sundays and holidays. Admission charge. 6 Via dei Benci (phone: 244661).

Museo Marini – Housed in the exquisitely remodeled, 9th-century Church of San Panrazio, this museum is devoted to the works of Marino Marini, considered to be one of the finest sculptors of the 20th century. Open 10 AM to 6 PM; closed Tuesdays. Piazza San Pancrazio (phone: 219432).

Museo Primo Conti – Oil paintings, drawings, watercolors, prints, and sketches by Primo Conti, an artist of the avant-garde movement in the early 1900s. 18 Via G. Dupre (phone: 597095).

Museo Stibbert – Vast collection (about 50,000 pieces) of art objects, antiques, arms from all over the world, and other curiosities left by the English collector Stibbert, with his villa and gardens. Open from 9 AM to 1 PM, Sundays from 9 AM to 12:30 PM. Closed Thursdays. Admission charge. 26 Via Federico Stibbert (phone: 486049).

Museo di Storia delle Fotografia (History of Photography Museum) – An impressive collection of 19th-century daguerreotypes and photographs housed in a 15th-century palace designed by Alberti. Open mornings only from 10 AM to 7 PM. Closed Mondays. Admission charge. 16 Via delle Vigna Nuova (phone: 213370).

Museo di Storia Naturale (Museum of Natural History) – Also known as "La Specola," it has a weird but interesting collection of wax anatomical models from the late 18th century. There also is an exhibit of waxed and stuffed animals. Open daily except Sundays from 9 AM to noon; second Sunday of the month from 9:30 AM to 12:30 PM. No admission charge. 17 Via Romana (phone: 222451).

Museo di Storia della Scienza (Museum of the History of Science) – Scientific instruments, including Galileo's telescopes, and odd items documenting the development of modern science from the Renaissance to the 20th century. Open Tuesdays, Thursdays, and Saturdays from 9:30 AM to 1 PM; Mondays, Wednesdays, and Fridays from 9:30 AM to 1 PM and from 2 to 5 PM. Admission charge. 1 Piazza de' Giudici (phone: 293493).

Ognissanti (All Saints' Church) – Built in the 13th century and rebuilt in the 17th, it contains extraordinary frescoes by Ghirlandaio and Botticelli and is the burial place of the latter as well as of the family of Amerigo Vespucci. 42 Piazza d'Ognissanti (phone: 239870).

Palazzo Davanzati – A well-preserved 14th-century palace with 15th-century furniture, tapestries, and ceramics, also known as the *Museo della Casa Fiorentina Antica*

(Florentine House Museum). Open from 9 AM to 1 PM. Closed Saturdays. Admission charge. 13 Via Porta Rossa (phone: 216518).

Palazzo Strozzi – This masterpiece of Renaissance architecture is the scene of a biennial international antiques show, held in the fall (in odd-number years). Open from 9:30 AM to 1 PM and 3 to 7 PM. Closed Mondays. Admission charge. Piazza Strozzi (phone: 215990).

Santa Maria del Carmine – Dating from the second half of the 13th century, this Carmelite church was mostly destroyed in a fire in 1771, but the Corsini and Brancacci chapels were spared. The latter, reopened after 10 years of restoration, contains the recently restored Masaccio frescoes that inspired Renaissance painters from Fra Angelico to Raphael. Piazza del Carmine.

Santa Trinita (Church of the Holy Trinity) – One of the oldest churches in Florence, built in the 11th century with a 16th-century façade. See the Ghirlandaio frescoes in the Sassetti Chapel — one shows the church with its original Romanesque façade. Piazza Santa Trinita.

Santi Apostoli (Church of the Holy Apostles) – Built in the 11th century, redecorated in the 15th and 16th centuries, and restored in the 1930s, it holds the flints said to have been brought back from Jerusalem during the Crusades and still used to light the Holy Fire in the Duomo for the *Scoppio del Carro* at *Easter* (see *Special Events*). Piazza del Limbo.

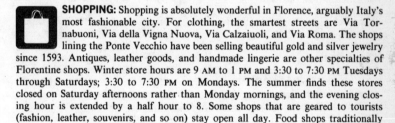 **SHOPPING:** Shopping is absolutely wonderful in Florence, arguably Italy's most fashionable city. For clothing, the smartest streets are Via Tornabuoni, Via della Vigna Nuova, Via Calzaiuoli, and Via Roma. The shops lining the Ponte Vecchio have been selling beautiful gold and silver jewelry since 1593. Antiques, leather goods, and handmade lingerie are other specialties of Florentine shops. Winter store hours are 9 AM to 1 PM and 3:30 to 7:30 PM Tuesdays through Saturdays; 3:30 to 7:30 PM on Mondays. The summer finds these stores closed on Saturday afternoons rather than Monday mornings, and the evening closing hour is extended by a half hour to 8. Some shops that are geared to tourists (fashion, leather, souvenirs, and so on) stay open all day. Food shops traditionally close on Wednesdays.

Those in search of designer clothing will not be disappointed in this fashion-conscious city. One of the largest selections of fine leather goods can be found at *Bottega Veneta* (3-4r Piazza Ognissanti; phone: 294265). At *Enrico Coveri* (35r Via della Vigna Nuova; phone: 284478) bright colors are the trademark. *Emilio Pucci Boutique* (6 Via dei Pucci; phone: 287622) continues to offer fashionable women's wear in vibrant hues. Casual clothing can be found at *Emporio Armani* (34r Via Pellicceria; phone: 212081), which features upscale, ready-to-wear by Giorgio Armani. At *Ferragamo* (12-16r Via Tornabuoni; phone: 292123) the offspring of famous shoemaker Salvatore Ferragamo produce the largest selection of wonderfully crafted shoes, leather goods, and clothing in Italy. Another name known the world over is *Gucci* (57-73-75r Via Tornabuoni; phone: 264011), for chic leather goods and men's and women's wear clothing. *Mario Buccellati* (71r Via Tornabuoni; phone: 296579) offers exceptional hand-crafted jewelry and silverware in traditional Florentine designs. *MaxMara* (890 Via Tornabuoni; phone: 214133 and 28r Via Brunelleschi; phone: 287761) offers both classic and contemporary togs in fine fabrics. Luxurious, classic, minimalist, and chic are the watchwords at *Prada* (26-28r Via Vacchereccia; phone: 213901), whose merchandise also includes handbags, shoes, and accessories. *Valentino* (47r Via della Vigna Nuova; phone: 293142) offers elegant women's wear.

After Dark Bookstore – Hard-to-find English books, comics, and magazines. 86r Via del Moro (phone: 294203).

Alex – The best in designer clothes for women — Gianni Versace, Yamamoto,

Byblos, Claude Montana, Basile, Thierry Mugler. 19r and 5r Via della Vigna Nuova (phone: 210446).

Alinari – Housed in Palazzo Ruccelai, this shop sells photographs of Italy from the turn of this century and photography books. 46-48r Via della Vigna Nuova (phone: 218975).

Alvar – Classics of modern design — van der Rohe, Breuer, Le Corbusier, Mackintosh, and more in this stylish showroom. 38 Via Cavour (phone: 2302265).

Antico Setificio Fiorentino – Fabulous fabrics, all handloomed. 97r Via della Vigna Nuova (phone: 282700).

A. Ugolini – Classic Italian men's and women's wear, including Brioni suits. 65-68r Via Calzaiuoli (phone: 214439).

Befani & Tai – Quality gold craftsmanship at good prices. 13r Via Vaccherreccia (phone: 287825).

Beltrami – A chain of elegant, expensive leatherwear shops: shoes, bags, jackets, pants, and other items. 31r, 44r, and 202r Via Calzaiuoli (phone: 212418); 1r Via dei Pecori (phone: 216321); 11r Via Calimala (phone: 212288); and 28 Via Tornabuoni (phone: 287779).

Benetton – Colorful, reasonably priced casualwear for the young at heart. 66-68r Via Por Santa Maria (phone: 287111) and 2r Via Calimala (phone: 214878), and other locations.

Bijoux Cascio – Moderately priced jewelry, particularly in gold; the designs are the shop's own. 32r Via Tornabuoni (phone: 284709) and other locations.

Bisconte – Natural hide leather bags, cases, and small leather goods — all stamped with designer Wanny di Filippo's trademark buffalo. 31r Via del Parione (phone: 25722).

BM – An English-language bookstore. 4r Borgo Ognissanti (phone: 294575).

Bojolo – Leather and canvas bags, luggage, and umbrellas and canes with a sporty look crowd this shop. 25r Via Rondinella (phone: 21155).

Cagliostro – A beautiful and original collection of jewelry that includes antique, baroque, Art Deco, and modern pieces. 5r Piazza San Giovanni (phone: 283862).

Cartier – Fantastic jewelry. 1 Piazza Santa Trinita (phone: 292347).

Casa de' Tessuti – *The* place to go to find wonderful Italian fabrics, including wool, silk, and linen. 20-24r Via de' Pecori (phone: 215961).

Cellerini – High-quality bags and suitcases made by a craftsman in a workshop above the store. 9 Via del Sole (phone: 282533).

Cirri – Lovely linen. 38-40r Via Por Santa Maria (phone: 296593).

C.O.I. – Gold jewelry sold by weight at affordable prices. 8 Via Por Santa Maria (phone: 283970 or 293424).

David – Leather bags, luggage, shoes, clothes. 11-13r Via Roma (phone: 211884).

Dodo – Painted cats, rabbits, and piglets adorn wooden frames, chairs, pins, earrings, and barrettes in this eccentric shop. 32r Borgo SS. Apostoli (phone: 282022).

Emilio Paoli – Straw market with class — locally produced gift articles and imports. 26r Via della Vigna Nuova (phone: 214596).

Falai – Florence is known for its jewelry shops, but this one will also copy much-loved items or help you design new ones from drawings or descriptions. 28r Via Por Santa Maria (phone: 261688).

Feltrinelli – Art books. 12-20r Via Cavour (phone: 219524).

Frette – Fine bed and table linen decorated with delicate embroidery. 8-10 Lungarno Amerigo Vespucci (phone: 292367).

Gants – Gloves of the highest quality; they make their own. 78r Via Porta Rossa.

Gerard – Way-out, punk, and exotic fashions for men and women. 18-20r Via Vaccherreccia (phone: 215942).

Gherardini – A century-old leather shop, also selling sunglasses and perfume, run by an old Florentine family (the subject of the *Mona Lisa* was a Gherardini). 57r Via della Vigna Nuova (phone: 215678) and other locations.

Giulio Giannini e Figlio – This father-and-son store is one of the oldest selling the famous hand-crafted Florentine paper products, and its selection is one of the best in town. 37r Piazza Pitti (phone: 215342).

Gori Boutique – Santa Croce Leather School products, as well as articles by Italy's top-name designers. 13r Piazza Santa Croce (phone: 242935).

Happy Jack – A good men's boutique; alterations done quickly. 7-13r Via della Vigna Nuova (phone: 284329).

International Calico Lion – Romantic children's clothes; it's a great shop for grandmothers. 15 Borgo SS Apostoli (phone: 217647).

Libreria Franco Maria Ricci – Fine books selected by the publishers of *FMR* magazine. 41r Via delle Belle Donne (phone: 283312).

Libreria Salimbeni – Specializes in art books. 14r Via Matteo Palmieri (phone: 2340904).

Lily of Florence – Italian shoes in American sizes. 2r Via Guicciardini (phone: 294748).

Lisio – Housed in a medieval tower, this shop sells an incredible selection of beautiful silks, damasks, and brocades for upholstery, all handwoven on 17th-century looms. 45 Via dei Fossi (phone: 212430).

L'Officina Profumo-Farmaceutica di Santa Maria Novella – A truly unique pharmacy and perfume shop that carries fine cosmetics and unusual products, such as anti-hysteria salts, from another era. 16 Via della Scala (phone: 216276).

Loretta Caponi – Exquisite handmade lingerie and linen by this second-generation shop that designs for Nina Ricci and Dior. 38-40r Borgo Ognissanti (phone: 213668).

Lori Clara e Lorenzo – A vast selection of fine men's and women's clothing sold at discount prices. 15 Viale Enrico de Nicola (phone: 6503204).

Luisa – International fashion boutique full of trendy clothes, shoes, and accessories for men and women. 19-21r Via Roma (phone: 217826).

Luisa Spagnoli – Women's high-quality clothing, made from the purest cotton and wool, at moderate prices. 20 Via Strozzi (phone: 211978).

Madova – Italy's most competent and incomparable glovemaker. 1r Via Guicciardini (phone: 296526).

Mario Buccellati – Fine jewelry and silverware in traditional Florentine designs. 71r Via Tornabuoni (phone: 296579).

Mario Valentino – Designer shoes and bags. 67r Via Tornabuoni (phone: 261338).

Melli – Antique jewelry, ivory, silver, and clocks. 48 Ponte Vecchio (phone: 211413).

Mercato Nuovo (Straw Market) – The covered market, with all sorts of items made of straw, wood, and leather, as well as goods from Florence's growing immigrant community. Piazza del Mercato Nuovo.

Mujer – Original fashions for the adventurous woman. 6r Via Vacchereccia (phone: 210057).

Neuber – British and Italian wools. 32r Via Strozzi (phone: 215763).

Oli-Ca – Colorful cardboard boxes in all shapes and sizes, and a wrapping service so visitors can avoid the complexities of the Italian postal system. 27r Borgo SS Apostoli (phone: 296917).

Paperback Exchange – New and used books, plus a wide selection of travel guides. 31r Via Fiesolana (phone: 247854).

Papiro – *Papier à cuve,* or marbled paper, a method of hand-decoration invented in the 17th century; lovely stationery. 55 Via Cavour (phone: 215262) and other locations.

Parri's – Off-the-rack and custom-made leather clothing. 12-18r Via Guicciardini (phone: 282829).

Parson – Trendy women's boutique. 16-18r Via Tosinghi (phone: 282590).

La Pelle – Leather clothes made to order in two stores. 11-13r and 11-14r Via Guicciardini (phone: 292031).

Pineider – Italy's most famous stationers. 13r Piazza della Signoria (phone: 284655) and 76r Via Tornabuoni (phone: 211605).

Pitti Libri – Beautiful illustrated books on a wide range of subjects, as well as hand-embroidered *Christmas* stockings and small antique objects. 16 Piazza Pitti (phone: 212704).

Primi Mesi – Embroidered crib and carriage sets; maternity, infants, and toddlers wear. 23r Via dei Cimatori (phone: 296372).

Principe – A small but elegant department store. 21-29r Piazza Strozzi (phone: 216821).

Quaglia & Forte – Hand-carved cameos and reproductions of Etruscan gold jewelry are sold here. 12r Via Guicciardini (phone: 294534).

Renard – Leather, suede, and sheepskin clothing. 21-23r Via dei Martelli (phone: 284566).

Richard Ginori – Exquisite china, as well as fine crystal and silver. 17r Via Rondinelli (phone: 210041).

Rosetta Belli – Specializes in handbags, and at relatively reasonable prices. 9r Via dei Fossi (phone: 293567).

Santa Croce Leather School – Top-quality leather goods (boxes, gloves, handbags, wallets, clothing, and shoes) from the school and shop inside the monastery of Santa Croce. 16 Piazza Santa Croce or (through the garden) 5r Via San Giuseppe (phone: 244533 or 2479913).

Sbigoli – Attractive, rustic earthenware ceramics; shipping can be arranged. 4r Via San Egidio (phone: 2479713).

Schwicker – Quality gifts by Florentine artisans. 40r Piazza Pitti (phone: 211851).

Seeber – English-language bookshop. 70 Via Tornabuoni (phone: 215697).

Stefanel – Colorful casualwear. Via Borgo San Lorenzo (phone: 312578).

Tanino Crisci – The most stylish shoe shop (for men and women) in town. 43-45 Via Tornabuoni (phone: 216741).

Il Torchio – Well-priced, handmade Florentine marbleized paper, books, pencils, desk sets, and more. 17 Via dei Bardi (phone: 2342862).

Torrini – Exquisite jewelry. 10r Piazza Duomo (phone: 284506).

U. Gerardi – Best selection of coral jewelry in town. 5 Ponte Vecchio (phone: 211809).

Ugo Poggi – Florentine handicrafts in silver, china, glass. 26r Via degli Strozzi (phone: 216741).

Ungaro Parallèle – High fashion for women. 30r Via della Vigna Nuova (phone: 210129).

UPIM – A large, moderately priced department store. Piazza della Repubblica (phone: 298544).

Valmar – Tapestry items perfect for everything from upholstery to women's belts. 53r Via Porta Rossa (phone: 284493).

Viceversa – New-wave, high-tech, and classic designer tableware and gift items. 53r Via Ricasoli (phone: 298281).

Zanobetti – Classic clothing and leather goods for men and women. 20-22r Via Calimala (phone: 210646).

SPORTS AND FITNESS: Check with your concierge to find out which sports facilities currently are open to the public. Most are private clubs, but a day visit often can be arranged for a fee.

Fitness Centers – *Gymnasium* (49r Via Palazzuolo; phone: 293308); *Il Vortice* (16 Via Lambertesca; phone: 280212); *Indoor Club* (15 Via Bardazzi; phone: 430275); *Narcisus Club* (6 Via Ponte Sospeso; phone: 709903); *Palestra Savasana* (26

Via J. da Diaccetto; phone: 287373); *Sauna Finlandese* (108 Via Cavour; phone: 587246); *Swan* (28 Via Pepi; phone: 240802); *Tropos* (20/A Via Orcagna; phone: 661581).

Golf – There is a good 18-hole course (closed Mondays) at *Golf dell'Ugolino,* in nearby Impruneta, 3 Via Chiantigiana (phone: 230-1096).

Horseback Riding – For information, call *Piazzale Cascine* (phone: 360056) or *Agriturist* (phone: 287838). Just outside the city is *Badia Montescalari* (129 Via Montescalari at La Panca; phone: 959596).

Jogging – The best place to run is the Cascine, a very long, narrow park along the Arno west of the center. To get there, follow the river to Ponte della Vittoria.

Soccer – See the *Fiorentina* in action from September to May at the *Stadio Comunale,* designed by Pier Luigi Nervi. 4-6 Viale Manfredo Fanti (phone: 572625).

Squash – Courts can be reserved at the *Centro Squash Firenze;* 24-29 Viale Piombino (phone: 710055).

Swimming – Swimmers will do best to stay at one of the following hotels: *Crest, Croce di Malta* (although the pool is very small), *Jolly Carlton, Kraft, Minerva, Park Palace, Villa Belvedere, Villa Medici,* or *Villa sull'Arno* or, outside the city, at the *Grand Hotel Villa Cora, Villa La Massa, Villa San Michele,* or the *Villa Villoresi.* There also are a few indoor and outdoor public pools, including *Piscina Costoli* (Viale Paoli; phone: 669744); *Piscina Le Pavoniere,* an outdoor pool in a pleasant park (Viale degli Olmi; phone: 367506); and *Zodiac Sport* (2 Via A. Grandi; phone: 2022847).

Tennis – Play tennis at the semi-public *Circolo Tennis alle Cascine* (1 Viale Visarno; phone: 356651); *Circolo Tennis Torrigiani* (144 Via de' Serragli; phone: 224409); *Assi-Giglio-Rosso* (64 Viale Michelangelo; phone: 6812686 or 687858); *Il Poggetto* (24/B Via Michele Mercati; phone: 460127); *Match Ball* (Via della Massa; phone: 631752); and *Tennis Pattinaggio Piazzale Michelangelo* (61 Viale Michelangelo; phone: 6811880).

 THEATER: If you'd like to see a play in Italian, the principal theaters in Florence are the *Teatro della Pergola* (32 Via della Pergola; phone: 247-9651); the *Teatro Niccolini* (5 Via Ricasoli; phone: 213282); and *Tenda Città di Firenze* (Via de Nicola; phone: 650-4112). *Teatro Variety* (47 Via del Madonnone; phone: 660632) offers singers and humorous contemporary pieces. Films in English are shown frequently at the *Cinema Astro* (Piazza San Simone near Santa Croce; phone: 222388).

 MUSIC: Opera begins earlier in Florence than in most Italian cities. The season at the *Teatro Comunale* (Corso Italia; phone: 27791), the principal opera house and concert hall, runs from October to early January, with ballet in July. The annual *Maggio Musicale Fiorentino* festival, which attracts some of the world's finest musicians and singers, also is held here in May and June. Tickets can be purchased at the theater; *Universal Turismo* (7r Via Speziali; phone: 217241); or *Box Office* (10Ar Via della Pergola; phone: 241881). The *Teatro della Pergola* (see *Theater*) is the scene of Saturday afternoon concerts from autumn through spring. The *Orchestra da Camera Fiorentina* (Florentine Chamber Orchestra; 6 Via E. Poggi; phone: 470027) regularly stages classical concerts. Open-air concerts are held in the cloisters of the *Badia Fiesolana* (in Fiesole) and of the *Ospedale degli Innocenti* on summer evenings, and occasionally in other historic monuments such as the restored Church of Santo Stefano al Ponte Vecchio, now the seat of the *Regional Tuscan Orchestra.*

 NIGHTCLUBS AND NIGHTLIFE: A Florentine evening usually begins with an *aperitivo* at one of the cafés on Piazza della Signoria (such as *Rivoire,* an elegant watering hole with wood-paneled walls and marble-top tables) or Piazza della Repubblica, at *Harry's Bar* (22r Lungarno Amerigo Vespucci;

phone: 296700), or at *Bar Donatello,* on the main floor of the *Excelsior* hotel, the pre-dinner gathering place for Florence's smart set. Because nightspots come and go so quickly — and since most are closed at least 1 night of the week — it always is a good idea to check with your hotel concierge before going out. Discos and piano bars are among the most popular forms of evening entertainment, and tops among the former are *Tenaz* (46 Via Pratese; phone: 373050) and *Jackie-O'* (24A Via dell'Erta Canina; phone: 2342442). Other discos include *Yab Yum* (5r Via Sassetti; phone: 282018); *Full-Up* (21r Via della Vigna Vecchia; phone: 293006); and *Plegyne* (26r Piazza Santa Maria Novella; phone: 211590). *Andromeda* (13 Via Cimatori; phone: 292002) is a small disco near Piazza della Signoria; *Capitale* (2 Via Fossi Macinante; phone: 332723) is a hip disco located in Cascine park that features outdoor dancing in the summer. For the very young crowd, dancing happens at *Space Electronic* (37 Via Palazzuolo; phone: 293082). The *Domino Club* (23r Borgo Santa Croce; phone: 244897) provides après-disco entertainment for young Florentines, with video clips, dancing, gelato, snacks, and breakfast at dawn. *Energia* (574 Via Verdi; phone: 2345842), near Santa Croce, is a singles spot that attracts an international crowd, as does *Maramao* (79r Via dei Macci; phone: 2444341). If a quieter evening is called for, there are numerous lovely piano bars from which to choose, such as the elegant *Loggia Tornaquinci,* nestled atop a 16th-century Medici building (6r Via Tornabuoni; phone: 219148). Others include the *Caffè* (9 Piazza Pitti; phone: 296241); *Oberon* (12r Via dell'Erta Canina; phone: 216516); *Petit Bois* (Via Ferrucci; phone: 59578); and *Prezzemolo* (5r Via della Caldaie; phone: 211530), a champagne bar for night owls. The elegant *Oliviero* (51r Via della Terme; phone: 287643) is a restaurant with piano bar, the place for a romantic evening. There also are piano bars at some of the hotels, such as the *Anglo-American,* the *Londra,* the *Majestic,* and the *Savoy. Il Salotto* is a "private" club open to everyone. Situated in a 15th-century palazzo at 33 Borgo Pinti, it's not surprising that it boasts a clientele of Florentine nobility, artists, and wealthy merchants. Popular for drinks is the *Cotton Club* (15 Via Porta Rossa; phone: 288138), and the *Caffè Strozzi* (16-19 Piazza Strozzi; phone: 212574), with outdoor tables for good people watching. Three other local favorites are *Gilli,* a Belle Epoque café with a lively outdoor terrace (39r Piazza della Repubblica; phone: 296310); *Giacosa* (83 Via Tornabuoni; phone: 296226), where the elite meet over truffle-paste sandwiches; and *Procacci* (33 Via Tornabuoni), a café/bar serving white truffle-paste sandwiches and other elegant snacks to a chic local crowd.

BEST IN TOWN

CHECKING IN: The Italian Government Travel Office (ENIT) offers lists of hotels in Florence, giving the class of each, its address, and a few other details (such as the existence of a restaurant, air conditioning, parking facilities, and so on), but no telephone numbers. One-star, or fourth class, hotels are not listed, and price ranges for individual hotels are not given, but a general range of prices for each of the four hotel categories is included.

The rates posted in Italian hotel rooms include service charges and value added tax (VAT — 19% in five-star hotels, 9% in others), so receiving the bill at the end of a stay rarely is a cause for shock. If the locality imposes a visitor's tax (a minimal amount, called the *imposta di soggiorno*), that, too, usually is included in the posted price. No surcharge may be made for central heating, but a surcharge (often per person) for air conditioning is allowed.

In Italy, a single room is a *camera singola;* a double room is a *camera doppia.* If you request a single and are given a double, it may not cost more than the maximum price for a single room. If you specify a double, you may be asked whether you prefer a *camera a due letti* (twin-bedded room) or a *camera matrimoniale* (with a double bed). A single room to which an extra bed has been added may not cost more than a double room, and a double room to which an extra bed has been added may not increase in price by more than 35%. And the price of a double usually holds whether it's occupied by one or two people.

If you are traveling on a shoestring, you will be interested to know that a great many rooms that do not have a private bath or shower (*bagno privato* or *doccia privata*) do have a sink with hot and cold running water (occasionally cold water only) and often a bidet. Sometimes there even is a toilet. Thus you can save money by denying yourself the luxury of a private bathroom and still not be totally without convenience. Some places have showers or baths down the hall that guests may use — often free or for a nominal fee.

Rentals – An attractive alternative for the visitor planning to stay in Florence for a week or more is to rent an apartment or villa. These offer a wide range of luxury and convenience, depending on the price you want to pay. One of the advantages to staying in a house, apartment (usually called a "flat" overseas), or other rented vacation home is that you will feel much more like a visitor than a tourist.

Known to Europeans as a "holiday let" or a "self-catering holiday," a vacation in a furnished rental has both the advantages and disadvantages of living "at home" abroad. It can be less expensive than staying in a first class hotel, although very luxurious and expensive rentals are available, too. It has the comforts of home, including a kitchen, which means potential savings on food. Furthermore, it provides a sense of the country that a large hotel often cannot. On the other hand, a certain amount of housework is involved because if you don't eat out, you have to cook, and though some rentals (especially the luxury ones) include a cleaning person, most don't. (If the rental doesn't include daily cleaning, arrangements often can be made with a maid service.)

For a family, two or more couples, or a group of friends, the per-person cost — even for a luxurious rental — can be quite reasonable. Weekly and monthly rates are available to reduce costs still more. But best of all is the amount of space that no conventional hotel room can equal. As with hotels, the rates for properties in Florence are seasonal, rising during the peak travel season, while for others they remain the same year-round. To have your pick of the properties available, you should begin to make arrangements for a rental at least 6 months in advance.

There are several ways of finding a suitable rental property. Most provincial and local tourist boards in Italy have information on companies arranging rentals in their areas. US branches of the Italian Government Travel Office have lists of agents who specialize in villa and apartment rentals, and the Florence board issues a guide to villas and flats for rent that meet some range of minimum standards.

Many tour operators regularly include a few rental packages among their offerings; these generally are available through a travel agent. In addition, a number of companies specialize in rental vacations. Their plans typically include rental of the property (or several properties, but usually for a minimum stay per location), a rental car, and airfare.

The companies listed below rent properties in Florence. They handle the booking and confirmation paperwork, and can be expected to provide more information about the properties than that which might ordinarily be gleaned from a short listing in an accommodations guide.

Castles, Cottages and Flats (7 Faneuil Hall Marketplace, Boston, MA 02109; phone: 617-742-6030). Handles apartments in the city; some villas outside the city. Small charge ($5) for receipt of main catalogue, refundable upon booking.

Europa-Let (PO Box 3537, Ashland, OR 97520; phone: 800-462-4486 or 503-482-5806). Offers apartments and villas.

Grandluxe International (165 Chestnut St., Allendale, NJ 07401; phone: 201-327-2333). Rents apartments in the city and farmhouses and villas on the outskirts of the city.

Interhome (124 Little Falls Rd., Fairfield, NJ 07004; phone: 201-882-6864). Apartments in the city, farmhouses on the outskirts of the city.

International Lodging Corp. (300 1st Ave., Suite 7C, New York, NY 10009; phone: 212-228-5900). Rents flats.

Rent a Vacation Everywhere (*RAVE;* 328 Main St. E., Suite 526, Rochester, NY 14604; phone: 716-454-6440). Rentals include moderate to luxurious apartments and houses.

Vacanze in Italia (PO Box 297, Falls Village, CT 06031; phone: 800-533-5405). This organization has moderate to luxury apartments.

Villas International Ltd. (605 Market St., Suite 510, San Francisco, CA 94105; phone: 800-221-2260 or 415-281-0910). Rents apartments, in the city; villas on the outskirts of the city.

And for further information, including a general discussion of all forms of vacation rentals, evaluating costs, and information on rental opportunities in Florence, see *A Traveler's Guide to Vacation Rentals in Europe.* Available in general bookstores, it also can be ordered from Penguin USA (120 Woodbine St., Bergenfield, NJ 07621; phone: 800-526-0275 and ask for cash sales) for $11.95, plus postage and handling.

In addition, a useful publication, the *Worldwide Home Rental Guide,* lists properties throughout Europe, as well as the managing agencies. Issued twice annually, single copies may be available at larger newsstands for $10 an issue. For a year's subscription, send $18 to *Worldwide Home Rental Guide,* PO Box 2842, Sante Fe, NM 87504 (phone: 505-988-5188).

When considering a particular vacation rental property, look for answers to the following questions:

● How do you get from the airport to the property?
● What size and number of beds are provided?
● How far is the property from whatever else is important to you, such as a golf course or nightlife?
● How far is the nearest market?
● Are baby-sitters, cribs, bicycles, or anything else you may need for your children available?
● Is maid service provided daily?
● Is air conditioning and/or a phone provided?
● Is a car rental part of the package? Is a car necessary?

Home Exchanges – Still another alternative for travelers who are content to stay in one place during their vacation is a home exchange: The Smith family from Chicago moves into the home of the Rossi family in Florence, while the Rossis enjoy a stay in the Smiths' home. The home exchange is an exceptionally inexpensive way to ensure comfortable, reasonable living quarters with amenities that no hotel possibly could offer; often the trade includes a car. Moreover, it allows you to live in a new community in a way that few tourists ever do: For a little while, at least, you will become something of a resident.

Several companies publish directories of individuals and families willing to trade homes with others for a specific period of time. In some cases, you must be willing to list your own home in the directory; in others, you can subscribe without appearing in it. Most listings are for straight exchanges only, but each directory also has a number of listings placed by people interested in either exchanging or renting (for instance, if they own a second home). Other arrangements include exchanges of hospitality while owners are in residence or youth exchanges, where your teenager is put up as a guest in return for your putting up their teenager at a later date. A few house-sitting opportunities also are available. In most cases, arrangements for the actual exchange take place directly between you and the foreign host. There is no guarantee that you will find a listing in the area in which you are interested, but each of the organizations given below includes Italian homes among its hundreds or even thousands of foreign listings.

Home Base Holidays (7 Park Ave., London N13 5PG, England; phone: 81-886-8752). For $48 a year, subscribers receive four listings, with an option to list in all four.

Intervac US/International Home Exchange Service (Box 190070, San Francisco, CA 94119; phone: 415-435-3497). Some 8,000 listings. For $45 (plus postage), subscribers receive copies of the three directories published yearly, and are entitled to list their home in one of them; a black-and-white photo may be included with the listing for an additional $11. A $5 discount is given to travelers over age 62.

Loan-A-Home (2 Park La., Apt. 6E, Mt. Vernon, NY 10552; phone: 914-664-7640). Specializes in long-term (4 months or more — excluding July and August) housing arrangements worldwide for students, professors, businesspeople, and retirees, although its two annual directories (with supplements) carry a small list of short-term rentals and/or exchanges. $35 for a copy of one directory and one supplement; $45 for two directories and two supplements.

Vacation Exchange Club (PO Box 820, Haleiwa, HI 96712; phone: 800-638-3841). Some 10,000 listings. For $50, the subscriber receives two directories — one in late winter, one in the spring — and is listed in one.

World Wide Exchange (1344 Pacific Ave., Suite 103, Santa Cruz, CA 95060; phone: 408-476-4206). The $45 annual membership fee includes one listing (for house, yacht, or motorhome) and three guides.

Worldwide Home Exchange Club (13 Knightsbridge Green, London SW1X 7QL, England; phone: 71-589-6055; or 806 Brantford Ave., Silver Spring, MD 20904; no phone). Handles over 1,500 listings a year worldwide. For $25 a year, you will receive two listings, as well as supplements.

Better Homes and Travel (formerly *Home Exchange International*), with an office in New York, and representatives in Los Angeles, London, Paris, and Milan, functions differently in that it publishes no directory and shepherds the exchange process most of the way. Interested parties supply the firm with photographs of themselves and their homes, information on the type of home they want and where, and a registration fee of $50. The company then works with its other offices to propose a few possibilities, and only when a match is made do the parties exchange names, addresses, and phone numbers. For this service, *Better Homes and Travel* charges a closing fee, which ranges from $150 to $500 for switches from 2 weeks to 3 months in duration, and from $300 to $600 for longer switches. Contact *Better Homes and Travel* at 30 E. 33rd St., New York, NY 10016 (phone: 212-689-6608).

■**A warning about telephone surcharges in hotels:** A lot of digits may be involved once a caller starts dialing beyond national borders, but avoiding operator-assisted calls can cut costs considerably and bring phone rates down to a somewhat more reasonable range — except for calls made through hotel switchboards. One of the most unpleasant surprises travelers encounter in many foreign countries is the amount they find tacked onto their hotel bill for telephone calls, because foreign hotels routinely add on astronomical surcharges. (It's not at all uncommon to find 300% or 400% added to the actual telephone charges.)

Until recently, the only recourse against this unconscionable overcharging was to call collect when phoning from abroad or to use a telephone credit card — available through a simple procedure from any local US phone company. (Note, however, that even if you use a telephone credit card, some hotels still may charge a fee for line usage.) Now *American Telephone and Telegraph (AT&T)* offers *USA Direct,* a service that connects users, via a toll-free number, with an *AT&T* operator in the US, who will then put the call through at the standard international rate. Another new feature of this service is that travelers abroad can reach US toll-free (800) numbers by calling a *USA Direct* operator, who will connect them. Charges for all calls made through *USA Direct* appear on the caller's regular US phone bill. To reach this service in Italy, dial 172-1011. For a brochure and wallet card listing the toll-free number for other European countries, contact International Information Service, *AT&T Communications,* 635 Grant St., Pittsburgh, PA 15219 (phone: 800-874-4000).

AT&T also has put together *Teleplan,* an agreement among certain hoteliers that sets a limit on surcharges for calls made by guests from their rooms. As we went to press, *Teleplan* was in effect in Italy only in selected hotels in Rome. *Teleplan* agreements stipulate a flat, low rate for credit card or collect calls, and a flat percentage on calls paid for at the hotel. For further information, contact *AT&T*'s International Information Service (address above).

Until these services become universal, it's wise to ask for the surcharge rate *before* calling from a hotel. If the rate is high, it's best to use a telephone credit card, make a collect call, or place the call and ask the party to call right back. If none of these choices is possible, to avoid surcharges make international calls from the local post office or one of the special telephone centers located throughout Italy.

Hotels – Florence is well organized for visitors, with more than 400 hotels to accommodate more than 20,000 travelers. Still, somehow, it's hard to find a room in high season. The hotel count above and the list below include former *pensioni,* something like boardinghouses, but now officially designated as "hotels." A few still require that some meals be taken, a feature that is specified for those that do. (Half board means you must take breakfast and either lunch or dinner at the establishment.) Expect to pay more than $500 a night for a double room at those places listed as very expensive. At an expensive hotel, plan on spending from $210 to $470. Moderate-priced establishments cost between $95 and $210; inexpensive lodging ranges from $60 to $95. All telephone numbers are in the 55 city code unless otherwise indicated.

Villa Cora – A neo-classical villa built during the period when Florence was the capital of Italy. The name comes from one of the many former owners, an ambassador. As a private villa, it hosted Napoleon's widow, Eugénie, as well as Tchaikovsky's patron, the Baroness Von Meck. It offers spacious rooms and suites (56 rooms) decorated in the original style, grand public rooms, and a magnificent garden with heated pool, all about 2 miles (3 km) from the chaotic city center. On the other side of the Boboli Gardens. Business facilities include 24-hour room service, meeting rooms for up to 120, an English-speaking concierge, foreign currency exchange, secretarial services in English, audiovisual equipment, photocopiers, computers, cable television news, translation services, and express checkout. 18 Viale Machiavelli (phone: 229-8451; fax: 229086; telex: 570604). Very expensive.

Villa San Michele – Dramatically set about 5 miles (8 km) from Florence, on the slopes below Fiesole. Originally an ancient monastery, built by the Davanzati family in the late 15th century with a façade designed by Michelangelo, it became a private villa during Napoleon's day and was transformed into one of Tuscany's most romantic hotels in the 1950s. (Brigitte Bardot honeymooned here in the 1960s.) Restored to its former glory, it now has 28 exquisitely appointed rooms with canopied beds and 7 suites (most with Jacuzzis), intimate dining indoors or in the open-air loggia, fragrant gardens with splendid views, a pool, and limousine service into the city. Half board in the elegant restaurant, which serves wonderful Tuscan fare, is required. Business facilities include 24-hour room service, meeting rooms for up to 40, an English-speaking concierge, foreign currency exchange, secretarial services in English, audiovisual equipment, photocopiers, computers, cable television news, translation services, and express checkout. Open from March to mid-November. 4 Via Doccia, Fiesole (phone: 59451; in the US, 800-237-1236; fax: 598734; telex: 570643). Very expensive.

Baglioni – A traditional hotel in refined Tuscan taste: parquet floors, solid furnishings, handsome carpets, sober — even somber — atmosphere and service, with nearly 200 rooms. It's near the railway station and only a short walk from the best shopping. The roof garden restaurant has an enviable view of the historic city. Business facilities include 24-hour room service, meeting rooms for up to 210, an English-speaking concierge, foreign currency exchange, secretarial services in English, audiovisual equipment, photocopiers, computers, cable television news, translation services, and express checkout. 6 Piazza dell'Unità Italiana (phone: 218441; fax: 215695; telex: 580525). Expensive.

Brunelleschi – With its own terra cotta piazza off a quiet back street near the Duomo, this elegant 94-room hostelry has been recently restored with great style. A 6th-century Byzantine tower has been incorporated into this complex, originally three hotels; there's a rooftop terrace with exceptional views of the city. Business services include an English-speaking concierge. 3 Piazza S. Elisabetta (phone: 562068). Expensive.

Excelsior – Beside the Arno, just a short walk from the city center, traditional in both style and service. Part of the reliably luxurious and efficient CIGA chain. The excellent terrace restaurant, *Il Cestello,* has a splendid view when the stained glass windows are opened. The 205-room hotel is a favorite of Florentines and their guests. Newly remodeled rooms, many of which overlook the Arno, are charmingly appointed. The lobby, a vision of marble and gilt, is reminiscent of bygone days. Business facilities include 24-hour room service, meeting rooms for up to 350, an English-speaking concierge, foreign currency exchange, secretarial services in English, audiovisual equipment, photocopiers, computers, cable television news, translation services, and express checkout. 3 Piazza Ognissanti (phone: 264201; fax: 210278; telex: 570022). Expensive.

Grand – Across the street from the *Excelsior,* this 109-room hostelry was renovated in 1990 to re-create its original 15th-century elegance. Brunelleschi is said to have designed the palazzo as a residence for one of Florence's noble families. Part of the CIGA chain, it has meeting and banquet rooms and a restaurant. Business facilities include 24-hour room service, meeting rooms for up to 230, an English-speaking concierge, foreign currency exchange, secretarial services in English, audiovisual equipment, photocopiers, computers, cable television news, translation services, and express checkout. 1 Piazza Ognissanti (phone: 278781; fax: 217400; telex: 570055). Expensive.

Helvetia & Bristol – Considered one of Florence's best in the 19th century, this hotel has now been restored to all its former glory, with antique furniture, velvet drapes, and original oil paintings. All 50 rooms and suites are decorated in different styles, ranging from chinoiserie to Art Nouveau, and the beautiful marble bathrooms all have Jacuzzis. Ideally located on a tranquil street behind the Piazza della Repubblica. Business facilities include 24-hour room service, meeting rooms for up to 70, an English-speaking concierge, foreign currency exchange, secretarial services in

English, audiovisual equipment, photocopiers, computers, cable television news, translation services, and express checkout. 2 Via dei Pescioni (phone: 287814; fax: 288353; telex: 572696). Expensive.

Hotel de la Ville – Dark, quiet, and somber, the perfect place for light sleepers. Its double doors and storm windows provide a peaceful oasis in the center of Florence, just off the elegant Via Tornabuoni. There are 96 rooms. Business facilities include 24-hour room service, meeting rooms for up to 75, an English-speaking concierge, foreign currency exchange, secretarial services in English, audiovisual equipment, photocopiers, computers, cable television news, translation services, and express checkout. 1 Piazza Antinori (phone: 261805; fax: 261809; telex: 570518). Expensive.

Regency – Small (31 rooms) patrician villa set in a quiet residential area and decorated with exquisite taste. Like its sister in Rome (the *Lord Byron*), it offers calm and privacy, discreetly displaying its Relais & Châteaux crest at the entrance. There is a charming garden and an excellent restaurant (see *Eating Out*). Business facilities include 24-hour room service, meeting rooms for up to 20, an English-speaking concierge, foreign currency exchange, secretarial services in English, audiovisual equipment, photocopiers, computers, cable television news, translation services, and express checkout. 3 Piazza Massimo d'Azeglio (phone and fax: 245247; telex: 571058). Expensive.

Savoy – A classic gem in the heart of Florence, with most of its 100 rooms decorated in Venetian style. It also has a popular piano bar. Business facilities include 24-hour room service, meeting rooms for up to 150, an English-speaking concierge, foreign currency exchange, secretarial services in English, audiovisual equipment, photocopiers, computers, cable television news, translation services, and espress checkout. 7 Piazza della Repubblica (phone: 283313; fax: 284840; telex: 570220). Expensive.

Sheraton – Situated 3 miles (5 km) south of Florence, this 321-room member of the worldwide chain has tennis courts and an outdoor swimming pool (perfect for a dip after a hot day's sightseeing). A van transports guests into the city. Business facilities include 24-hour room service, meeting rooms for up to 1,300, an English-speaking concierge, foreign currency exchange, secretarial services in English, audiovisual equipment, photocopiers, computers, cable television news, translation services, and express checkout. Just off the Firenze Sud autostrada exit. 33 Via G. Agnelli (phone: 64901; fax: 680747; telex: 575860). Expensive.

Torre di Bellosguardo – The majestic, cypress-framed site on a hill with an unforgettable view of Florence's terra cotta roofs makes this handsome 16-room hostelry a special place to stay. A sunny verandah, lush gardens, and a swimming pool — plus rooms whose ceilings are punctuated by rough hewn beams and each of which is individually decorated with antiques — add to the charm. There is an English-speaking concierge and 24-hour room service. 2 Via Roti Michelozzi (phone: 229-8145). Expensive.

Villa Carlotta – Located on a quiet residential street only minutes away from Porta Romana is this modernized villa with Oriental rugs, antique reproductions, and 48 charmingly decorated rooms. Breakfast on the lovely terrace is a real treat. Business services include 24-hour room service, a meeting room that holds up to 40 people, an English-speaking concierge, foreign currency exchange, audiovisual equipment, photocopiers, and translation services. 3 Via Michel di Lando (phone: 220530; fax: 233-6147). Expensive.

Villa Medici – A reconstruction of the 18th-century Sonnino de Renzis Palace, halfway between the railroad station and the Arno. Many of the 110 charming, spacious rooms have balconies affording panoramic views. The grand public rooms, tranquil gardens, and elegant service all are worthy of a hotel of this class.

The swimming pool is a bow to contemporary tastes. Business facilities include 24-hour room service, meeting rooms for up to 100, an English-speaking concierge, foreign currency exchange, secretarial services in English, audiovisual equipment, photocopiers, computers, cable television news, translation services, and express checkout. 42 Via del Prato (phone: 261331; fax: 261336; telex: 570179). Expensive.

Anglo-American – Between the train station and the river, very near the *Teatro Comunale,* with 118 refurbished rooms. Business facilities include 24-hour room service, meeting rooms for up to 150, an English-speaking concierge, foreign currency exchange, secretarial services in English, audiovisual equipment, photocopiers, computers, cable television news, translation services, and express checkout. 9 Via Garibaldi (phone: 282114; fax: 268513; telex: 570289). Expensive to moderate.

Croce di Malta – Housed in a former convent close to Santa Croce, the site actually harks back to Roman times — you'll see Roman columns and an ancient brick vaulted roof, all carefully restored by the hotel's architect-owner. There are 98 rooms, a pretty garden, and a small swimming pool — a luxury for a hotel in the center of town. Business facilities include 24-hour room service, meeting rooms for up to 70, English-speaking concierge, foreign currency exchange, secretarial services in English, audiovisual equipment, photocopiers, computers, cable television news, translation services, and express checkout. 7 Via della Scala (phone: 282600 or 211740; fax: 287121; telex: 570540). Expensive to moderate.

Fenice Palace – Recently renovated and restored, the 67 guestrooms occupy 4 floors in a 19th-century palazzo near the Duomo. The accommodations offer considerable comfort and some magnificent views of the city's major monuments. Business facilities include 24-hour room service, an English-speaking concierge, foreign currency exchange, secretarial services in English, audiovisual equipment, photocopiers, computers, translation services, and express checkout. 10 Via Martelli (phone: 289942; fax: 210087; telex: 575580). Expensive to moderate.

Jolly Carlton – Large and modern, this 167-room member of the efficient Jolly chain has a pool and a wonderful view from the terrace. It's near the Cascine park. Business facilities include 24-hour room service, meeting rooms for up to 120, English-speaking concierge, foreign currency exchange, secretarial services in English, audiovisual equipment, photocopiers, computers, cable television news, translation services, and express checkout. 4A Piazza Vittorio Veneto (phone: 2770; fax: 292794; telex: 571523). Expensive to moderate.

Kraft – This modern 66-room hotel in a nice area near the *Teatro Comunale* has a roof-garden restaurant sporting umbrella pines and a cypress tree, as well as a splendid panorama and a rooftop swimming pool. Business facilities include 24-hour room service, meeting rooms for up to 60, an English-speaking concierge, foreign currency exchange, secretarial services in English, audiovisual equipment, photocopiers, computers, translation services, and express checkout. 2 Via Solferino (phone: 284273; fax: 571723). Expensive to moderate.

Lungarno – Comfortable, functional, and cheerful. Set between the Ponte Vecchio and the Ponte Santa Trinita on the Oltrarno side of town, with 70 modern rooms, the best of which have terraces and balconies overlooking the Arno (be sure to book one of these in advance). There also is a garage. Business facilities include 24-hour room service, meeting rooms for up to 60, an English-speaking concierge, foreign currency exchange, secretarial services in English, audiovisual equipment, photocopiers, computers, cable television news, translation services, and express checkout. 14 Borgo San Jacopo (phone: 264211; fax: 268437; telex: 570129). Expensive to moderate.

Minerva – The 107 rooms here are large and comfortably furnished, all with private modern baths. The staff is pleasant, and the hotel is near the train station, convenient to shopping and the major museums. Business facilities include 24-hour room service, meeting rooms for up to 70, English-speaking concierge, foreign currency exchange, secretarial services in English, audiovisual equipment, photocopiers, computers, cable television news, translation services, and express checkout. 16 Piazza Santa Maria Novella (phone: 284555; fax: 268281; telex: 570414). Expensive to moderate.

Palazzo Antellesi – Visitors planning at least a 1-week stay in Florence might want to consider renting an apartment in this exquisite palazzo on Piazza Santa Croce. The owners have converted it into several self-contained units that can sleep from two to five people. It is one of the few buildings in the city with a frescoed façade and some of the apartments also have frescoes. All are beautifully furnished, most have fireplaces, and some have terraces. There also is a garden and several courtyards, making this place an oasis of peace when Florence is at its hottest and most crowded. 21-22 Piazza Santa Croce (phone: 244456; fax: 234-5552). Expensive to moderate.

Park Palace – With its lovely garden and swimming pool, and a knockout view overlooking the city from the south, this charming, small hotel was once a private villa. 5 Piazzale Galileo (phone: 222431). Expensive to moderate.

Tornabuoni Beacci – This delightful former pensione occupies the top floors of a 14th-century palace on Florence's most elegant street. It's traditional yet cheerful and sunny, provides excellent service, and has a charming terrace. Drinks at sunset on the terrace overlooking a sea of Florentine tile roofs is delightful. Guests are required to take breakfast and another meal (half board) during high season. 3 Via Tornabuoni (phone: 212645; telex: 570215). Expensive to moderate.

Aprile – Few establishments in Italy are as romantic as this place, located in a 15th-century Medici palace embellished with frescoes and vaulted ceilings. The 17 rooms and 2 suites are well appointed, and those located in the back overlook a quiet courtyard. 6 Via della Scala (phone: 216237). Moderate.

Continental – In an ideal, albeit sometimes noisy, spot overlooking the Ponte Vecchio, this is as efficient as its sister hotel across the river, the *Lugarno*, which you can see from the terrace. No restaurant. Business facilities include 24-hour room service, an English-speaking concierge, and cable television news. 2 Lugarno Acciaiuoli (phone: 282392; fax: 268557; telex: 580525). Moderate.

Monna Lisa – On a tiny side street, this hostelry in an old renovated building offers Old World charm and style with modern comforts. Some of the 20 guestrooms have Jacuzzis. There is private parking for no extra charge during low season. 27 Borgo Pinti (phone: 247-9751). Moderate.

Villa Villoresi – About 5 miles (8 km) from the center of Florence, it's another noble home away from home. It dates from the 12th century, but for the last 200 years it has been the property of the Villoresi family, who turned it into a hotel in the 1960s. With only 28 rooms, they manage to impart a sense of family as well as history. Bedroom walls have frescoes and meals are good. There is a pool in the garden among the olive trees. 2 Via Ciampi, Località Colonnata, Sesto Fiorentino (phone: 448-9032; telex: 580567). Moderate.

Loggiato dei Serviti – Well located on the charming Piazza SS Annunziata, the 20 rooms in this Renaissance palazzo are a bargain, especially by Florentine standards. Most are furnished with antiques. Be sure to book well in advance. 3 Piazza SS Annunziata (phone: 219165; telex: 575808). Moderate to inexpensive.

Balestri – A clean, no-frills stopping place overlooking the Arno. It has 50 rooms, no restaurant. 7 Piazza Mentana (phone: 214743). Inexpensive.

Bencistà – This 35-room 15th-century villa, an inn among the olive trees near Fiesole, is a beautiful bargain for those whose shoestrings do not stretch as far as the *Villa San Michele*. Half board is required. No phones in the rooms. A free minibus service is available to take guests into Florence. Open mid-March to November. 4 Via Benedetto da Maiano, between Fiesole and San Domenico (phone: 59163). Inexpensive.

La Residenza – A small, renovated hotel, with a lovely terrace, on Florence's best shopping street. Its 24 rooms, located on the top floors of a Renaissance palazzo, are lovely, and the staff is unusually helpful. Half board is required during high season. 8 Via Tornabuoni (phone: 284197; telex: 570093). Inexpensive.

Liana – A 10-minute walk to the city center, this onetime site of the British Embassy is an oasis of calm. It boasts 20 nicely decorated rooms; try for one facing the garden. 18 Via Vittorio Alfieri (phone: 245303). Inexpensive.

Morandi alla Crocetta – A small but charming 15-room establishment, run by an Englishwoman and her Italian-born son, and situated in a section of what used to be a 16th-century Dominican convent. Rooms are furnished with Tuscan antiques and many guests become friends of the family, returning year after year. 50 Via Laura (phone: 234-4747; fax: 248-0954). Inexpensive.

Norma – Guests keep coming back to Signora Norma and her husband, who own and run this tiny 11-room pensione in a 14th-century building that has a terrace, a tower as tall as the Duomo, and unbelievable views. 8 Borgo SS Apostoli (phone: 239577). Inexpensive.

Pendini – An old-style, family-run place, in operation for over 100 years in a building far older, but renovated. 2 Via degli Strozzi (phone: 211170; fax: 282179; telex: 570007). Inexpensive.

Porta Rossa – Said to be one of Florence's oldest (14th century, with a 13th-century tower), and perhaps in need of a little sprucing up. Balzac and Stendhal, they say, slept here. It has Renaissance public rooms (good for meetings in the commercial center of the city) and a terrace overlooking the Ponte Vecchio. 19 Via Porta Rossa (phone: 287551). Inexpensive.

Quisisana Ponte Vecchio – Between the Ponte Vecchio and the *Uffizi*, with an unparalleled view of the former from a charming terrace. This was the setting for the film *A Room with a View*, adapted from E. M. Forster's novel. 4 Lungarno Archibusieri (phone: 216692; fax: 268303). Inexpensive.

Silla – A charming, friendly place, with 3 large newer rooms on the third floor and a quiet courtyard. Its large flowered terrace overlooks the river and a park on the Oltrarno side of town. No restaurant; usually closed in December. 5 Via dei Renai (phone: 234-2888). Inexpensive.

 EATING OUT: Back in the 16th century, Catherine de' Medici married King Henry II of France, and her cousin Maria de' Medici married Henry IV. The women took their cooks and their recipes for creams, sauces, pastries, and ice creams to the French court — along with their trousseaus. As an Elizabethan poet once said, "Tuscany provided creams and cakes and lively Florentine women to sweeten the taste and minds of the French."

Following their departure, the fanciness went out of Florentine food, and French cooking began to shine. But today, Florentine cooking, while simpler and more straightforward than during the Renaissance, is still at the top of the list of Italy's many varied regional dishes. No small contributing factor to this culinary art is the quality of the ingredients. Tuscany boasts excellent olive oil and wine, exquisite fruits and vegetables, good game in season, fresh fish from its coast, as well as salami, sausages, and every kind of meat. A *bistecca alla fiorentina*, thick and juicy on the bone and traditionally accompanied by new potatoes or white beans drenched in pure golden olive oil, is a meal fit for the fussiest of kings. A typical meal can begin with salami, frequently flavored with fennel, and rounds of bread spread with chicken liver sauce. *Fettunta*, toasted bread rubbed with garlic and soaked in freshly pressed, extra virgin olive oil, is another glorious Florentine appetizer. Meat is simply prepared; it is either grilled, deep-fried, or subjected to long *stracotto* (extra cooked) braising. Beans are a staple in the Florentine diet, flavored with sage and dressed with olive oil. Raw vegetables are served with a small bowl of salt and olive oil for dipping (the technique is known as *pinaimonio*). A plate of hard almond cookies, *biscotti* or *cantucci,* is served with a squat glass of *vin santo,* into which the cookies are dipped. Diners can roughly gauge the price of a restaurant before entering by the cost per kilo (2.2 pounds) of its Florentine steaks on the menu displayed outside. Fortunately, one steak is usually more than enough for two persons, and it is not considered a gaffe to order one steak for two or more.

Mealtimes in Florence begin earlier than in Rome, beginning by 12:30 or 1 PM for lunch, and by 8 PM for dinner. Many of the typical *mamma 'n' papà* restaurants are small, popular, and crowded. If you don't book, be prepared to wait and eventually share a table (single guests are often seated at a communal table — a respectable way of meeting residents). Also unlike Rome, you won't be encouraged to linger over your dessert wine if there are people waiting for your table. Food, like most everything else in Florentine life, is taken seriously; do your business and socializing elsewhere. A meal for two at the very expensive *Enoteca Pinchiorri* will vary (but will be at least $200), depending on what you eat and what wine you select. A full meal for two, including the house wine or the low-priced (but excellent) local chianti, at an expensive restaurant will cost between $95 and $180. Expect to pay between $60 and $95 at a moderate restaurant and under $60 at an inexpensive one. All telephone numbers are in the 55 city code unless otherwise indicated.

Enoteca Pinchiorri – In the 15th-century Ciofi-Iacometti Palace, with a delightful courtyard for dining alfresco, this is possibly Italy's best restaurant and certainly the place for that grand dinner in Florence. The service, however, can be very unfriendly — a major minus, considering the size of the check. The four chefs prepare exquisite traditional and nouvelle dishes with a Franco-Italian flavor, perhaps a mosaic of sweet and sour fish, sweetbread salad with shrimp sauce, ricotta and salami pie, or medallions of veal with capers and lime. The wine collection (60,000 bottles) is outstanding, understandably so, since the restaurant actually began as a wine showroom. Closed Sundays, Mondays at lunch, and August. Reservations necessary. Major credit cards accepted. 87 Via Ghibellina (phone: 242777). Very expensive.

Campidoglio – White tablecloths and elegant service set this attractive place apart from most Florentine trattorias, and the excellent Italian fare makes it worth the tab. Closed Thursdays. Reservations advised. Major credit cards accepted. 8r Via Campidoglio (phone: 287770). Expensive.

Il Cenacolo – "The Last Supper" continues to be the rage in refined restaurants. The ambience is ultra-cool, with a lovely garden for alfresco dining in fine weather. The cuisine is both traditional and new, featuring some old Florentine recipes with an innovative flair and a light touch for today's health-conscious patrons. There also is a bar in which to drown your sorrows after you settle the tab. Closed Sundays and Mondays at lunch. Reservations necessary. Major credit cards accepted. 34 Borgo Ognissanti (phone: 219493). Expensive.

Coco Lezzone – Classic Florentine fare, white-tile trattoria decor, and attentive service are the major pluses of this unpretentious establishment. Don't miss the *pappa al pomodoro* or *ribollita,* hearty, bread-thickened soups. A pontential drawback is that it is often crowded, so don't expect to linger over a meal. Closed Tuesday evenings and Sundays. Also closed in August and from late December through early January. Reservations advised. Most major credit cards accepted. 6r Via del Parioncino (phone: 287178).

Harry's Bar – No relation to the famed eatery in Venice, but Americans tend to flock here just the same. Italian specialties are best, though it's also the place to find a hamburger and French fries. Closed Sundays and mid-December to mid-January. Reservations advised. Major credit cards accepted. 22r Lungarno Amerigo Vespucci (phone: 296700). Expensive.

Ottorino – This chic establishment, with its welcoming ambience, serves beautifully prepared, classic Italian specialties — mostly fresh pasta and fish — served with fine wines. Closed Sundays and in August. Reservations advised. Major credit cards accepted. 12r Via delle Oche (phone: 218747). Expensive.

Quattro Stagioni – Perfectly executed, simple Italian dishes are served to a crowd of regulars for lunch; a few tourists come here in the evening. Fresh pasta, homemade spinach gnocchi (dumplings), and wonderful fish and meat dishes are served with flair. Closed Sundays, Saturdays in summer, and August. Reservations advised. Most major credit cards accepted. 61 Via Maggio (phone: 218906). Expensive.

Relais le Jardin – Located in the *Regency Umbria* hotel, well-heeled Florentines like to dine here, especially in summer when the tables are moved into the garden. The tone is one of understated elegance, with first class service and faultless Florentine cooking. The menu changes frequently, and the chef turns out some interesting pasta variations. Open daily. Reservations advised. Major credit cards accepted. 3 Piazza Massimo d'Azeglio (phone: 245247). Expensive.

Sabatini – Once Florence's top dining room, but thoroughly outclassed in recent years. It's still quiet, dignified, and noted for its traditional fare, but the quality has slipped. Some may find the standard menu far less interesting than those of less expensive trattorias. Closed Mondays. Reservations advised. Major credit cards accepted. 9A Via Panzani (phone: 211559 or 282802). Expensive.

Bibe – In a buccolic setting along the Bagnese River, this establishment specializes in simple trattoria fare. Homemade pasta and soup, grilled meat and poultry, Florentine fried foods, and tasty desserts grace the menu. Closed Wednesdays and Thursdays for lunch. Reservations advised. Most major credit cards accepted. 1r Via delle Bagnese (phone: 204-9085). Expensive to moderate.

Cantinetta Antinori – Not quite a restaurant, but a typically rustic (yet fashionably chic) cantina, with food designed to accompany the Antinori wines. Perfect for a light lunch of salami, or *finocchiona,* with bread, *crostini* (chicken liver canapés), soup, or a modest hot dish such as tripe or *bollito misto* (mixed boiled meat). Closed weekends and August. Reservations unnecessary. No credit cards accepted. 3 Piazza Antinori (phone: 292234). Expensive to moderate.

Cibreo – Also named after a historic Florentine dish, one so good it is said to have given Catherine de' Medici near fatal indigestion from overeating. Although the menu offers interesting old Tuscan dishes, it does not limit itself to the traditional Florentine fare it does so well. Genoese minestrone, eggplant parmesan from the south, polenta from the Veneto, plus savory appetizers such as walnut and *pecorino* cheese salad, soups, seafood with an unusual twist (mussel terrine, squid stew), and homemade desserts are all available, as are good wines. In summer, there's alfresco dining. Closed Sundays and from late July to mid-September. Reservations necessary. Major credit cards accepted. 118r Via de' Macci (phone: 234-1100). Expensive to moderate.

Taverna del Bronzino – Rustic yet elegant, set in a 16th-century palazzo furnished with antiques and a garden for alfresco dining in season. *Crostini ai funghi porcini* (wild mushroom canapés), *tortelloni al cedro,* and renowned Florentine beef with green peppers are specialties. Closed Sundays. Reservations advised. Major credit cards accepted. 25-27r Via delle Ruote (phone: 495220). Expensive to moderate.

La Vecchia Cucina – A bit out of the way, but offering *nuova cucina* worth trying when you've had your fill of wonderfully traditional Tuscan food. The innovative menu of a half-dozen first and second courses and three desserts is recited by the owner (tricky if you don't speak Italian), and it changes every week. Interesting wine list. Closed Sundays and August. Reservations advised. Major credit cards accepted. 1r Viale Edmondo De Amicis (phone: 660143). Expensive to moderate.

Acqua A Due – Once a vegetarian restaurant, this place now offers a selection of both fowl and fish, but most diners come here for the *assaggi* tasting menu of pasta and desserts, which change daily. Closed Mondays. Reservations advised. No credit cards accepted. 40r Via della Vigna Vecchia (phone: 284170). Moderate.

La Baraonda – Hearty Tuscan dishes, as well as rice cooked with lettuce, meat loaf, vegetable timbale, and Baraonda apple pie are expertly prepared here. Closed Sundays and August. Major credit cards accepted. 67 Via Ghibellina (phone: 234-1171). Moderate.

Buzzino – The perfect place for lunch or dinner after a cultural feast at the *Uffizi*, which is just a block away. The setting is warm, the waiters friendly, and the food good enough to put tired museumgoers back on their feet. The bill is sweetened by the arrival of the free *vin santo* (a sweet dessert wine). Open daily. Reservations advised. Major credit cards accepted. 8 Via dei Leoni (phone: 2398013). Moderate.

Cammillo – An appealing, bustling spot near the Ponte Santa Trinita, offering authentic dishes such as tripe *alla fiorentina* and, in season, pasta with white truffles. Closed Wednesdays and Thursdays. Reservations unnecessary. No credit cards accepted. 57r Borgo San Jacopo (phone: 212427). Moderate.

Cantina Barbagianni – This "white owl" is a new Tuscan eatery with an interesting, original menu. From the wonderful soup to the delicious grilled meat and fish, each meal is a completely satifying experience. A complimentary vegetable terrine is served to diners while they wait for their first course to arrive. The desserts are attractive, and the wine list is quite good. Closed Sundays. Reservations advised. Most major credit cards accepted. 13r Via Sant'Egidio (phone: 248-0508). Moderate.

La Carabaccia – Named after an antique Florentine dish (none other than onion soup) loved by the Medicis, the menu changes daily according to what's good at the market. Five starters and five main courses generally are offered, occasionally featuring parts of an animal you never thought you could eat (don't ask!). Very popular, informal, and unrushed. Closed Sundays, Mondays at lunch, and August. Reservations advised. No credit cards accepted. 190r Via Palazzuolo (phone: 214782). Moderate.

Le Cave – A delightful stop in Fiesole and sheer magic in early summer and fall, when it's great to lunch under the linden trees and gaze out over the splendid valley. Indoors is warm, cozy, and rustic, as is the country-style cooking, beginning with excellent prosciutto, *finocchiona* and other local salami, chicken and truffle croquettes, canapés of mozzarella and mushrooms, *crespelle* or ravioli, and the house specialty, *gallina al mattone*, spring chicken grilled on an open fire and seriously seasoned with black pepper and the purest of virgin olive oils. Closed Thursdays, Sunday evenings, and August. Reservations necessary. No credit cards accepted. 16 Via delle Cave, Località Maiano, Fiesole (phone: 59133). Moderate.

Cinghiale Bianco – This cozy, hospitable, and popular lunch spot with whitewashed walls and contrasting dark wood decor is near the Ponte Vecchio. It serves great pasta and tasty Florentine specialties such as spinach and ricotta dumplings called "priest-stranglers," veal scallops, cured beef with arugula, and simple desserts, all at reasonable prices. Closed Tuesdays and Wednesdays. Reservations advised. Major credit cards accepted. 43r Borgo San Jacopo (phone: 215706). Moderate.

Da Ganino – Long a Florentine favorite, this typically tiny Tuscan trattoria is family-run. It still is small and cozy in the winter, with alfresco dining on the small square in fine weather. Here is some of the best Florentine *cucina,* including fresh mushrooms and truffles in season and a justifiably famous cheesecake. Closed Sundays, 3 weeks in August, and *Christmas.* Reservations advised. Major credit cards accepted. 4r Piazza dei Cimatori (phone: 214125). Moderate.

Garga – The unusual specialties of this eatery that recently moved into larger quarters from a former butcher shop include *zuppa di cavoli neri* (soup of a bitter green local vegetable), risotto of leeks and bacon, and *gnocchetti verdi* (pasta of spinach and ricotta) — all exquisitely prepared, and absolutely terrific. Closed Sundays and Monday lunch. Reservations necessary. No credit cards accepted. 48-52 Via del Moro (phone: 239-8898). Moderate.

Il Latini – This popular eatery, in the former stables of the historic Palazzo Rucellai, serves such solid and abundant fare as hearty Tuscan soup, unpretentious meat platters, grilled fish, fresh vegetables, and traditional desserts. Not for romantic evenings, here you sit at long communal tables and the food keeps arriving. Good value. Closed Mondays and Tuesday lunch. Reservations unnecessary. No credit cards accepted. 6r Via Palchetti (phone: 210916). Moderate.

La Loggia – On the most spectacular site in Florence, with a view over the entire city, it's run by some former *Sabatini* waiters who, by employing traditional Tuscan cuisine and efficient service despite the crowds, have transformed a once-mediocre restaurant into a Florentine favorite. The panorama from the terrace makes it especially pleasant during the summer. Closed Wednesdays. Reservations advised. Major credit cards accepted. 1 Piazzale Michelangelo (phone: 287032 or 2342832). Moderate.

Monkey Business – An unusual eatery with jungle decor and creative dishes with lovely sauces. Worth trying are the fresh pasta and risotto, and the Bavarian cream with chocolate sauce for dessert. Closed Mondays. Reservations advised. Major credit cards accepted. 11r Chiasso dei Baroncelli (phone: 288219). Moderate.

Omero – The menu here hasn't changed in decades, and all the regulars who flock to this eatery are grateful. In the front is a grocery store where Florentines buy staples or stop for a glass of wine. The restaurant in the back has beautiful views of the Tuscan hills, and the small garden downstairs is wonderful for summer dining, although the service tends to be slow and the sound of the insect zapper may be distracting. Still, the exceptional *fettunta* (Tuscan garlic bread), ravioli, grilled chicken, ubiquitous *bistecca alla fiorentina,* fried artichokes or zucchini blossoms (in season), and meringue dessert are worth the wait. Closed Tuesdays and August. Reservations advised. Major credit cards accepted. 11r Via Pian dei Giullari (phone: 220053). Moderate.

Osteria da Quinto – A longtime favorite with Florentines, in large part because owner Leo Codacci is a great music lover and often treats customers to bursts of song when the mood strikes him. The *bistecca alla fiorentina* is among the biggest and best in town. It's always packed, so be sure to reserve ahead. Closed Mondays. Major credit cards accepted. 5 Piazza Peruzzi (phone: 213323). Moderate.

Pallottino – One of Florence's newest, this rising star on the gastronomic scene offers a good selection of Tuscan food, including many hard-to-find dishes. Specialties like spaghetti with fresh tomatoes and arugula, stuffed chicken neck (tastes much better than it sounds), and *bistecca alla fiorentina* are not to be missed. Closed Mondays and Tuesdays for lunch. Reservations necessary. Major credit cards accepted. 1r Via dell'Isola delle Stinche (phone: 289573). Moderate.

Pennello – An exciting antipasto table (as with dim sum, you're charged for how much you eat) with a wide array of salads, marinated fish, olives, and vegetables. While the pasta and other entrées are good, they are anticlimatic after the splendid appetizers. The ambience is pure trattoria, with a tiny dining terrace in back for outdoor dining in summer. Closed Sunday evenings, Mondays, and August. Reservations advised. Most major credit cards are accepted. 4r Via Dante Alighieri (phone: 94848). Moderate.

Pierot – The specialty is seafood, especially on Tuesdays and Fridays. The menu is long and ever-changing, depending on the availability of ingredients, but if you spot the traditional squid and beet dish called *inzimino di calamari e bietoline,* try it; ditto the chestnut ice cream for dessert. Open later than most. Closed Sundays and the last 3 weeks of July. Reservations advised. Major credit cards accepted. 25r Piazza Taddeo Gaddi (phone: 702100). Moderate.

La Sostanza – Popularly called *Troia,* literally a hog (also a woman of easy virtue), this is one of Florence's oldest and most cherished trattoria, serving some of the best steaks in town. If you haven't had a *bistecca alla fiorentina* with Tuscan beans, get here early. The place is picturesquely plain and tiny, the turnover as fast as the service (which can be rude if you try to linger). Communal tables. Closed Saturday evenings, Sundays, and August. Reservations necessary. 25r Via del Porcellana (phone: 212691). Moderate.

Trattoria del Francescano – Lovers of hearty Florentine fare such as *tagliatelle con funghi porcini* (wide noodles with mushrooms) and *pappa al pomodoro* (thick fresh tomato and bread soup) will appreciate this family-run place. Great store is set by fresh ingredients and time-honored recipes. Closed Wednesdays. Reservations necessary. Major credit cards accepted. 26r Via San Giuseppe (phone: 241605). Moderate.

Tredici Gobbi – Once known for Hungarian cooking, which still simmers on the back burner, Tuscan specialties have come to the fore. The name translates as "Thirteen Hunchbacks." Closed Sunday evenings, Mondays, and August. Reservations advised. Major credit cards accepted. 9r Via del Porcellana (phone: 298769). Moderate.

Antico Fattore – In the shadow of the *Uffizi,* it's famous for its *ribollita,* a vegetable soup so thick with broccoli, bread, and white beans a spoon stands up in it. The rest of the menu is equally hearty peasant fare. Closed Sundays, Mondays, and mid-July to early August. Reservations advised. Major credit cards accepted. 1r Via Lambertesca (phone: 261215). Moderate to inexpensive.

Belle Donne – This establishment is so tiny that it's easy to miss from the street. There's a communal marble table with butcher-paper placemats — perfect for a quick lunch or complete meal. Closed Saturdays and Sundays. Reservations advised. No credit cards accepted. 16r Via delle Belle Donne (phone: 262609). Moderate to inexpensive.

Osteria Tre Panche – This eatery has only three tables (which means communal seating) in the winter, in addition to a few outdoor tables in the spring and summer, but it offers homemade pasta, interesting salads, and a menu larger than you'd dream possible for the infinitesimal kitchen. Closed Sundays. Reservations advised. Most major credit cards accepted. 32r Via Paccinotti (phone: 583724). Moderate to inexpensive.

Trattoria del Cibreo – The no-frills backroom of *Cibreo* serves food here from the same kitchen at a fraction of the cost. Closed Sundays, Mondays, and July 15 through August. Reservations advised. Most major credit cards accepted. 35 Piazza Ghiberti (phone: 234100). Moderate to inexpensive.

Vecchia Bettola – Quality home-style Tuscan cooking in a typical trattoria, with marble tabletops and butcher-paper placemats. Chicken liver canapés, soups and pasta, hearty meat dishes, and some unexpectedly good wines fill the menu. Uncomfortable seating is the only drawback to this pleasant old dive. Closed Sundays and Mondays. Reservations unnecessary. No credit cards accepted. 34r Viale Ariosto (phone: 224158). Moderate to inexpensive.

Angiolino – Very good potluck and very economical. This is on the Pitti side of the river and the ambience is cozy. Closed Sundays and Mondays. Reservations unnecessary. No credit cards accepted. 36r Via di Santo Spirito (phone: 239-8976). Inexpensive.

La Casalinga – Neighborhood workers, artisans, and shop-owners congregate daily at this simple trattoria to eat on white paper tablecloths and discuss everything from international affairs to philosophy. Closed Sundays and August. No reservations. No credit cards accepted. 9r Via Michelozzi (phone: 218624). Inexpensive.

Cinghiale Bianco – Cozy and hospitable, this trattoria serves great pasta and other tasty Florentine specialties at very reasonable prices. Don't miss the *fettunta farcita,* an old peasant recipe of garlic-rubbed bread layered with spinach and white beans. Closed Tuesdays, Wednesdays, and January. Reservations advised. No credit cards accepted. 43r Borgo San Jacopo (phone: 215706). Inexpensive.

Da Rocco – Tasty food and low prices are the trademarks. They also prepare take-out dishes, as well as fine vegetarian meals. Open for lunch only. Closed Sundays. No reservations. No credit cards accepted. *Sant'Ambrogio Market.* Inexpensive.

Fagioli – A cheery, rustic ambience and a full bar. Enjoy the *passato di fagioli con pasta,* a thick soup of white beans and pasta. Closed weekends and August. No reservations. No credit cards accepted. 47r Corso Tintori (phone: 244285). Inexpensive.

Le Mossacce – Still largely frequented by habitués, it's filled with long paper-covered tables and serves good country cooking. Try the *ribollita,* a thick and hearty vegetable soup. Closed Saturday nights, Sundays, and August. Reservations unnecessary. No credit cards accepted. 55r Via del Proconsolo (phone: 294361). Inexpensive.

Nerbone – Perfect for a quick midday bite and a glass of wine. The ambience may be less than elegant, but it is quite cheerful and the prices are extraordinarily low. Open for lunch only. Closed Sundays. No credit cards accepted. *San Lorenzo Market.* Inexpensive.

Osteria Di Guiseppe Alessi – Now a private club, this is still one of the great bargains in the city, featuring fast service and simple Tuscan cooking. Visitors can purchase a 1-year membership on the spot for 7,000 lire, which covers the entrance fee and admits them to other inexpensive restaurant clubs in Florence. Closed Sundays. Reservations advised. No credit cards accepted. 26r Via di Mezzo (phone: 241821). Inexpensive.

Ruggero – This simple trattoria serves some of the best Florentine food in the city — well-prepared rustic fare. The *pasta alla carrettiera* (in a spicy tomato sauce), the traditional *pappa al pomodoro* (thick tomato soup), *ribollita,* and meat dishes are all tasty. The tables are filled with members of the Florentine nobility at Sunday lunch. Closed Tuesdays, Wednesdays, and July 7 to August 7. Reservations necessary. No credit cards accepted. 89 Via Senese (phone: 220542). Inexpensive.

Trattoria da Graziella – When you are tired of Florentine fare, head to this eatery in Fiesole where Sardinian-born Ugo Salis offers well-cooked island dishes, such as the spectacular and mouth-watering suckling pig. There are good Sardinian wines to wash down the meal, though chianti fans also will be satisfied. There is a large terrace for alfresco dining. Closed Mondays. Reservations advised. Major credit cards accepted. 20 Via Cave di Maiano, Fiesole (phone: 599963). Inexpensive.

Vecchia Bettola – A typical Tuscan trattoria with quality home-style cooking and marble tabletops. Closed Mondays and Tuesdays. Reservations unnecessary. No credit cards accepted. 32-34r Viale Ariosto (phone: 224158). Inexpensive.

PIZZA: Although pizza isn't a traditional Florentine dish, when it emerges fresh from a wood-burning oven and melting with mozzarella, it is still one of the glories of Italy. Variations on the simple pie can range from a minimalist *marinara* (tomato, garlic, and oregano) to the classic *margherita* (mozzarella, tomato, and basil) to more ornate creations such as the *capricciosa,* whose ingredients are based on the whims of the pizza maker. In restaurants, pizza is generally the size of a dinner plate and has a thinner, crisper crust than most American pies. Beware of the indigestible rectangles of pizza perched in snack bar windows which seem appealing and are utterly ignored by city denizens. The following places serve up tasty creations with flair: *Al Pescatore* (54 Via Ponte alle Mosse; phone: 353974); *Borgo Antico* (6r Piazza Santo Spirito; phone: 210437); *Yellow* (39r Via Proconsolo; phone: 211766); and *Danny Rock* (13 Via Pandolfini; phone: 234-0307).

CAFFÈS: Just as Parisians religiously congregate in little outdoor cafés to read a newspaper or discuss politics with friends, the Italians regard the *caffè* as a home away from home. Here life slows to a romantic standstill as patrons leisurely sip cappuccino or Campari.

Dolce Vita – *The* hangout for beautiful people in Florence. Convivial chatter rarely ceases here, and the bar stays open until 2 AM. Closed Sundays. No reservations. No credit cards accepted. Piazza del Carmine (phone: 284595).

Giacosa – Located on Via Tornabuoni, this *caffè* is the perfect place for a tasty snack or a stand-up lunch; have a cup of tea at one of the tiny tables in the corner or try a Negroni, which was invented here in the 1920s by Count Negroni. A combination of Campari, vermouth, and gin, it is a potent potable. Closed Sundays. No reservations. No credit cards accepted. 83r Via Tornabuoni (phone: 296226).

Gilli – Easily the most beautiful *caffè* situated in the wide expanse of Piazza della Repubblica, its Belle Epoque decor is especially charming in the summer, when an orchestra plays music in the background and all seems right with the world. Order a *caffè normale* if you need a shot of energizing espresso, or sample a *caffè correto*, into which a generous dash of brandy is added. Closed Tuesdays. No reservations. No credit cards accepted. 13-14r Piazza della Repubblica (phone: 212280).

Paszkowski – Right next door to the *Gilli* is this lively place, *the* spot in the piazza for people watching. If you arrive early enough and are longing for some home cooking, try their filling American breakfast. Closed Mondays. No reservations. No credit cards accepted. 6r Piazza della Repubblica (phone: 210236).

Rifrullo – Just by the San Niccolo gate, this bar attracts a young, international crowd. Aside from its extensive menu of aperitifs, it also offers delectable crêpes and some sandwiches. Don't forget to visit its gelateria around the corner, one of the best places in the city to satisfy your sweet tooth. Closed Wednesdays. No reservations. No credit cards accepted. 55r Via San Niccolò (phone: 234-2621).

Rivoire – An inspiring view of the Palazzo Vecchio combined with a cup of fragrant hot chocolate is the antidote to even the most exhausted sightseer. Although its prices are rather steep, its location in Florence's loveliest piazza more than compensates for the inflated tab. Closed Mondays. No reservations. No credit cards accepted. 54 Piazza della Signoria (phone: 214412).

GELATO: No one should leave Italy without at least a taste of this treat. Far lighter than ice cream (it's made without cream), it has a creamy consistency. Fruit flavors are composed of fresh fruit, sugar, and water, and other flavors — such as chocolate, coffee, hazelnut, and vanilla — have a milk or custard base. *Semifreddo* is a milk-based gelato that has whipped cream folded in; the chocolate flavor is known as mousse. In any case, it is always delicious!

Badiani – Number one on the gelato list for Florentine cognoscenti, these creamy, original flavors include Buontalenti, an extra-rich custard named after the Florentine architect/artist. According to legend, Buontalenti was the inventor of gelato. Closed Tuesdays. No reservations. No credit cards accepted. 20r Viale dei Mille (phone: 578682).

Cavini – This establishment has a loyal cult following. Its fruit flavors are first-rate. Closed Mondays. No reservations. No credit cards accepted. Piazza della Cure (phone: 587489).

Frilli – This tiny latteria (milk shop) is known for its fine *semifreddo*, especially the chocolate mousse and *amarena* (sour cherry). Closed Wednesdays. No reservations. No credit cards accepted. 57 Via San Niccolò (phone: 23621).

Gelateria dei Neri – Virtually open around the clock, this new gelateria has won the hearts of many Florentines. The ambience is elegant, and the tasty ice cream is served in fancy cones. 20-22r Via dei Neri (phone: 210034).

Perchè No? – This establishment is located on a side street near Piazza della Signoria. The fruit flavors offered here are a bit less sweet than most Florentine gelato. Closed Tuesdays. No reservations. No credit cards accepted. 19r Via dei Tavolini (phone: 239-8969).

Pomposi – Right on the corner of Piazza della Signoria, this place is considered by many Florentines to have the finest gelato in the land. Try the chocolate or coffee — they're true standouts. Closed Mondays. No reservations. No credit cards accepted. 9r Via Calzaiuoli (phone: 216651).

Vivoli – A venerable and adored institution, this is regarded as the oldest and best gelateria in town, although some find its ice cream to be slightly too sweet. The rice pudding-ish *riso* is a knockout. Closed Mondays. No reservations. No credit cards accepted. 7 Via dell'Isola delle Stinche (phone: 292334).

■ **A Taste of Home:** And if for some reason your tastebuds get homesick, head for *CarLie's* (12r Via delle Brache; phone: 215137). Started by two Smith College graduates, these Yankees offer brownies, cupcakes, strawberry shortcake, and at *Thanksgiving,* pumpkin or apple pie.

DIVERSIONS

For the Experience

Quintessential Florence

Florentines tend to be a bit more reserved than their southern counterparts in Rome and Naples, but that doesn't mean they have less to be excited about.

For the most part, Florentines' attitude toward their rich inventory of culture and heritage is dignified — but nonetheless full of pride. Perhaps this attitude is a by-product of waking each morning to greet all the abundant relics of Michelangelo and Da Vinci — to say nothing of virtually every other Renaissance master. It's tough not to take this extraordinary bounty for granted.

But that doesn't mean that Florence isn't full of all sorts of earthier entities that delight both spirit and body. This rare combination of ancient and modern is what makes Florence unique. What follow are some of the best ways to quickly get in touch with the soul of Florence.

THE VIEW — PIAZZALE MICHELANGELO AND FORTE BELVEDERE: An elevated view of the city from the surrounding hills is one of the purest forms of pleasure that Florence offers. The distinctive architecture of the city's main monuments is easy to pick out in the sea of terra cotta tile roofs, divided by the Arno River, and punctuated with bridges. Piazzale Michelangelo is a favorite with visitors for its wonderful panorama. It also is the setting for copies of Michelangelo's *David, Dawn,* and *Dusk* — all stuck incongruously in the center of a parking lot.

But the best vista of Florence is from Forte Belvedere, built in the late 1500s by Florentine Mannerist architect Buontalenti for Grand Duke Ferdinand I de' Medici. The locale, with its hillside views of domed, terra cotta Florence, is far more evocative than Piazzale Michelangelo because there are virtually no souvenir stands or tour buses. A good time to go is early morning or before sunset, when the light is best, although clouds and fog can make the entire city disappear in a carpet of mist at any time. Forte Belvedere's terraces are the site of frequent exhibitions of Italian creativity, and everything from modern sculpture to Ferraris have been shown off with the city as a backdrop.

AN APERITIVO AT RIVOIRE: The ambience at this café is typically Florentine, and with Piazza della Signoria in the background it's ideal for people watching. Sit outdoors when the weather permits (watch out for the pigeons) and gaze out on the bustling scene of one of the world's most beautiful piazze. Take in the copy of Michelangelo's *David* and the Renaissance palazzi that surround the square. On a brisk fall day, the tiny tables in the paneled, Old World interior offer the same vista, as well as warmth. *Rivoire*'s bright-red house *aperitivo* is laced with Campari, garnished with an orange wedge, and quite tasty. Even Florentine dialect becomes comprehensible after three of these. Perfect in the cooler weather is the pudding-like hot chocolate or the *crema cioccolata,* a chocolate-hazelnut cream with a fudge-like consistency that will thrill chocoholics. Packaged in a rectangular red box, the *crema* comes complete with its own demitasse spoon engraved with the café's name.

STROLLING THE PONTE VECCHIO: The oldest bridge spanning the Arno River, this is the only one the Nazis left standing when they retreated from Florence in 1944. Destroyed by floods and rebuilt many times over the centuries, its current incarnation was reinforced in 1345. Since then, it has withstood many of the river's overflowings. Rows of shops specializing in gold jewelry line both sides of the ancient span. The displays of earrings, rings, bracelets, necklaces, and brooches — made from semi-precious stones and set in gold — can be mesmerizing, even if you don't want to buy. Visit before 8 AM, when old-fashioned shutters still conceal shop windows, creating a romantic atmosphere of another era, and when the lack of crowds will enhance enjoyment of the statues in the bridge's center and the tranquil flow of the river. The views from both sides — of towering cypresses and the Church of San Miniato, and of the graceful curves of the Ponte Santa Trinita — are fantastic. (Be sure to return later in the day for an 18-karat shopping spree.) Nighttime is special, too, when the twinkling lights along the river give the whole city an ethereal feeling.

THE THREE DAVIDS: One of the world's best-known sculptures, Michelangelo's *David* has been endlessly reproduced, displayed in phalanxes on souvenir shop shelves, yet is still capable of inspiring awe. Carved out of one huge piece of white marble that other sculptors had discarded, this was the first *David* (unlike those by Donatello and Andrea del Verrocchio) that depicted this biblical figure in full height in all his anatomical perfection. It artfully expresses the Greek quality of resistance to tyranny. Two copies — one in Piazzale Michelangelo and one in its original location outside the Palazzo Vecchio (it was moved in 1873 when it was feared that the elements would destroy the statue) — only hint at the glory of this masterpiece, now housed in the *Accademia.* The recently broken (by a lunatic) toe of the original was being repaired as we went to press.

LA FIORENTINA: The name for both a juicy T-bone steak and the city's soccer squad, *La Fiorentina* appeals to both serious carnivores and sports fans. The thick steak, sold in 100-gram units and grilled rare over a charcoal fire, is usually big enough for two or three diners, and is found in most traditional restaurants, including *Omero* and *Pallottino.* Purists may want to hold out for the local, hard-to-find Chianina beef. Soccer, Italy's national sport, is followed with an almost religious fervor by fans, and the Sunday afternoon *partita* is a rite. During the 2 hours when these games are played, an eerie hush — broken only by periodic shouts of joy — falls over the city. After Florence wins a home game and the stadium empties, triumphant fans drape themselves in team colors, cheering and waving banners from buses and cars; the streets are raucous with the honking of car horns. Buy a purple-and-white *Fiorentina* scarf and root for the home team. Tickets for a soccer match can be purchased at the sports bar next to the central post office in Piazza della Repubblica, or from your hotel concierge. It seems fitting that the *1990 World Cup* was held in Italy — matches took place in 12 cities throughout the country (including Florence), although Italy placed only a heartbreaking third.

SAN LORENZO MARKET: A microcosm of Florentine commerce, the *Mercato di San Lorenzo* offers wares including sweaters, T-shirts, underwear, Italian Army-Navy wear, leather goods, costume jewelry, and much, much more, in an outdoor bazaar surrounding the huge, cast-iron building where Florentines shop indoors for groceries 6 mornings a week. Take the escalator to the fruit and vegetable stands on the top floor — closer to the wonderful glass-and-cast-iron ceiling — for a whiff of freshly picked produce and a view of Florentine shoppers and vendors locked in daily combat.

MADE-TO-ORDER-BY-HAND GLOVES: The artisan tradition in Florence still runs strong — in a city known for leather goods, *Madova* is the last glove manufacturer and sells more than any other store. It also makes custom gloves for hard-to-fit hands, and caters to the whims of color-conscious clients. Choose from more than 40 different shades of supersoft kid, and a wealth of styles and linings. Prices range from $10 to $12 for simple gloves to over $100 for exotic leathers.

LUNCH AT CANTINETTA ANTINORI, DINNER AT OMERO: Lunch at *Cantinetta Antinori*, with its traditional menu and clubby atmosphere (dark wood, high ceilings, muted lighting, and white linen placemats on wooden tables), attracts locals and visitors in the know. Antinori wines from the Chianti region are served by the glass or bottle. Politicians, fashion designers, and nobility all hang out here, soaking up the *Antinori* extra virgin olive oil on country-style bread.

Dinner at *Omero* never strays from Florentine classics, especially the grilled chicken or incredibly tender Chianina steaks. Marcello Mastroianni, Julia Child, and Raymond Burr are all fans. Passing through the local grocery store to reach the restaurant is part of the experience. Inside, windows on three sides overlook the Florentine countryside, and landscape paintings typical to trattorie hang on the walls. Food lovers can purchase fine extra virgin olive oil ladled from a terra cotta urn to take home — the quintessential Florentine gastronomic souvenir.

Florence's Most Memorable Hostelries

Sooner or later, whenever the world was too much with them, the Greta Garbos and Winston Churchills, Richard Wagners and Liz Taylors, of every era slept here.

None of this should come as a surprise to anyone who has ever experienced the pleasures of the best Florentine hotels. Like one big room with a view, Florence and the surrounding area is full of princely villas, magnificent monasteries, and other handsome accommodations lovingly and lavishly ransomed from the past. These historic hostelries supply the perfect excuse to avoid the anonymous glass-and-concrete business domes of postwar Italy.

EXCELSIOR: The halls of this 205-room hotel are truly elegant — marble, gilt, mirror, and chandeliers all representing the style and ambience of the days of the Grand Tour. A recent restoration has dressed it up with 18th-century Florentine furnishings, and the service lives up to the setting. Elegant appointments, such as marble bathrooms and linen sheets, are hallmarks of the CIGA luxury hotel chain. Many rooms overlook the Arno River, and a drink at the bar at sunset is an unforgettable experience. Details: *Excelsior*, 3 Piazza Ognissanti, Firenze 50125 (phone: 55-264201; fax: 55-210278).

GRAND: Across the way from the *Excelsior* is this recently restored, but smaller and more intimate 109-room hostelry. The guestrooms in this 15th-century palazzo are luxurious and the public spaces elegant. Head concierge Signor Barbacci is said to be the best in Florence, capable of procuring a ticket for almost any event, and able to handle almost any eventuality. Details: *Grand*, 1 Piazza Ognissanti, Firenze 50123 (phone: 55-278781; fax: 55-217400).

HELVETIA & BRISTOL: Newly restored to all its 19th-century splendor, this lovely place has 52 individually decorated rooms and suites. All are furnished with antiques and boast the most spectacular marble bathrooms in the city (with the added luxury of Jacuzzis). Conveniently located on a quiet street right off the Piazza della Repubblica, its winter garden, with an Art Nouveau stained glass ceiling, is the perfect setting for a drink; its restaurant serves elegant Tuscan cuisine. Details: *Helvetia & Bristol*, 2 Via dei Pescioni, Firenze 50123 (phone: 55-287814; fax: 55-288353).

LOGGIATO DEI SERVITI: Located in one of the most beautiful piazze in the city, this 20-room hostelry in a Renaissance palazzo has quickly become a Florentine favorite, which is why booking ahead is definitely recommended. The suites are spacious, the decor simple but well done, with old (not antique by Florentine standards, which measure in centuries) furniture, and the staff extremely helpful. Some rooms overlook the piazza, others the terra cotta roofs and the courtyard of the *Accademia*. Details: *Loggiato dei Serviti,* 3 Piazza SS Annunziata, Firenze 50122 (phone: 55-219165.)

REGENCY: Housed in a former Florentine villa, this charming member of the prestigious Relais & Châteaux chain enjoys a garden-like setting not far from the center of town. Small (only 31 rooms), it offers the ultimate in luxury — exquisitely furnished rooms, a first-rate restaurant — and personalized service in a serene environment reminiscent of a country estate. Details: *Regency,* 3 Piazza M. d'Azeglio, Firenze 50121 (phone and fax: 55-245247; telex: 571058).

TORRE DI BELLOSGUARDO: Up a narrow country lane just a 10-minute drive from the center of Florence, this lovely, understated, exceptional hotel is the next best thing to owning a fully staffed Florentine villa. Terra cotta floors, beamed ceilings, antiques, and intimate sitting rooms are part of the charm of Baron Franchetti's villa-turned-hostelry. Its 10 rooms and 6 suites are individually decorated, and the views are amazing, especially from the swimming pool. The baron, his wife, and the staff are helpful and friendly; stroll through the gardens and feel like Florentine nobility. Details: *Torre di Bellosguardo,* 2 Via Roti Michelozzi, Firenze 50124 (phone: 55-229-8145; fax: 55-229008).

VILLA SAN MICHELE: Michelangelo designed the façade for a spartan monastery, but this 28-room hostelry in Fiesole, in the hills above Florence, under the same careful ownership as the *Cipriani* in Venice, is a place of aristocratic dinners by candlelight in an open-air restaurant, state-of-the-art Jacuzzis, manicured gardens, canopied beds and other antiques, and princely prices. A limousine is available to whisk guests back and forth to see Michelangelo's other creations in the museums and churches of Florence. Art critic Bernard Berenson's famed villa and painting collection, *I Tatti* — now the property of Harvard University — is only a Titian's throw away. Closed mid-November through February. Details: *Villa San Michele,* 4 Via Doccia, Fiesole (Firenze) 50014 (phone: 55-59451; in the US, 800-237-1236; fax: 55-598734).

Buon Appetito: The Best Restaurants of Florence

While all those mad dogs and Englishmen are running around in the noonday sun, Florentines are lolling in the shade of a spaghetti tree in a piazza beside the banks of the Arno. Every afternoon, they sit happily and hungrily at table for 3 or 4 hours. Almost every evening, dinner is the principal entertainment. The city is full of family trattorie that make the most of their comestible bounties, wonderful establishments that offer a mix of hominess, sophistication, and generally superb food made from whatever was in the market that morning (usually written in purple ink in an almost indecipherable scrawl). At places like these, it's great fun to share the Italians' zest in their culinary heritage — those below are just the *crema della crema.*

La cucina creativa — Italy's answer to the nouvelle cuisine of France — is firmly established. Old-fashioned cereal staples like barley and *faro* are new culinary fashions; give them a try. With 5,000 miles of coastline, there are plenty of fish in Italian seas that are served in grand style in Florentine restaurants. There are more pasta dishes in Florence than there are forks. We suggest making an effort to try them all. (Be sure to phone ahead for reservations.) And if you overeat, a shot of the pungent little herbal horror known as Fernet-Branca, available in most bars and restaurants, normally will chase away all evil abdominal spirits. *Buon appetito!*

CANTINETTA ANTINORI: The atmosphere here is more like a Florentine club than a restaurant, with a crowd of regulars who frequent what was originally the Antinori family wine bar. The menu has been expanded to include some interesting Tuscan classics, in addition to the dishes that have been prepared with great success for years. There is a wide range of splendid Antinori wines that can be had by the glass or bottle and the extra virgin olive oil is also from the family estates. *Fettunta* (garlic bread), *pappa al pomodoro,* and *biscotti* with the sweet wine (*vin santo*) are a must. Closed weekends and August. No credit cards accepted. Details: *Cantinetta Antinori,* 3r Piazza Antinori, Firenze 50123 (phone: 55-292234).

CIBREO: Three differently priced restaurants (one kitchen prepares the food for all) serve dishes that please Florentine regulars and visitors alike, despite the absence of pasta. In the elegant front room, there is wooden wainscotting, paintings, tablecloths, stemware, and long tables displaying serious antipasti and desserts; for those in a hurry, the back room is crowded, has no frills, and you can't reserve ahead. The bell pepper soup, polenta with herbs, squid and swiss chard, and boned duck are classics. The café around the corner serves an inexpensive light lunch, drinks, coffee, and dessert. All three choices are fine, and are among the best eateries in the city. Closed Sundays and late August to mid-September. Major credit cards accepted. Details: *Cibreo,* 118r Via dei Macci, Firenze 50122 (phone: 55-234-1100).

ENOTECA PINCHIORRI: Michelangelo, Botticelli, and this restaurant make a perfect Florentine day. The edible art here changes with the market's offerings, but often exhibits such masterworks as foie gras with pomegranate salad, sole with onion-and-parsley purée, tiny gnocchi (potato dumplings) with basil, veal with caper-and-lime sauce, and duck in red wine. The charming 15th-century-palace setting and the flawlessly appointed tables complete the picture. An *enoteca* is a kind of wine merchant's showroom — that's how the restaurant got its start — and red, white, and rosé are still its flying colors. One ingredient that should be left out: Service is very stuffy these days, and the $300 check for two does make you think twice before being snubbed by Italy's haughtiest waiters. Closed Sundays, Mondays at lunch, and August. Details: *Enoteca Pinchiorri,* 87 Via Ghibellina, Firenze 50122 (phone: 55-242777).

GARGA: The Canadian and Florentine wife-and-husband owners moved their tiny, highly successful restaurant into a larger space down the street, but the food is the same — Tuscan with a twist of fantasy. Fresh pasta with a spicy tomato sauce, or delicately dressed with a lemony mint as homage to the Medicis, are specialties, and the wonderful meat dishes are flavored with fresh herbs. The decor of wildly colorful frescoes, large plants, and antique tables creates a wonderful bohemian atmosphere. Closed Sundays and Mondays for lunch. No credit cards accepted. Details: *Garga,* 48-52 Via del Moro, Firenze 50123 (phone: 55-239-8898).

OMERO: It's easy to see why this eatery has a steady stream of regulars — it's in a beautiful setting outside the city and the menu hasn't changed in decades, for which the regulars who flock here are grateful. There is a grocery store in front where locals can purchase salt, olive oil, other Tuscan staples, salami and other meat, or stop in for a glass of wine. The restaurant in the back has lovely views of the countryside, and there is alfresco dining in the summer. The service, however, can be slow, and the anti-insect machine annoying. Still, the exceptional *fettunta* (garlic bread), ravioli, flattened grilled chicken, *bistecca alla fiorentina* (Chianina beef when they can get it), fried artichokes or zucchini flowers (in season), and meringue dessert are worth the wait. Extra virgin olive oil is the house dressing. Closed Tuesdays and August. Major credit cards accepted. Details: *Omero,* 11r Via Pian dei Giullari, Firenze 50125 (phone: 55-220053).

PALLOTTINO: One of the city's newest, with stone floors, yellow tablecloths, tiled walls, and a comfortable feeling. Seating is mostly on benches and stools, with colorful fabric cushions adding zest to the simplicity. Spaghetti with fresh tomatoes and arugula, stuffed chicken neck (tastes far better than it sounds), and *bistecca alla fiorentina* (of Chianina beef) are among the wonderful selections of strictly Tuscan food that is not to be missed. It's hard to resist the lure of gelato at *Vivoli* next door, but the cakes here are also tasty. Closed Mondays and Tuesday lunch. Major credit cards accepted. Details: *Pallottino,* 1r Via dell'Isola delle Stinche, Firenze 50122 (phone: 55-289573).

Florence's Best Cafés and Confections

Perhaps no other institution reflects the relaxed Italian lifestyle as much as the ubiquitous café (or bar, as it is most often called in Italy). From small emporia with three tin tables where locals perpetually argue the Sunday soccer results, to the sprawling outdoor drawing rooms of the cafés in Piazza della Repubblica, life slows to a sit-and-sip. Florentines order Campari or cappuccino and put the world on hold. Inside, Florentine cafés are for receiving friends and suitors, reading the paper, and writing the great Italian novel. Some regulars even get their mail at their local café. Outside, in summer, the café is for appraising and supervising the spectacle. There was good reason why Puccini set a whole act of his opera *La Bohème* in a café.

When you visit those below — a few of the most evocative of the breed — remember that cafés are not necessarily inexpensive. Table prices are usually far higher than what you pay for the same items when standing at the bar. So when you're charged $5 for an espresso, don't grumble — just think of it as rent. Pastries and gelato also play a large role among Florentines with a sweet tooth. Those listed are among the best.

BADIANI: The first choice of many Florentines for gelato, especially for the flavor Buontalenti, named for the Mannerist architect-artist-sculptor and supposed inventor of gelato. The chocolate is rich and dark, and the hazelnut is outstanding, but an out-of-the-way location may deter all but the most determined fans. Closed Tuesdays. 20r Viale dei Mille (phone: 55-578682).

CARLIE'S: Expatriates, students abroad, and savvy Florentines flock here for American-style chocolate-chip cookies, brownies, muffins, cheesecake, and apple pie freshly baked by two Smith College graduates. Closed Tuesdays. 12r Via delle Brache (phone: 55-215137).

COSI: Crowded all day, this pastry shop and bar serves one of the best classic *cornetto* (croissant) and cappuccino breakfasts in town. Sandwiches are fresh and well made and the pastries are tasty. Closed Sundays. 9r Piazza Salvemini (phone: 55-248-0367).

DOLCE DOLCEZZA: This out-of-the-way shop is said to have the tastiest nontraditional desserts in the city by those in the know. Chocoholics thrill to the dense icing-like chocolate cake or the chocolate hazelnut *torta Ilaria.* The tangy lemon tart also has its fans. Those not interested in traveling to the edge of town can sample these desserts at *Coco Lezzone* (6r Via del Parioncino; phone: 55-287178) and *Il Bronzino.* Closed Sunday afternoons and Mondays. 8r Piazza Beccaria (phone: 55-234-5458).

GELATERIA DEI NERI: A relative newcomer on the scene is already making its mark on the taste buds of gelato lovers. The elegant decor, fancy cones, and flavors such as *mitica* (mythical) chocolate-nut-praline and *tiramisù semifreddo* will please even the most jaded palates. Open daily. 20-22r Via dei Neri (phone: 55-210034).

GIACOSA: The bar where the Negroni (Campari, gin, and a twist of orange peel) was invented is now under the same ownership as *Rivoire*. Sandwiches and pastry are first rate, and many locals eat a light, stand-up lunch at the counter. Closed Mondays. 83 Via Tornabuoni (phone: 55-2962260).

GILLI: It might be hard to decide whether to enjoy a coffee or *aperitivo* amidst a Belle Epoque interior or outside where a band plays old-time music in summer months. Either way, you win. Closed Tuesdays. 13-14r Piazza della Repubblica (phone: 55-212280).

MARINO: The *cornetto* (croissant) and cappuccino breakfast here is one of the most wonderful in town. The *cornetti* are always fresh from the oven, both in the morning and at 4 PM. Closed Mondays. 19r Piazza N. Sauro (phone: 55-212657).

RIVOIRE: Established over 100 years ago, this café is across the square from the stern façade of the Palazzo Vecchio. From its outdoor tables, you may contemplate the austere architecture of the fortress-like palace and the copy of Michelangelo's *David* while literally spooning up the decidedly wicked creamed chocolate confection that is the specialty of the house. It was in this piazza that the charming Lucy in Forster's *A Room with a View* fell in love, beneath "a pillar of roughened gold." Closed Mondays. Piazza della Signoria (phone: 55-214412).

VIVOLI: The most famous place in Florence for gelato, although some purists sometimes find its ice cream overly sweet. Still, the fruit flavors are out of this world — banana gelato actually tastes better than bananas, and the rice pudding–like *riso* is justifiably famous. Closed Mondays. 7 Via dell'Isola delle Stinche (phone: 55-292334).

Shopping in Florence

In the beginning, Italians created marble statues, stone palazzi and alabaster altarpieces. In our era, the national talent has turned from the eternal to the ephemeral, from the permanent to the portable. As a result, the descendants of Cellini and Michelangelo lavish their genius for design, their sure instinct for what is simply beautiful, on the creation of objects for daily use that delight the senses. The result has come to be known as "Italian style."

Most shops practice the Anglo-Saxon rite of *prezzi fissi* (fixed prices). Or at least they claim to. But it never hurts to try for the traditional *sconto* (discount) on the grounds that you're paying in cash, that you're buying in quantity, that the price is outrageous, or that you were sent by the owner's brother-in-law in Buffalo.

For information about the best buys in gold, leather, and silk, and where to find them, read on.

WHERE TO SHOP

PONTE VECCHIO: It is the oldest bridge in Florence — built by the Romans where the river was narrowest — and the first to span the Arno River. The Ponte Vecchio was destroyed many times by floods, but somehow it was spared by the Germans when they retreated from Florence in 1944 (although the other bridges in the city were not). In 1594 Ferdinand I, a Medici grand duke, decided to substitute goldsmiths and other jewelers for the shops selling common wares along the bridge. Thirty-eight tiny stores are now wedged on both sides of the Ponte Vecchio, with a bust in the center of the bridge commemorating famed Florentine goldsmith Benvenuto Cellini. Many of the stores have been here for centuries.

Burchi – Classic gold settings and precious stones. 54r Ponte Vecchio (phone: 55-287361).

Fratelli Piccini – Large stones in modern gold settings, as well as antique silver. 23r Ponte Vecchio (phone: 55-294768).

U. Gherardi – The best selection of coral in the city. 5 Ponte Vecchio (phone: 55-211809).

Della Loggia – Modern designs, using precious and semi-precious stones, in steel and gold settings. 52r Ponte Vecchio (phone: 55-296028).

Manelli – Semi-precious stones are the specialty here. 14 Ponte Vecchio (phone: 55-213759).

Melli – An exceptional collection of antique jewelry, silver, clocks, porcelain, and more. 44-46r Ponte Vecchio (phone: 55-211413).

Rajola – Modern jewelry made with precious and semi-precious stones, as well as some heavy handmade chains. 24 Ponte Vecchio (phone: 55-215335).

T. Ristori – Jewelry is more modern here — both precious and semi-precious stones are placed in unusual settings. 1-3r Ponte Vecchio (phone: 55-21557).

Tozzi – A blend of modern and older, not-quite-antique pieces. 19 Ponte Vecchio (phone: 55-283507.)

Vaggi – Classic jewelry at low prices. 2r Ponte Vecchio (phone: 55-215502).

OFF THE BRIDGE: Although Florence is reknowned for its gold jewelry, the city has an abundance of many other beautiful things to purchase. From kitchenware to women's wear, Florentine craftspeople are among the most creative in the world. The stores and markets listed are just a small sampling of the city's abundance.

Alex – The European selection of fashions at both locations is the most *au courant* in the city. Merchandise is well chosen and beautifully displayed. Romeo Gigli, Byblos, Genny, and Complice, as well as Gaultier and Montana, are well represented, as are less well-known brands by the stars of tomorrow. The window decor is usually provocative; it's worth strolling by even if the clothes aren't your style. 5r and 19r Via della Vigna Nuova (phone: 55-210446).

Alinari Books – Members of the Alinari photographer family were the first to capture everyday Italian life on film. Their massive archives are a national treasure, and include a wealth of painting and fresco reproductions and 19th-century Italian subjects; prints, books, catalogues, postcards, and posters of these images are for sale here. Next door is the *Alinari Photography Museum* — a must for photographers and devout Italophiles. 46-48r Via della Vigna Nuova (phone: 55-218975).

Antica Setificio Fiorentino – Thanks to Marchese Emilio Pucci, the 550-year-old Florentine tradition from the San Frediano artisans' quarter has remained alive. The shop at 97r Via della Vigna Nuova (phone: 55-282700) sells silk fabrics that are woven on 17th-century handlooms, but a visit to the showrooms at 4 Via Bartolini, with the clattering of the looms in the background, is more of a thrill.

Athos – Classic and elegant, the leather goods here are among the joys of Florentine shopping. Quality leather goods by Celine, Chanel, Hermès, and other famed designer almost-look-alikes are finely made and sell for far less than the real thing, which may even be produced in their factory. Crocodile and reptile goods are well priced. Custom-made attaché cases, in all sizes and shapes, are a specialty, and they'll monogram your purchase. 6r Borgo SS. Apostoli (phone: 55-262896).

Bottega Veneta – The advertising suggests that your own initials are enough. But the firm's buttery soft, basket-weave leather is their own unmistakable statement, as you can see for yourself. 3-4r Piazza Ognissanti (phone: 55-294265).

Emilio Pucci – The tiny ground-floor boutique in the noble Pucci family palace offers only a small sampling of the collection housed one flight up, where perfume and costume jewelry, as well as women's wear in the distinctive psychedelic prints that were fashionable in the 1960s, can be found. They're back with a vengeance, in new, cleaner shapes that bring out the best in these innovative designs. 6r Via dei Pucci (phone: 55-283061).

Ermenegildo Zegna – A full range of men's wear combines tailoring that outdoes the English with textiles of the finest quality, all in enduringly elegant clothes. The Zegna family started weaving in 1910, carefully choosing the raw materials for their fabrics from all over the world. Cashmere, alpaca, and mohair are the finest. King Juan Carlos of Spain is a fan. 4-7 Piazza dei Rucellai (phone: 55-211098).

Ferragamo – Neapolitan Salvatore Ferragamo established his reputation in Hollywood by creating shoes for the stars, and went on to become the first well-known exporter of fine Italian shoes. His flagship store is located in the Palazzo Feroni-Spini, a medieval fortress that just underwent an extensive restoration, bringing the Ferragamo image totally up to date, yet taking full advantage of its illustrious history. Shoes are known for their comfort, bags and small leather goods are beautifully made, and the clothes are of fine-quality fabric and classic design. The scarves are simply stunning. 12-16r Via Tornabuoni (phone: 55-292123.)

Gucci – Founded in 1904 by Guccio Gucci (from whom the trademark of two interlocking Gs comes), who made saddles and harnesses for the local nobility's horses, the now-famous Gucci empire turns out a wide range of designer goods, all noted for the same quality workmanship as that of Guccio's saddlery. The line was expanded after World War II and Gucci's wares were among the first wave of fine Italian exports. Many of the classic items (such as their loafers that are in the costume collection of New York's *Metropolitan Museum of Art*) are still in production. The entire line has recently been given a face-lift and is now looking quite stylish. The selection at the two Via Tornabuoni stores is beyond comparison, and room after room contains a wealth of items — more Gucci than you've probably ever seen. Prices are high, but less than in the US. 57-73-75r Via Tornabuoni (phone: 55-264011).

Loretta Caponi – If inheriting heirloom linen isn't in the offing, this shop is the next best thing. A favorite with European nobility, wares include crêpe-de-Chine, damask brocade, and linen, all delicately embroidered in the finest Italian tradition. The pastel-colored nightgowns, peignoirs, and robes of lace-trimmed silk or cotton are exquisite, and slips and camisole tops come in classic colors. Signora Caponi also does custom work — table linen can be embroidered to match your china, bath towels to match your wallpaper. All work is done by hand by women who embroider in the sunny back room, so don't expect bargain prices. 12r Borgo Ognissanti (phone: 55-2139668).

Lori Clara e Lorenzo – This huge fashion warehouse is a well-kept Florentine secret; few Americans shop here. Those who love Max Mara quality and style will be overwhelmed by the huge selection — room after room of women's and men's clothes, including countless Max Mara labels, samples, and a smattering of other designer goods. Fendi, Missoni, Kenzo, and Valentino pieces are often found on the seemingly endless racks. Salespeople (who usually won't speak English) escort customers through the labyrinth of garment-filled rooms. However, Clara, who works behind the sales desk and personally prices all garments, will be pleased to speak English. 15 Viale Enrico de Nicola (phone: 55-6503204).

Madova – This tiny shop, across the street from the Ponte Vecchio on the Oltrarno side, houses a wealth of gloves, and seems to have sold them to practically everyone all over the world. Elbow up to the olive green velvet cushion and try to make a decision: Kid or suede? Lined (cashmere, wool, or silk) or unlined? What length? Design? And as for color, there is an entire rainbow of gloves. All are sold with washing instructions. The staff speaks English and can tell your glove size at a glance. The yearly catalogue is barely a substitute for a visit here. 1r Via Guicciardini (phone: 55-296526).

Naj Oleari – Cotton fabrics decorated with whimsical but contemporary designs are treated to quilting, coated with plastic, sold by the meter, or made up into a wide variety of articles including umbrellas, baby clothes, women's wear, boxer shorts, ties, bookbags, and more. Other specialties are the natural floral scents and cosmetics. 37r Via della Vigna Nuova (phone: 55-219688).

L'Officina Profumo-Farmaceutica di Santa Maria Novella – Although it's not easy to find (look for the vertical sign on the side of the building), this onetime pharmacy (from the 17th century) is a unique experience for the visitor. A whiff of perfumed essences (is it frankincense and myrrh?) in the entrance hall will set you up for the main room of frescoed ceilings, patterned marble floors, dark wood cabinets containing flasks of perfumes, scents of all types, potpourri, soaps, talc, and products that seem to have been created for another era — anti-hysteria salts, cosmetic vinegars, and strange digestive liqueurs. 16 Via della Scala (phone: 55-216276).

Pampaloni – Table accessories, kitchen tools, and classic and modern housewares all reflect the very personal taste of this shop's owners. The selection is original, and includes local, imported, and even some handmade traditional crafted items like the miniature Neapolitan crèche fruit baskets. But without a doubt, the most wonderful objects in this store are made from silver. Frames, candlesticks, and bowls, whether Art Deco, baroque, or post-modern, are all finely crafted in the store's workshop outside town. *Tiffany* is a client. 47r Borgo SS Apostoli (phone: 55-263094).

Pineider – The most elegant paper and calling cards are made here for the most elegant Florentines. Some items for purchase include pale, pastel-colored deckle or straight-edged paper in different finishes, and featherweight onionskin airmail paper, as well as writing cards that come in a host of colors (with matching envelopes). Refined business cards can be ordered and shipped, and desktop accessories — fashioned with the same attention to detail — are also available. 76r Via Tornabuoni (phone: 55-211605).

Pitti Libri – A huge Venetian glass chandelier hangs over tall, lacquered bookshelves that are neatly lined with an impressive selection of beautiful books on a wide variety of subjects. Specialties include decorative arts, Florence and Tuscany guide and photo books, cookbooks, and small antique objects of great fascination — old-fashioned lacy stationery, fans, hand-embroidered *Christmas* stockings, select posters, and special postcards — all perfect souvenirs of a Florentine visit. The staff is as special as the book selection. 16 Piazza Pitti (phone: 55-212704).

Prada – High-quality classics — shoes, bags, belts, and small leather goods — have been given a new twist in a wealth of materials, styles, and colors. Reptile, crocodile, and ostrich items all have a modern look. The same new vision is given to the somewhat classic minimalist clothes made from beautiful materials. Fabric bags, totes, and luggage are especially attractive. The new perfume is not for everyone, but it does have its fans. 26-28r Via Vacchereccia (phone: 55-213901).

Richard Ginori – The vast selection of porcelain at this flagship store includes the entire *Richard Ginori* line, as well as fine crystal and silver. The staff is helpful and will order and ship all items. 17r Via Rondinelli (phone: 210041).

Sbigoli – A lovely selection of handmade, hand-decorated terra cotta pottery will make for difficult choices. Bean pots, casseroles, speckled ware, and the yellow bird of Montelupo are some of the specialties of this shop. Custom orders are considered a challenge; be forewarned, they take some time to be made. If you want more *Sbigoli* dishes or have broken a favorite piece, send a photograph and Signora Adami will be happy to make a new one. Shipping can be arranged. 4r Via San Egidio (phone: 55-2479713).

MARKETS: Florence's markets offer a vision of Italians intent on everyday commerce, buying foodstuffs and being distracted by a colorful collection of stalls selling a wealth of goods, from leather jackets to souvenirs. Some markets are ambulatory, setting up in neighborhoods once a week. Others have been in business at the same spot for decades and make an exhilarating contrast to the sober beauty of the narrow streets. The following are some of the most colorful.

Mercato delle Cascine – Located outside the *centro storico* (historic center) in Le Cascine — a tree-filled park — this is the best of the roving markets. Fans insist that they find boutique clothing and fabrics at discount prices, but it takes some hunting. The best stands are easy to spot — they're crowded with well-dressed Florentines. Elbow in and shop like a native, but watch your purse. Open Tuesday mornings from 8 AM to 1 PM. It's along the Arno River between the Ponte dell'Indiano and the Ponte D. Vittoria.

Mercato Nuovo – The *Straw Market* or *Il Mercato del Porcellino* — centrally located on Via Calimata — is covered over and graced with a bronze wild-boar fountain. On sale here are all the usual fake Fendi, Gucci, and Gherardini handbags and belts, and a medley of souvenir items — straw hats, bags, baskets, and placemats (once locally produced, now made in the Far East), tablecloths, tooled leather trays, and a wide range of African wares. It's open daily from 9 AM to 5 PM.

Mercato delle Pulci – Within walking distance of the *Mercato di Sant'Ambrogio,* this flea market sells goods that look like pickings from an Italian attic. The market consists of cramped stands housed in semi-enclosed glass and iron shacks that have a provisional look. Prices seem high, but avid collectors are bound to find something they just can't live without. It's open Tuesdays through Saturdays from 8 AM to 1 PM and from 3:30 to 7 PM; and the first Sunday of each month from 9 AM to 7 PM. Piazza dei Ciompi.

Mercato di San Lorenzo – The *San Lorenzo Market* has changed its location several times in the city's history. The food part moved from the Ponte Vecchio to an early Renaissance site where the Piazza della Repubblica now stands to its present location centered around the Church of San Lorenzo (off Via del Canto dei Nelli). However, about 15 years ago, the city decided to relocate the farmers once again from their outdoor stands to indoor stalls in a glass-domed, cast-iron building, where they sell all kinds of comestibles. Outside, the exhuberant market teems with low-cost temptations — mohair and Shetland sweaters, prim and practical underwear, costume jewelry, brilliantly colored scarves. Although the quality may not be the highest, the prices are usually right, and shrewd bargainers will be able to cut a better deal. *San Lorenzo* is open every morning except Sunday; the outdoor, nonfood part of the market is open daily from 8 AM to 8 PM.

Mercato di Sant'Ambrogio – Smaller, but more manageable than *San Lorenzo, Sant'Ambrogio* has perishables that are sold indoors, while produce, clothes, and plant stalls are outdoors under an awning. The clothing isn't up to the same standard as *San Lorenzo,* but food is the main draw here. Open Mondays through Fridays in the morning. Piazza Ghiberti.

For something out of the ordinary: If you've fallen in love with a corner of Florence and can't quit your job or leave your entire life behind you to live in this most captivating of cities, contact local artist Roberto Menchiari (4 Via delle Pinzochere; phone: 55-241400). His realistic micro-architectural modules of Florence — palaces, doorways, trattorie, tabernacles, and more — reflect his personal perspective of the city, and come complete with litter, scaffolding, and graffiti. Commission your favorite Florentine angle or purchase a set of Roberto's *Trattorie Tascabile,* his pocket-size postcard restaurant series.

HELP! MY SUITCASE WON'T CLOSE

If your suitcase won't close or you're tempted to buy something that won't even fit in a trunk, *Fracassi* (11 Via Santo Spirito; phone: 55-289340) will probably be the answer to your dreams. They'll pick up excess luggage from your hotel and wrap, ship, or airmail it to you in the US. If you visit their offices, check out the Gio Pomodoro sculpture and an impressive wisteria in the garden behind the courtyard.

Cooking Schools

Until recently, every Italian kitchen was a cooking school, *la professoressa* was *la Mamma,* and the student body was restricted to family members. However, Italians have discovered the pleasures of their own nation's regional cooking right along with the rest of the world: Neapolitans now eat Tuscan food at home and Venetians down Sicily's cannoli and cannelloni — foods which, as often as not, *Mamma's mamma* told her nothing about at all. Enter the cooking school.

Some classes are taught by superstars of Italian cooking like Giuliano Bugialli and Lorenza de' Medici, and all are in English. Some schedule courses at specific times, and most cooking schools offer customized arrangements. Some of the best include the following:

IN FLORENCE

COOKING IN FLORENCE: Giuliano Bugialli is well known as the author of four definitive books on Italian cuisine. Every year in Florence, however, he also offers hands-on courses for both professional and nonprofessional cooks that cover the culinary delights of all Italy. Each class in a given course involves supervised preparation of a complete meal planned by Bugialli — a different menu for each class. Students spend the morning with Giuliano working on the day's recipes in small groups, then enjoy a lunch of the prepared dishes. Market tours and sightseeing are part of the experience, and dinners are in local restaurants. Students are awarded a diploma at the end of the course. Week-long programs are held in May, July, September, and October, and cover about 35 recipes a week. Details: *Giuliano Bugialli's Cooking in Florence,* PO Box 1650, Canal Street Station, New York, NY 10013 (phone: 212-966-5325).

ITALIAN CUISINE IN FLORENCE: Teacher Masha Innocenti offers classes on haute Italian cuisine, as well as special pastry and dessert courses. Most last 4 to 5 days and are held year-round in Signora Innocenti's apartment. Course organizers will help students find suitable lodgings. Details: *William Grossi,* RD 1, Ancramdale, NY 12503 (phone: 518-329-1141).

MANGIA: Judy Witts teaches Tuscan cooking to American college students, but private lessons can also be arranged if you call in advance. Her straightforward recipes, easygoing manner, and enthusiasm make these classes enjoyable — and the food is tasty. Details: *Mangia,* 31 Via Taddea, Firenze, 50100 (phone: 55-292578.)

SABINE BUSCH'S DESSERTS: The restaurant *Da Noi* — once considered one of the city's finest — is now only a memory, but Sabine Busch, one of its owners, teaches her special dessert recipes and techniques to pre-arranged small groups. The classes are low-key, and a lesson or two can easily be worked into a Florentine stay. It's the only way to taste these not-too-sweet desserts, and you'll be able to duplicate them at home — a never-ending souvenir of legendary pies, cakes, gelati, and *sorbetti.* Details: *Sabine Busch,* 46r Via Fiesolana, Firenze 50100 (phone: 55-242917).

OUTSIDE THE CITY

RUFFINO TUSCAN EXPERIENCE, near Florence: Chefs (such as Maria Salcuni and Rosario Santoro) who demonstrate their culinary expertise and a group of sommeliers including Ruffino Wine Company owner Ambrogio Folonari Ruffino) are the lure of this adventure in the wine and food of chianti country. In English. Accommodations are in the *Excelsior* hotel in the heart of Florence. Details: *Annemarie Victory Organization, Inc.,* 136 E. 64th St., New York, NY 10021 (phone: 212-486-0353).

VILLA ARCENO COOKERY SCHOOL, Castelnuovo Berardenga: The newly restored 17th-century Villa Arceno in chianti country — with 25 luxurious bedrooms and suites — is the setting for one of Tuscany's newest cooking courses, taught by Betsy Newell and Italian cooking expert and author Anna del Conte. The courses run 5 to 6 days, and lessons are only part of the experience — there also are visits to Florence, Siena, and Pienza. Details: *Villa Arceno Cookery School,* c/o Betsy Newell, 3 St. James Gardens, London W11 4RB, England (phone: 71-6033907).

VILLA TABLE, Coltibuono: This week-long cooking experience permits total immersion in the way of life on a 2,000-acre wine making estate in the heart of chianti country. Lorenza de' Medici, author of many cookbooks published in Italy, teaches cooking using simple ingredients; the estate's produce, extra virgin olive oil, and wines are featured. Mornings are spent in the kitchen with Lorenza, followed by a five-course lunch. Afternoon excursions include visits to local producers of meat, cheese, pastry, and bread, and tours of nearby cities. In the evening, participants dine at private villas and castles. An extensive library, swimming pool, and sauna complete the experience. Live and dine like Tuscan royalty. Students sleep in the 15th-century villa's guestrooms. In English. Details: *The Villa Table,* Badia a Coltibuono, Gaiole in Chianti (Siena) 53013 (phone: 577-749498); or *The Villa Table,* Judy Terrell, 2405 Clublake Trail, McKinney, TX 75070 (phone: 214-542-1500).

For the Body

Good Italian Golf

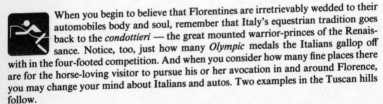

The British brought golf to Italy around the turn of the century, but it was another 50 years or so before the game acquired any degree of popularity — and then it remained an activity of the very social or the very rich.

For complete information about golf in Italy and Italian golf clubs, contact the *Italian Golf Federation*, 388 Via Flaminia, Roma 00196 (phone: 6-323-1825; fax: 6-322-0250).

One golf destination near Florence — nestled in the Chianti hills — is the *Dell'Ugolino* layout. Though not very long, its many trees, bushes, and bunkers require concentration and accuracy. The 4th hole is a long, downhill par 3, the 5th a long par 4 through an olive grove. Wine tasting before a round is not advised. Closed Mondays. Details: *Circolo Golf dell'Ugolino*, 3 Via Chiantigiana, Grassina (Firenze) 50015 (phone: 55-230-1009).

Horsing Around, Italian Style

When you begin to believe that Florentines are irretrievably wedded to their automobiles body and soul, remember that Italy's equestrian tradition goes back to the *condottieri* — the great mounted warrior-princes of the Renaissance. Notice, too, just how many *Olympic* medals the Italians gallop off with in the four-footed competition. And when you consider how many fine places there are for the horse-loving visitor to pursue his or her avocation in and around Florence, you may change your mind about Italians and autos. Two examples in the Tuscan hills follow.

RENDOLA RIDING, Montevarchi, Tuscany: The proprietor of this pastoral riding center goes by the very Anglo-Saxon name of Jenny Bawtree. But the setting, the food, and the gracious simplicity of the farmhouse accommodations are pure Tuscan, and the bridle paths rise and fall over the vineyard-clad hills of Chianti itself. This is art and wine country, and Arezzo, Florence, and Siena are comfortable day trips away — by motorized horsepower for the saddle-weary. In the sunbaked summer months, the party moves to a mountain lodge in the cool woods of Vallombrosa, and the excursions wind through forests and greener pastures. Beginners start with a few lessons in the training ring (*maneggio*), before going out for brief outings; experts join 2- to 5-day trips around the area. *Rendola Riding* has 20 horses and can house 15 people in 7 bedrooms year-round. Details: *Rendola Riding*, Rendola Valdarno (Arezzo) 52020 (phone: 55-9707045); in summer, *Centro Equitazione Vallombrosa*, Saltino (Firenze) 50060 (phone: 55-862018).

VALLEBONA, Pontassieve, Tuscany: Visitors to Vallebona can spend mornings on horseback and afternoons on foot exploring Florence, only a 20-minute drive away. A maximum of 15 guests stay in the simple rooms in this restored Tuscan farmhouse, help care for one of the 25 horses, putter in the garden, and generally participate in the busy, informal life on the farm. The center also organizes 3- to 10-day excursions to Etruscan sites, mountain trail rides, and sightseeing along the river valleys between Siena and Grosseto. Accommodations along these routes are in tents or on farms. Details: *Centro Ippico Vallebona,* Fattoria Lavaccho, 32 Via di Grignano, Pontassieve (Firenze) 50064 (phone: 55-839246).

Biking

 Around Florence, there's not a great deal of flat terrain for leisurely pedaling. But this is a nation of great bicycling tradition, and every Sunday on country roads all over the boot, legions of capped and uniformed bicyclists hunch over their handlebars, pretending to be Saronni or Fausto Coppi. But a word to the two-wheeled: Italian automobile drivers consider cyclists more a nuisance than folks entitled to a share of the roadway. Ride with extreme caution — and a sturdy helmet.

For serious cyclists, an interesting circuit of about 50 miles (80 km) starts in the busy medieval city of Prato, not far from Florence. Take the road to Figline, Schignano, Migliana, Vernio, and Montepiano, all charming country towns way off the tourist track. From Montepiano the road passes through green and golden farmland to Barberino, Calenzano, and back to Prato, itself worth a good long look. You'll find many suggested itineraries for trips all over the country in *Cicloturismo,* a monthly biking magazine in Italian, available at newsstands.

Spas

 In Italy, real water-immersion addicts wouldn't even think about a trip to the Riviera or the Greek isles when they could wallow happily in the mud of Salsomaggiore. Consequently, Italy's water — and its mud — are the base of one of the country's most lucrative industries. There are *terme* (spas) all over the country. Some flourish on the sites of thermal springs first exploited by those imperial water-worshipers, the ancient Romans, who built baths with great fervor. Others trace their origins to antique legends of healing streams spurting from the warm blood of slain princes and miraculous geysers gushing forth from the tears of abandoned maidens.

Happily, visitors to Florence who are 'taking the waters'' can indulge themselves at a spa just an hour away at Montecatini Terme. Time passes with Olympian calm in this most celebrated of Italian spas, an elegant enclave that once belonged to the Medicis and that has hosted princes and pashas, dukes and duchesses, marquises and their betters, since it became popular in the late 19th century. Giuseppe Verdi wrote the last act of *Otello* while taking the waters here, Samuel Barber readied his opera *Vanessa* for production between sips, and André Kostelanetz, Cole Porter, and Herbert von Karajan all found inspiration in the soothing routines. Visitors stop at the grandest of the grand spa pavilions, the Tettuccio Terme, all columns, caryatids, and ceramic tile murals, and then stroll for hours in the splendid and serendipitous gardens, sipping the medicinal waters before lunch as many a Henry James character has done on the pages of his period novels, and peregrinating past the seven other pavilions — they look more like castles, palaces, and monasteries. The straight, tree-lined streets are silent as a siesta for much of the afternoon. Only in the evening do the crowds emerge, glowing and rested — the provincial grocer's liver purified, the jet-lagged nerves of the overfed nobility untangled. The cultural calendar that attracts this cross section of Italian society is chockablock with theater, films, concerts, dance performances, and even auctions, after which the refreshed spa-goers find their way to little cafés where they sip an espresso to the waltzes of a local orchestra. Details: *Azienda Autonoma di Cura e Soggiorno,* 66 Viale Verdi, Montecatini (Pistoia) 51016 (phone: 572-70109).

For the Mind

Twenty-Five Centuries of History: Florence's Museums and Monuments

 Napoleon determinedly exported a significant portion of Italy's art treasures to France, but even so, what remains easily could fill a planet or two. Parochial museums house ancient booty from local excavations. Villas from the 17th century overflow with 16th-century paintings, 1st-century sculptures, and quite a bit from all the centuries in between. The massive state museums have basements stuffed with the national artwork of 2,500 years ago.

Faced with all this, a visitor to Florence is well advised to master the fine art of museumgoing. There is something essentially numbing about the means by which we normally view the world's greatest art, so when visiting the Florentine warehouses of beauty, stop first to thumb through the catalogue or finger the postcards to get an idea of what the collection includes — and where to find it. Determine in advance what you want to see most, and don't try to cover everything. If you attempt a single heroic sweep of the many rooms of the *Uffizi,* you may well develop a case of the dread Giotto-fusion, where all the Madonnas blend into one polychromatic blur. And when you look at paintings at random, study a picture before you inspect the nameplate — that's the best way to quickly determine what you really like, as opposed to what you're supposed to like. And try to give luncheons and Leonardos equal attention.

Break away from the gargantuan museums in any way you can. Don't forget that single altarpiece in a small church, the grouping of portraits adorning the fireplace of the ancient mansion — art in the environment for which it was created.

And visit a gallery or an auction house occasionally, just to remind yourself that once it was *all* for sale.

Note: The opening and closing times listed here should be right most of the time. But museum hours in Florence are often rearranged because of personnel shortages, labor disputes, surprise restorations, and as many other causes as there are paintings in the *Palazzo Pitti.* Caveat visitor!

GALLERIA DELL'ACCADEMIA: Unlike the great, and often bewildering, warehouses that hold more than 700 years of art, this compact museum provides a single, unified experience — of perfection. Its core is the 19th-century hall built especially to fit around Michelangelo's majestic *David.* No matter how many postcards and reproductions you may have seen of this gigantic boy, relaxed and self-confident in the moment before dispatching Goliath, the first in-person vision of him is always intensely dramatic. (A hammer-wielding lunatic smashed one of *David*'s toes last fall, but he was getting a pedicure as we went to press.)

Don't ignore the rest of the rich collection. Retrace your steps through the hall to enter the tortured world of *The Slaves.* Originally intended for the tomb of Pope Julius II, these figures try desperately to wrench themselves out of the rough stone blocks that

Italian composers like Rossini and Puccini. Some of the concerts are held in the magical Boboli Gardens — lovely and quintessentially Italian, especially on a June evening. Despite a name that translates as "Florentine Musical May," the goings-on continue right through June. Details: *Maggio Musicale Fiorentino, Teatro Comunale,* Corso Italia, Firenze 50123 (phone: 55-277-9236).

IL PALIO, Siena: On July 2 and August 16 every year, the whole city of Siena comes alive with *Palio* fever for this wild and exciting medieval horse race around the central Piazza del Campo. The pageantry is incomparable, from the chapel blessing of the steed a couple of days before the event to the monumental costumed procession that kicks off the celebration the night before to the post-race all-night celebration of the victorious neighborhood *contrada,* where the beast dines at a jubilant open-air banquet. The jockeys are notorious for their treachery, and there are absolutely no rules — even a riderless horse can finish in the money. Details: *Azienda Autonoma di Soggiorno e Turismo,* 43 Via di Città, Siena 53100 (phone: 577-42209). For further details, see *Drive 1: Siena and San Gimignano,* DIRECTIONS.

An Antiques Lover's Guide to Florence

Though Italy preserves some of the finest collections of antiquities in the world, buying genuine antiques is not an easy matter. Plenty of dealers are willing to sell small relics of ancient Rome or Etruscan civilization, but even if these items were genuine, the strict control on exporting antiquities would make it impossible for foreign purchasers to take them out of the country legally. At the same time, the kinds of handsome household items of later periods that predominate in the antiques trade of countries like England and Scotland are uncommon in Italy; poorer than other European nations, it never had a large middle class to demand luxury goods in quantity. The objects of value that do exist were almost always made for large noble families who have passed them down — or sold them at prices far beyond the means of the average buyer.

WHAT TO BUY

Italian antiques do exist, however, in several categories. Candlestick holders and marionettes, Sicilian puppets, and lamps made from opaline are good finds, as are figurines from the traditional *Christmas presepe* (nativity scene). Also look for the following:

CHINA AND GLASS: There is a lot of Venetian glass about, but it is very hard to tell its age without expert advice (there are some master glassblowers who make excellent reproductions). The original Venetian crystal tended to be of a darker, smoky hue.

COPPER AND BRASS: You don't have to be an expert to find good pieces of domestic copper and brass. These metals were used for domestic utensils and, therefore, no imprints were used. The oldest pieces were shaped with a hammer and are of irregular thickness.

FURNITURE: Most genuinely old Italian furniture is very heavily restored or extremely expensive. What is available is often not nearly as beautifully finished as pieces made in England or France; design was generally considered more important. Renaissance furniture is particularly sought after and difficult to find at reasonable prices. Popular versions of *barocchetto* (baroque) furniture, however, as well as *rustico* (rustic furniture), are still available.

JEWELRY: Though Italy is one of the world's major centers of modern goldsmithing, much antique jewelry sold here is imported. However, the market offers some very beautiful and ornamental earrings — mostly produced in Gaeta in Lazio. Serving as a constant reminder of the beloved, these were traditionally used instead of engagement rings by peasant girls who worked in the fields, where a ring would have been a nuisance. Many shops also sell old cameos.

PAINTINGS: Since Italians are the world's experts at restoration, there are plenty of appealing pictures on the market. But don't automatically assume they'll be as authentic (or as valuable) as they are handsome. Also be sure to ask first about export restrictions.

PICTURE FRAMES: Gilded-and-carved wood-and-glass frames can still be found fairly easily — though you need a very large wall to hang them and a large bank account to pay for those made during the Renaissance. More practical are the little dressing table frames made in mahogany. They are not outrageously expensive and are widely sold.

POTTERY: Production of majolica — the tin-glazed and richly colored and ornamented earthenware pieces Italians know as *maiolica* or faïence — reached its zenith in the northern Italian towns of Deruta, Faenza, and Gubbio, and in Urbino (the Marches) and Castelli (Abruzzo), during the Renaissance. In the middle of the 16th century, potters in Faenza introduced a lacy, baroque style of "white" pottery, called *bianchi di Faenza,* which remained popular well past the middle of the 17th century. Both types of pottery are much sought after. There are many clever copies, and antiques dealers tell of colleagues who commission pieces and then have them joined together with copper wire so that the finished vessel looks authentically old. Another trick is to glaze century-old bricks to give them an aged look before turning them into Castelli pottery.

PRINTS: The mapmaker of the medieval world, Italy created maps by the score beginning in the 14th century. Prints were also widely issued. Many of those available today have been reproduced on old paper or pulled out of old books.

WHERE TO SHOP

For a comprehensive listing of antiques dealers by region and specialization and of major fairs, consult the *Guida OPI dell'Antiquariato Italiano,* published by Tony Metz, and the *Catalogo dell'Antiquariato Italiano,* published by Giorgio Mondadori. Both are in Italian.

There are dozens of antiques shops in Florence, and the concentrations are highest along Via dei Fossi, Via Maggio, the Ponte Vecchio, and Borgo Ognissanti.

Some good dealers include the following:

Antichità Santoro – The best antiques shop in Italy for Occidental fabric, embroidery, and costumes. 8r Via Mazzetta (phone: 55-213116).

Berto Berti – An eclectic selection of antique silver, paintings, sculpture, furniture, and more. 29r Via dei Fossi (phone: 55-294549).

Botticelli Antichità – Incredible statues (medieval to Renaissance), some furniture, and an interesting selection of European glass. 40r Via Maggio (phone: 55-294229).

Carlo Carnevali – Majolica. 64 Borgo San Jacopo (phone: 55-295064).

Fallani Best – European and Italian 19th-century Art Deco and Art Nouveau (known as Liberty in Italy) furniture, paintings, and objects. 15r Borgo Ognissanti (phone: 55-214986).

Funghini – Italian paintings from the 14th through the 18th centuries, furniture from the 17th and 18th centuries, and occasional antique sculptures. 32r Via dei Fossi (phone: 55-294216).

Galleria Luigi Bellini – The doyen of local dealers, selling 13th- to 17th-century Gothic and Renaissance pieces. 3-5 Lungarno Soderini (phone: 55-294626).

Galleria Parronchi – Paintings from the 19th century. 20r Via dei Fossi (phone: 55-215109).

Giorgio Albertosi – Neo-classical pieces from France and Italy — paintings, sculpture, clocks, and more. 1r Piazza Frescobaldi (phone: 55-213636).

Guido Bartolozzi e Figli – Furniture and works of art. 18r Via Maggio (phone: 55-215602).

Luzzetti Antichità – Italian Renaissance antiques in a 12th-century palace. Medieval pottery, 14th- to 16th-century furniture, sculpture, paintings. 28/A Borgo San Jacopo (phone: 55-211232).

Paolo Romano Antichità – Furnishings, paintings, and sculpture from the 1600s through the 1800s. 20r Borgo Ognissanti (phone: 55-293294).

Piero Betti Galleria – French Art Nouveau furniture and objects, although some Italian glassware has crept in. 46r Borgo Ognissanti (phone: 55-287725.)

The premier Italian antiques fair is Florence's *Mostra d'Antiquariato,* held in mid-September of odd-numbered years in the Palazzo Strozzi. Dealers come from all over the world to exhibit and acquire exquisite antiques. There won't be any bargains, but dedicated collectors shouldn't miss it.

There are junk markets in the Piazza dei Ciompi (Tuesdays through Saturdays) and Piazza Tasso (Saturdays). Bargains are there for the finding, and haggling is the rule. Curiosities are also commonly found in the early morning under the loggia of the *Mercato Nuovo* (Straw Market), near Piazza della Signoria.

RULES OF THE ROAD FOR AN ODYSSEY OF THE OLD

Buy for sheer pleasure, not for investment. Forget about the carrot of supposed retail values that dealers habitually dangle in front of amateur clients. If you love something, it will probably ornament your home until the Ponte Vecchio falls.

Buy the finest example you can afford of any item, in as close to mint condition as possible. Chipped or broken "bargains" will haunt you later with their shabbiness.

Train your eye in museums. These are the best schools for the acquisitive senses, particularly as you begin to develop special passions.

Get advice from specialists when contemplating major acquisitions. Much antique furniture and many paintings have been restored several times over, and Italian antiques salespeople often are more entertaining than knowledgeable. If you want to be absolutely certain that what you're buying is what you've been told it is, stick with the larger dealers. Most auction houses have an evaluation office whose experts will make appraisals for a fee. Even museums in some cities can be approached.

Don't be afraid to haggle. Only a few of the large dealers have *prezzi fissi* (fixed prices). The others will decide for themselves how much you can afford and charge accordingly. So the rule of thumb is to bargain wherever you don't see the *prezzi fissi* sign. A word of warning: While most larger dealers take credit cards, smaller shops do not.

When pricing an object, don't forget to figure the cost of shipping. Around 30% of the cost of the item is about right for large items. Italian firms are expensive, so the best idea is to stick to the bigger international shipping firms, which offer a door-to-door service to New York as well as advice about required export licenses. The store where you purchase the antiques is also a good source.

Note that the Italian government requires that any object of possible historical interest to the Italian state be declared and has levied an export tax on goods exported to the United States. Antiques certified to be at least 100 years old can be brought into the US duty-free, provided they aren't deemed an important part of Italy's artistic patrimony. Any respectable dealer can take care of necessary forms and practicalities.

Churches and Piazzas

 Whether it's a sleek designer space ringed with chic cafés or a rustic square sprouting vegetable stalls, Florence's piazze are the acknowledged centers of local activity. Revolutions are preached there, crowds harangued, heretics burned (figuratively), confetti sprinkled. Every day marks a new period in the perennial urchin-league soccer match. Every evening, tables and chairs are hauled onto the sidewalk, and a new hand is dealt in some card game that seems to have been in progress since the sacking of Rome. And every Sunday, at the end of mass in the late morning, a churchful of the faithful pours out onto the square for a round of gossip before lunch. The church, drawing its patrons from the teeming society just outside its portals and representing a supremely Italian mix of diversion and devotion, is the raison d'être of almost every piazza in Florence. Their styles range from plain to grandiose, from a small church tacked on as an afterthought to the dusty piazza of a Florentine suburb, to Santa Maria Novella, with its grassy square designed to allow optimum admiration of the church's façade.

Built for the greater glory of God, churches were centers of learning, preaching, healing, and redemption through commissions of art by nobles and wealthy merchants during the Middle Ages and Renaissance. They were architectural triumphs, neighborhood centers, and the city's spiritual backbone. Most churches are a layer cake of architectural styles, from the Romanesque (San Miniato) through the Gothic (Santa Maria Novella, Santa Croce) to the Renaissance (the Duomo, San Lorenzo, Santo Spirito), created over the centuries by master craftsmen, artists, and sculptors, each generation contributing a new era's idea of embellishment.

So when making a list of touristy tasks, put "sloth" and "idleness" very near the top and spend a large, lazy slice of as many days as possible doing as the Florentines do — sitting and sipping and stretching and strolling on a glorious Florentine piazza in front of a lush Italian church like those listed below. Here, indeed, the *far niente* (doing nothing) for which Italy is well known is truly *dolce* (sweet).

PIAZZA DELLA REPUBBLICA: Once a jumble of narrow lanes, this piazza was the site of the Jewish ghetto and market from the 1500s until the 1800s, when urban renewal cleared out the area to make a piazza. Five major bars — *Paszkowski* and *Gilli* on the north side of the piazza, *Donnini* and *Giubbe Rosse* on the south, and the *Gambrinus* under the arcade — offer ample leisure opportunities for those who wish to enjoy an *aperitivo* while watching the world go by.

PIAZZA DELLA SANTISSIMA ANNUNZIATA: With Brunelleschi's columned arcades on the Ospedale degli Innocenti (Hospital of the Innocents) marking the beginning of Renaissance architecture, this square is a wide, bright expanse across from the Giardino della Gherardesca. In the center of the piazza is a statue of Ferdinand I de' Medici — Giambologna's last work — and two small green fountains. On the corner is the Palazzo Grifoni, one of the few brick palaces in the city. There aren't any bars for lolling about — sit on the steps in the sun, or stroll under the arcades when it rains.

PIAZZA DELLA SIGNORIA: With the giant, needle-like tower of the Palazzo Vecchio shooting straight up from its base in Piazza della Signoria, this is a noteworthy spot, not least because of the towering, weathered copy of Michelangelo's *David,* the emblem of the city, that stands at its portal. It has also been the heart of Florence for a millennium. Over the troubled centuries of the Renaissance, the square was gradually expanded as powerful families razed the houses of the rivals they expelled. It was here, in the heart of what modern Italy knows as its prime magnet for consumer vanities, that the puritanical priest Savonarola organized his 1497 "Burning of the Vanities," a bonfire fed with purportedly lewd drawings, books, and other trinkets of worldly corruption. And it was also here that Savonarola himself was hanged and burned, on a spot now marked by an etched inscription. Now that the violence has given way to the peaceful ringing of the bells every quarter of an hour, which, along with the throaty cooing of the pigeons, is the dominant sound, the piazza is shiningly beautiful, all the more so because of the adjacent Loggia dei Lanzi — so called because Cosimo the Younger stationed mercenary guards known as *lanzichenecchi* under its overhanging roof, where a small collection of statues now stands.

PIAZZA AND CHURCH OF SANTA CROCE: Despite the church's overwhelming façade, tourist leather shops, and trinket stalls, a wonderful neighborhood feeling exists in this piazza. Take a seat at one of the stone benches and soak up the scene. The church was begun in 1294 so that Franciscan friars could spread their message to the neighborhood's woolworkers. Considered the Florentine *Pantheon* — Galileo, Michelangelo, Machiavelli, and other illustrious locals are buried here — its Giotto frescoes in the Peruzzi and Bardi chapels, now difficult to decipher, had an important influence on 15th-century artists, but were painted over in the 18th century. The Pazzi family's chapel, next to the church in a cloister from the 1300s, is a jewel of Florentine Renaissance architecture by Brunelleschi.

PIAZZA AND CHURCH OF SANTA MARIA NOVELLA: On Via della Scala near the main train station, this piazza, with its tiny formal lawns, benches, and twin obelisks, has long been a favorite of foreigners. Shelley, Henry James, Longfellow, and Emerson all lived here. The famed Gothic preaching church of the Dominicans has a 15th-century façade by Alberti, and Masaccio's powerful fresco of the Trinity and Ghirlandaio's biblical scenes inside are worth a visit.

PIAZZA AND CHURCH OF SANTO SPIRITO: In the Oltrarno, Santo Spirito is one of the city's loveliest piazze — small, simple, well proportioned, and outside the main tourist channels. It has a genuine neighborhood quality (no souvenir stands) and the stone benches, steps leading to the church, and numerous cafés and restaurants afford plenty of vantage points for anyone inclined to spend some leisure time in this favorite Left Bank area. The church, begun by Brunelleschi in 1436, is one of the finest examples of Renaissance architecture; its unadorned, unfinished façade takes on luminous tones in the early morning.

SAN LORENZO: The Medici's parish was northwest of the Duomo, and it was here that they commissioned Brunelleschi to build this beautiful Renaissance house of worship. The interior is notable for its mathematically precise design in harmony with Donatello's decorative works of art. Several of the Medicis are buried here. Michelangelo's plan to complete the façade was rejected, and it remains unfinished to this day. However, he was later commissioned to design the Biblioteca Laurenziana (Laurentian Library) next door (open by appointment only), as well as the New Sacristy of the Medici chapels.

SANTA MARIA DEL CARMINE: This church in the Oltrarno is a must-see for its newly restored Brancacci Chapel, with its monumental, emotive frescoes by Masaccio. The frescoes, much of which depict St. Peter's life, were begun by Masolino, Masaccio's mentor, worked on by Massacio, and completed by Filippino Lippi. They represent a turning point in the history of art — the style of painting revolutionized the way artists depicted the world through the innovative use of light and shade (chiaroscuro) and bold forms.

SANTA MARIA DEL FIORE AND PIAZZA DEL DUOMO: Henry James rhapsodized that this stupendous 13th-century structure — the fourth-largest cathedral in the world — was "the image of some mighty hillside enameled with blooming flowers." It is no less overwhelming today: A visit here is a series of vivid vignettes as unforgettable as Florence itself. Stand at the top of the cupola, and you're afloat in a realm of pink, green, and white marble, with a bird's-eye view of what look to be toy-size pigeons and equally tiny people in the double-sized piazza below. Or climb the endless steps to the top of the Campanile (bell tower) designed by Giotto, and look out over a sea of shingles — those of the cathedral's own lordly Brunelleschi dome blending with those of the rusty rest of the roofs of Florence. Come to earth through the poised and soberly decorated gray and white *pietra forte* interior — stopping, perhaps, for a haunting few minutes at the crypt — and, before you know it, the piazza's rousing rabble is all around you.

In front of the church is the Octagonal Baptistry of St. John the Baptist (San Giovanni Battista), which was Florence's cathedral from the time it was built (in perhaps the 4th century) until the construction of Santa Maria del Fiore. It was clothed in its present marble stripes in the 12th century and is still used for baptisms — Dante Alighieri was baptized here. The royal gilded bronze-relief doors on the east, which Ghiberti spent 27 years of his life creating, rang in the Renaissance and were dubbed by Michelangelo as worthy of being "the gates of paradise." Just to the rear of the Duomo (at 9 Piazza del Duomo) is the *Museo dell'Opera del Duomo* (Duomo Museum), which houses two masterworks of Renaissance sculpture — Donatello's gaunt and tormented (but elegant nonetheless) statue *Mary Magdalene* and an oddly powerful but unfinished Michelangelo *Pietà*, which the artist finally broke up in frustration. For further details, peruse the Duomo section in *Special Places*, THE CITY.

SAN MINIATO AL MONTE: A view of the San Miniato façade from the Ponte Vecchio in the early morning light is an unforgettable sight. With its perfect green-and-white Romanesque marble façade, it is one of Florence's oldest churches, set in the hills overlooking the city. The same marble is used inside, and the 13th-century floor has geometric patterns. There also are many masterpieces by artists such as Michelozzo, Luca della Robbia, and Taddeo Gaddi.

Genealogy Hunts

Unfortunately for modern-day pretenders to the throne, only a privileged few will find their ancestral roots reverently inscribed in the exclusive *Libro d'Oro della Nobiltà Italiana* (Golden Book of the Italian Nobility), published by the *Istituto Araldico Romano* (Via Santa Maria dell'Anima, Roma 00186; phone: 6-1395) and available in most genealogical libraries. This is just as well. The monarchy was outlawed in Italy in 1946, and having to check if you're listed in the *Libro d'Oro* is like wanting to know the price of a Lamborghini — if you have to ask, it's not for you. Also, be forewarned that there are no proven extant lines of descent extending back to the ancient Etruscans, Greeks, or Romans, despite many impassioned claims to the contrary. (However, if behavior is any indication of kinship, these claims may have some basis. The ancient Romans were so eager to prove that they had descended from the city's founding fathers that they had their *sacra gentilica* — family tree, Roman style — painted on the walls of their homes, and fake ancestor portraits and spurious pedigrees were not unknown even then. Rather than dusty canvases, though, these parvenus proudly displayed phony portrait busts, and Aeneas replaced the *Mayflower* as the preferred point of ancestral departure.)

Happily for contemporary ancestor worshipers, Italians have kept meticulous records, beginning as far back as the 13th century, and legitimate evidence of Italian forebears — no matter how humble their origins — usually is yours for the searching. With a little digging around, there's a good chance that you'll be able to visit the church where your Great Uncle Sal married your Great Aunt Rosa before leaving for America, or the port where your grandfather waved good-bye to the Old Country, or the cemetery where your mother's family has been resting quietly for centuries.

Constructing a family tree is a backward process: You need to start with your parents' dates and places of birth, their parents' dates and birthplaces, and so on —

as far back as your search will take you. It should be a considerable stretch since it's quite possible to trace Italian families to about 1500, when it became obligatory for baptisms to be registered in parish churches. To obtain the relevant documents, make sure you have the exact names of each ancestor (remember, many Italian surnames were irrevocably, if unwittingly, changed through clerical misspellings or requested alterations at Ellis Island and other ports of entry), as well as the names of any family members closely related to the ancestors you are researching. You can request many different types of documents that contain information about a previous generation: for example, birth and death certificates, marriage licenses, emigration and immigration records, and baptism and christening records.

PRELIMINARY RESEARCH: Try to gather as much information as possible before your trip. For example, check with your local library and state offices for local published records, regional archives, and local history. The US Library of Congress (Local History and Genealogy Room, Jefferson Building, Washington, DC 20540; phone: 202-707-5537) and the New York Public Library (Division of United States History, Local History, and Genealogy, Room 315N, 42nd St. & 5th Ave., New York, NY 10018; phone: 212-930-0828) both have extensive facilities for in-person research, but you may want to call these institutions in advance to find out if they do have material relevant to your search.

The Family History Library of the Church of Jesus Christ of Latter-Day Saints has more than 32,000 reels of Italian genealogical records on microfilm, available for consultation in person at its headquarters (35 North West Temple St., Salt Lake City, UT 84150; phone: 801-240-2331) or through any of its branch libraries. Using the Mormons' index reels, you can, for a small fee, borrow microfilm records of any Italian town from Salt Lake City. Film should arrive at the branch library in about 6 weeks, and loans are renewable for 2-week periods up to 6 months. There is no charge for reviewing a film at the headquarters in Salt Lake City.

The *Italian Cultural Institute* (686 Park Ave., New York, NY 10021; phone: 212-879-4242) publishes an information sheet on how to go about researching your Italian ancestry. Look in your library for T. Beard and D. Demong's *How to Find Your Family Roots* (McGraw-Hill, 1977), which contains an excellent list of genealogical resources available in both Italian and English.

An indispensable resource found in most libaries is the scholarly reference guide, *The World of Learning* (Europa Publications), which lists libraries and archives throughout Italy. *In Search of Your European Roots* by Angus Baxter ($12.95) contains an excellent chapter on Italy. Two other books worth consulting are the *International Vital Records Handbook* ($24.95) by Thomas Jay Kemp and *Do's and Don'ts for Ancestor-Hunters* ($10.95) by Angus Baxter. The last three titles are available from the Genealogical Publishing Company (1001 N. Calvert St., Baltimore, MD 21202-3897; phone: 301-837-8271).

Further tips can be provided by *Omnibus,* a publication of the *Augustan Society* (PO Box P, Torrance, CA 90508; phone: 213-320-7766). This magazine, which comes out once or twice a year, includes information on genealogy for those researching their family history in any of several European countries, including Italy. A 4-year subscription costs $40. You also may want to subscribe to the *Ancestry Newsletter,* edited by Robb Barr and published bimonthly by Ancestry Incorporated (PO Box 476, Salt Lake City, UT 84110; phone: 800-531-1790). It contains practical information on how to research your ancestry. A 1-year subscription costs $12.

REQUESTING RECORDS: Before 1865, personal records — baptism, confirmation, marriage, and death — were kept, as a rule, only by parish churches. Thus, to obtain information on your family prior to 1865, you should begin by writing either to the parish priest or to the bishop holding territorial jurisdiction. Since 1865, birth, marriage, death, and citizenship records have been kept by the *comuni* (municipalities), so you must write to the *comune* from which your ancestors came. Address your request to the Ufficio di Stato Civile, Piazza della Signoria, Firenze 50121. While the office may have English-speaking personnel, making a request in Italian usually will facilitate matters considerably. The form letter given below will be of great use in your research (send a separate letter for each ancestor).

In Italy, the Ministry of Foreign Affairs (Ministero degli Affari Esteri, 1 Piazzale Farnesina, Roma 00194; phone: 6-63691) has an Office for Research and Studies of Emigration (Ufficio Ricerche e Studi dell'Emigrazione), which may be of assistance.

DIGGING DEEPER: Once you've done your basic research, you might want to turn to some older records or even use them as duplicates to verify information you've already accumulated. The following are some of the records most readily available by mail or in person.

Certificates of Family Genealogy – Write to the Ufficio Informazione (Palazzo Vecchio, Firenze 50122) to obtain a certificate of your family genealogy *(certificato di stato di famiglia)* giving names, relationships, birthdates, and birthplaces of all living family members at the time of recording. These certificates usually date from about the turn of the century and can go back as far as 1869.

Emigration Records – Write to the prefecture of the province of the emigrant's birthplace or port of departure to obtain documentation of an ancestor's emigration from about 1869 to the present. Addresses of provincial prefectures are available from Unione delle Province d'Italia, 4 Piazza Cardelli, Roma 00186 (phone: 6-687-3672).

Draft Records – For draft records dating from 1869 to the present, write to the military district *(Distretto Militare)*, giving birthdates and birthplaces. Some conscription records go back to the Napoleonic era (as early as 1792).

Clerical Surveys – To obtain Catholic parish records *(status animarum),* contact the Central Office for Italian Emigration (UCEI, 3 Via Chiavari, Rome 00186; phone: 6-686-1200) for addresses of local parishes. Records of birthdates, marriage dates, and other biographical information exist, irregularly, from the beginning of the 18th century.

Protestant Parish Registers – Write to the Family History Library in Salt Lake City (address above) for the addresses of 16 Waldensian parishes in the Piedmont district. The parish records include information similar to Catholic clerical surveys and date from 1685.

Roman Catholic Parish Records – Write to the vicar-general of the diocese involved (you can get the address from the Central Office for Italian Emigration, above) for permission to consult the records, which usually are written in Latin. Baptism and christening records, as well as marriage records, date from 1545 (1493 in the town of Fiesole) to the present. Death and burial records go back to the beginning of the 17th century.

Tax Assessment or Census Registers – Write to the Istituto Centrale di Statistica (16 Via Cesare Balbo, Roma 00184; phone: 6-46731) to locate the old census data *(catasti),* also called *libri degli estimi.* Often dating from the 14th century, these contain so-called real estate records (actually tax records — census takers were no fools even then) of heads of households, subtenants, or taxpayers and their residences along with the amount of tax assessed. Most of the records are in the Archivio di Stato Civile in Florence (see above).

Ecclesiastical Records – For clerical records from the 13th to the 19th century, write to the Archivio Segreto, Città del Vaticano, Rome 00185 (phone: 6-6982).

Notarial Records – Contact the Ispettore Generale of the Archivio Notarile (89 Via Padre Semeria, Rome 00154; phone: 6-512-6951) for records concerning wills, donations, settlements, and land sales dating from about 1340. For similar records from Waldensian Protestant archives beginning in 1610, contact the Ispettore Generale of the Archivio di Stato di Torino, 165 Piazza Castello, Torino 10122 (phone: 11-540382).

Other Archives – Archivio Centrale dello Stato, the Italian national archives, are located in a central office (Piazzale degli Archivi, Roma 00144; phone: 6-592-6204);

more complete records are kept in the various former independent states that existed before the unification of Italy. There is a substantial archival center in Florence, the Archivio di Stato.

RESEARCH SERVICES: For those who would rather leave the digging to others, reputable genealogical societies in Italy will do it for you for a fee. Among them are the following:

> *Istituto Araldico Coccia* (Count Ildebrando Coccia Urbani, director; 6 Borgo Santa Croce, Palazzo Antinori, Casella Postale 458, Firenze 50122; phone: 55-242914). Write for their "international ready reckoner," which lists six programs for heraldic and genealogical research.
>
> *Istituto Araldico Genealogico Italiano* (Count Guelfo Guelfi Camaiani, director; 27 Via Santo Spirito, Firenze 50125; phone: 55-213090).
>
> *Istituto Storico Araldico Genealogico Internazionale* (Count Luciano Pelliccioni di Poli, director; 5 Via Pio VIII, Roma 00165; no phone).
>
> *Ufficio di Consulenza Tecnica* (Presso Collegio Araldico, 16 Via Santa Maria dell'Anima, Roma 00185; phone: 6-1395).

With the above information and a little *pazienza* (patience), you should have a firm grasp for a lengthy climb up your Italian family tree.

The following letter states that you wish to know the history of your family and therefore are requesting the document or documents specified regarding the person indicated by name, place of birth, and date of birth; it thanks the addressee in advance for his or her kind attention to your request.

Ufficio dei Registri di Stato Civile
Comune di (Name of municipality)
Provincia di (Name of province)
Italy

> Gentilissimi Signori:
> Desiderando conoscere la storia della mia famiglia, chiedo se cortesemente potreste inviarmi i seguenti certificati:
> (*Check the documents desired.*)
>
> _____ certificato di nascita (*birth certificate*)
> _____ certificato di matrimonio (*marriage certificate*)
> _____ certificato di morte (*death certificate*)
>
> riguardante la persona seguente:
> (*Fill in the appropriate information for your ancestor.*)
>
> (*for a man*) Il Signor: _____ (*name of man*)
> (*for a woman*) La Signora: _____ (*name of woman*)
> nato/a a: _____ (*place of birth*)
> il: _____ (*date of birth*)
>
> Ringraziando Vi anticipatamente per la Vostra cortese attenzione, spero di ricevere al più presto notizie.
>
> Distinti saluti,
> (*sender's signature*)
> (*name of sender*)

A Shutterbug's Florence

 The dramatic interplay of lustrous marble and terra cotta tile, crowded squares and romantic corners, these are Florence's photogenic stock in trade. Even a beginner can achieve remarkable results with a surprisingly basic set of lenses and filters. Equipment is, in fact, only as valuable as the imagination that puts it into use.

Don't be afraid to experiment. Use what knowledge you have to explore new possibilities. Don't limit yourself with preconceived ideas of what's hackneyed or corny. Because the Duomo has been photographed hundreds of times before doesn't make it any less worthy of your attention.

In Florence as elsewhere, spontaneity is one of the keys to good photography. If a sudden shaft of light bursting through the crowds in Piazza della Signoria, don't hesitate to shoot if the moment is right. If photography is indeed capturing a moment and making it timeless, success lies in judging just when a moment worth capturing occurs.

A good picture reveals an eye for detail, whether it's a matter of lighting, positioning your subject, or taking time to frame a picture carefully. The better your grasp of the importance of details, the better your results will be photographically.

Patience is often necessary. Don't shoot a wide-angle view of the Ponte Vecchio if a bus suddenly passes in front of it. A TV antenna in a panorama from the Campanile? Reframe your image to eliminate the obvious distraction. People walking toward a scene that would benefit from their presence? Wait until they're in position before you shoot. After the fact, many of the flaws will be self-evident. The trick is to be aware of the ideal and have the patience to allow it to happen. If you are part of a group, you may well have to trail behind a bit in order to shoot properly. Not only is group activity distracting, but bunches of people hovering nearby tend to stifle spontaneity and overwhelm potential subjects.

The camera provides an opportunity, not only to capture Florence's charm, but to interpret it. What it takes is a sensitivity to the surroundings, a knowledge of the capabilities of your equipment, and a willingness to see things in new ways.

LANDSCAPES: Florence's unique architectural style and the rolling hills surrounding the city are compelling photographic subjects. Getting the full sweep of the city's visual effect can be vital to a good photograph.

Color and form are the obvious ingredients here, and how you frame a picture can be as important as getting the proper exposure. Study the shapes, angles, and colors that make up the scene and create a composition that uses them to best advantage.

Lighting is a vital component in landscapes. Take advantage of the richer colors of early morning and late afternoon whenever possible. The overhead light of midday is often harsh and without the shadowing that can add to the drama of a scene. This is where a polarizer is used to best effect. Most polarizing filters come with a mark on the rotating ring. If you can aim at your subject and point that marker at the sun, the sun's rays are likely to be right for the polarizer to work properly. If not, stick to your skylight filter, underexposing slightly if the scene is particularly bright. Most light meters respond to an overall light balance, with the result that bright areas may appear burned out.

Although a standard 50mm to 55mm lens may work well in some landscape situations, most will benefit from a 20mm to 28mm wide-angle. Panoramic views taken of the Arno River fit beautifully into a wide-angle format, allowing not only the overview, but the opportunity to include other points of interest in the foreground.

To isolate specific elements of any scene, use your telephoto lens. This is the best way to photograph Santa Croce or get a detailed short of one of the panels on the Battistero (Baptitstry). The successful use of a telephoto means developing your eye for detail.

PEOPLE: As with taking pictures of people anywhere, there are going to be times in Florence when a camera is an intrusion. Your approach is the key: Consider your own reaction under similar circumstances, and you have an idea of what would make others comfortable enough to be willing subjects. People are often sensitive to suddenly having a camera pointed at them, and a polite request, while getting you a share of refusals, will also provide a chance to shoot some wonderful portraits that capture the spirit of the city as surely as the scenery does. For candid shots, an excellent lens is a zoom telephoto in the 70mm to 210mm range; it allows you to remain unobtrusive while the telephoto lens draws the subject closer. And for portraits, a telephoto lens can be effectively used as close as 2 or 3 feet.

For authenticity and variety, select a place likely to produce interesting subjects. Piazza della Repubblica is an obvious spot for visitors, but if it's local color you're after, visit the Oltrarno or stroll through the produce and fish markets early in the morning. Aim for shots that tell what's different about Florence. In portraiture, there are several factors to keep in mind. Morning or afternoon light will add richness to skin tones. To avoid the harsh facial shadows cast by direct sunlight, shoot in the shade or in an area where the light is diffused. The only filter to use is a skylight.

SUNSETS: The best place to be for a Florentine sunset is from Piazzale Michelangelo or Forte Belvedere — they afford a spectacular ancient backdrop at day's end.

When shooting sunsets, keep in mind that the brightness will distort meter readings. When composing a shot directly into the sun, frame the picture in the viewfinder so that only half of the sun is included. Read the meter, set, and shoot. Whenever there is this kind of unusual lighting, shoot a few frames in half-step increments, both over and under the meter reading. Bracketing, as this is called, can provide a range of images, the best of which may well be other than the one shot at the meter's recommended setting.

Use any lens for sunsets. A wide-angle is good when the sky is filled with color-streaked clouds, when the sun is partially hidden, or when you're close to an object that silhouettes dramatically against the sky.

Telephoto lenses also produce wonderful silhouettes, either with the sun as a backdrop or against the palette of a brilliant sunset sky. Bracket again here. For the best silhouettes, wait 10 to 15 minutes after sunset. Unless using a very fast film, a tripod is recommended.

Red and orange filters are often used to accentuate a sunset's picture potential. Orange will help turn even a gray sky into something approaching a photogenic finale to the day and can provide particularly beautiful shots linking the sky with the sun reflected on the water. If the sunset is already bold in hue, the orange may overwhelm the natural colors. A red filter will produce dramatic, highly unrealistic results.

NIGHT: If you think that picture possibilities end at sunset, you're presuming that night photography is the exclusive domain of the professional. If you've got a tripod, all you'll need is a cable release to attach to your camera to assure a steady exposure (which is often timed in minutes rather than fractions of a second).

For most nighttime situations, a strobe does the trick, but beware: Flash units are often used improperly. You can't take a view of the *Uffizi* with a flash. It may reach out 30 to 50 feet, but that's it. On the other hand, a flash used too close to your subject may result in overexposure, resulting in a "blown out" effect. With most cameras, strobes will work with a maximum shutter speed of 1/125 or 1/150 of a second. If you set the exposure properly and shoot within range, you should come up with pretty sharp results.

CLOSE-UPS: Whether of people or of details of buildings, close-ups can add another dimension to your photography. There are a number of shooting options, one of which is to use a 70mm or a 210mm lens at its closest focusable distance. Unless you're working in bright sunlight, a tripod will be worthwhile. If you are very near your subject and there is a good deal of reflective light, it may pay to underexpose a bit in relation to the meter reading.

If you do not have a telephoto lens, you can still shoot close-ups using a set of magnification filters. Filter packs of one-, two-, and three-time magnification are available, converting your lens into a close-up lens. Even better is a special macro lens designed for close-up photography.

■**Note:** Standing before some of Florence's most moving Botticellis you may feel an urge to capture the painting on film. Don't do it. Besides the fact that many museums and churches do not allow photography, the results are almost certain to be disappointing. In most of the museums and churches, the lighting is so bad or the painting so far away that a flash will not help. If you really want to bring the memory of the painting home with you, buy a prepared slide from the museum gift shop or a book that has the painting in it.

A SHORT PHOTOGRAPHIC TOUR

Art fans come back from Florence raving about the museums, architects go on about the palaces and piazze, shoppers relate their acquisitions, and photographers talk about the light. Early morning or before sundown are the very best times for pictures that glow. The Arno River, which usually looks murky, takes on a romantic look, almost silver, as it's been described in songs of old. Some photographers prefer a gray, cloud-covered sky. But no matter which light you choose, bring plenty of film, which is more expensive in Italy. Processing is also more costly. *Foto Levi* (12 Vicolo dell'Oro; phone: 55-294002), near the Ponte Vecchio, and *Carnicelli* (4r Piazza Duomo; phone: 55-214352) are both reliable, quick and centrally located.

For inspiration, look to Fulvio Roiter, one of Italy's most famed photographers, who is responsible for a truly beautiful book of Florence and Tuscany and to *Alinari*'s classic 19th-century Florentine photographs (see *Shopping*) which capture to perfection the Florence of another era.

THE VIEW: One of the most wonderful things about Florence is seeing it from above, from practically anywhere overlooking the city. Major monuments rise from a sea of terra cotta tile roofs filling the valley of Florence, edged by dark green cyprus trees on the surrounding hills. From this perspective, pollution, traffic, and chaos disappear. Piazzale Michelangelo, Fiesole, Forte Belvedere, and many other spots on the outskirts of the city offer wonderful photo opportunities, and many hotels have roof garden bars that are perfect for drinks and photographs.

SAN LORENZO AND SANT'AMBROGIO MARKETS: Inside the architecturally interesting edifice of the *Mercato di San Lorenzo,* the bustle of commerce, with a wealth of multicolored produce as a backdrop, is irresistible to a photographer. The market's outdoor stalls also offer some wonderful photo opportunities. The *Mercato di Sant'Ambrogio* is smaller, with more of a neighborhood feeling. For more about this cross-section of Florentine life, see *Markets.*

PONTE VECCHIO AT DAWN: Have a cappuccino and croissant and see the city before the rest of Florence gets up. In the early morning hours on the bridge, the Arno looks misty and the shops with their wooden and iron window-coverings seem straight out of the Middle Ages. It is touristless, the domain of pigeons and a few pedestrians. The views of the Church of San Miniato al Monte and of the Ponte Santa Trinita alone are worth rising early.

THE DAVID: You may think it's a cliché to photograph, until you see the real *David* in all its detailed majesty at the *Accademia.*

THE DUOMO: Green and white striped marble, innumerable impressive angles, and aerial views from its roof all add up to memorable photo possibilites at the Duomo, Campanile, and Baptistry complex.

PIAZZA DELLA SIGNORIA: Gray stone pavements, the imposing Palazzo Vecchio, the gracefully arched Loggia dei Lanzi, some of the best statuary in the world, and a different photo opportunity at different times of the day — the dawn domain of the pigeons, morning tourist crossroads, afternoon playground, or nighttime street theater with fire-eaters.

PIAZZA SANTO SPIRITO: Though not nearly as impressive as Piazza Santa Maria Novella or Piazza Santa Croce, lovely Piazza Spirito has its fans. The small morning market, Brunelleschi's unadorned façade of the Church of Santo Spirito, the graceful fountain in the middle of the oval piazza, complete with a cast of local characters, should satisfy the most demanding shutterbugs.

38 VIA CIMATORI WINE BAR: A shotglass of red wine and a simple sandwich or chicken-liver canapé are the staple fare at this closet-size, stand-up bar located on a side street just around the corner from Piazza Signoria. Locals flock here for lunch or snacks during the day, and the prevailing mood is jovial. Here you can capture some wonderful character studies, as the Florentines aren't averse to having their portraits snapped.

SCAFFOLDING: Somewhere on your trip something you want to photograph will be shrouded in scaffolding, under restoration, and therefore not in its most photogenic condition. Forgive the Italians; their keen sense of restoration is the reason why it's all still there. Think of the tinker-toy-like scaffolding as part of the work and snap away.

DIRECTIONS

INTRODUCTION

Florence is a city for walkers. Not only is it small, but most of its artistic treasures are located within the *centro storico* (historical center) — or within a half-hour's walk of it. Every step through the medieval streets and piazze brings yet another delight — multi-hued stones on magnificent buildings, soaring towers, and imposing bridges. Even for those who think they have seen it all, there is always an unexpected discovery, whether it is one of the less celebrated museums that grace the city, a surprising alleyway off a main thoroughfare, or perhaps one of the many unassuming — but nonetheless wonderful — neighborhood cafés.

It's easy to imagine the days when Dante and Michelangelo lived here; very little has changed in the past several hundred years, except for the addition of cars (and traffic is now prohibited from most of the center). But there are still many outdoor markets, the Arno River flows through the city, and buildings erected by the Medicis are mostly intact.

To explore this Renaissance gem, here are five walks that encompass some of the most interesting and accessible sites, each offering a different perspective on the city. The first four orient visitors to the special qualities of four main Florentine neighborhoods, each with its own traditions and loyalties. They follow a division of the city into quarters that was imposed in 1343, centered around the most important churches of the time — San Giovanni, Santa Maria Novella, Santa Croce, and Santo Spirito. North of the Arno River are San Giovanni (in the center), Santa Maria Novella (in the west), and Santa Croce (in the east). South of the Arno, in the part of Florence called the Oltrarno, is Santo Spirito. Rivalries among the four areas still exist to this day, as is dramatically demonstrated in the annual *Calcio in Costume,* when men in 16th-century costumes partake in a very rough medieval soccer game.

The fifth walk takes visitors out of Florence to the Piazzale Michelangelo and the lovely Church of San Miniato al Monte, where spectacular views of the city down below make the easy hike up worthwhile.

Each itinerary wends its way beside churches, museums, monuments, artisans' shops, boutiques, and restaurants, and steers a course through main piazze, side streets, back alleys, and hidden courtyards. The walks last anywhere from 2 hours (not counting leisurely meals or compulsive shopping) to an entire day — for those who succumb totally to the temptations of the city. It is better to embark on the San Giovanni or the Santa Croce walk in the morning, because both take in bustling markets that close at 2 PM. Work off lunch with the Santa Maria Novella or the Oltrarno itinerary, ideal for afternoon strolling. Although the Oltrarno walk does go past a small morning market, its focus is on local artisans' shops.

A note about the shops along these routes: Most open at 8:30 or 9 AM, close for lunch between 1 and 4 PM, and stay open till 7:30 PM. In summer, most shops are closed Monday mornings, as well as Saturday afternoons.

Also included are four drives through the Tuscan countryside surrounding Florence, with its lush green hills replete with lone, dark cypresses, centuries-old olive trees, and vineyards. The first drive explores the many villas built by the Medicis, who recognized Tuscany's beauty and built their homes in the rolling hills around Florence. The second itinerary visits cities — medieval and Renaissance Prato and Romanesque Pistoia — and the fashionable spa of Montecatini Terme. The bountiful area south of Florence produces chianti classico — the world-famous wine; the third drive goes through the area and includes some wineries that are open to visitors. Finally, the fourth route is to the medieval cities of Siena and San Gimignano. Each excursion could take a day, but for those who wish to set a more leisurely pace, hotels and restaurant recommendations are given.

Though some of the terrain will no doubt be familiar to repeat visitors, the point of these walks and drives is to wander and discover detours off the beaten track. The joy and challenge is to use these suggestions as a guide, and to add to them with a variation ot two on your own theme. Just think of yourself as an artist, with Florence as your palette of inspiration. And enjoy.

Walk 1: San Giovanni

As in most of Italy, markets play an important role in daily Florentine life. They offer not only things to buy — comestibles, clothing, and household goods — but a chance for people to socialize as well. Strolling through these vibrant scenes is a good way to observe the Italian character firsthand. Remember that bargaining is an integral part of any market experience; don't be shy, demand a lower price, and compromise if necessary — it's all part of the fun. This walk starts in the city's largest market — the *Mercato di San Lorenzo* (San Lorenzo Market), then goes past various Medici buildings to San Marco and Piazza Santissima Annunziata, and ends at the Duomo, Florence's magnificent cathedral.

Before starting, indulge in a breakfast of exceptional pastries — there's a window full of them — at the *Sieni* bar (on the corner of Via dell'Ariento and Via Sant'Antonino). Or opt for freshly made doughnuts (*bomboloni*) at *Luisa* (50r Via Sant'Antonino), a shop that specializes in all kinds of fried fantasies, including polenta squares, bread balls, and sweet treats.

After this internal fortification, stroll down Via dell'Ariento and the area surrounding Piazza San Lorenzo. Tempting bargains among the numerous stalls include handbags, gloves, belts, leather clothing, shoes, sweaters, T-shirts, sweatshirts, scarves, headbands, costume jewelry, sunglasses, and many other items, at prices lower than most formal retail shops (although the quality is usually inferior).

Move inside to the modern cast-iron and glass building, built in 1874 by Guiseppe Mengoni, architect of Milan's *Galleria.* It replaced the *Mercato Vecchio* (at the site of the current Piazza della Repubblica), which was torn down to convince Florentine merchants to relocate indoors after the city decided the old market was not only a health hazard, but aesthetically unpleasant as well. A veritable food emporium, ground-floor stands with marble counters offer meat (including horse's), game, fish, bread, pasta, beans, and dried fruit.

Walk the perimeter for an all-inclusive market tour. Although most produce is sold upstairs, don't miss Signor Conti's opulent selection of what seems to be every kind of fruit and vegetable available in Italy. Go to the center of the building and up the escalator (it always seems to be out of order) for a view of the produce — inhale the perfume of freshly harvested fruit and vegetables from the countryside. Purchase a basket of tender berries and admire the herb selection at *Gianni Fancelli* (No. 16).

Back downstairs, stop at *Nerbone* (located on the perimeter — look for the red-and-white sign), a snack or lunch stop featuring both counter and table dining, low prices, and a clientele of market regulars munching away on crispy rolls stuffed with boiled beef and green sauce and other tasty treats. Indulge in a *panino* (sandwich) or plan to return for a hearty lunch.

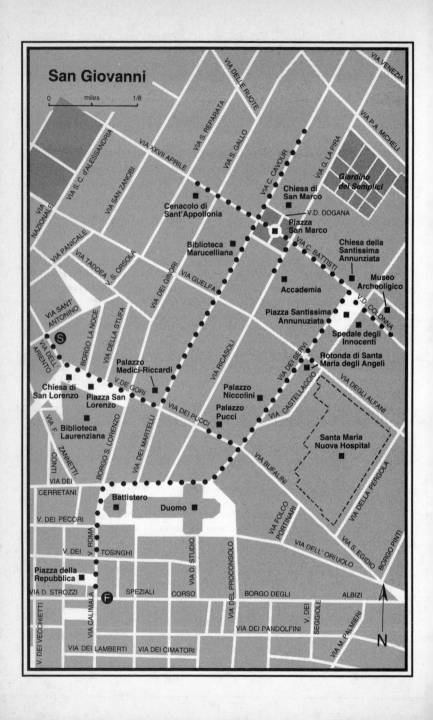

San Giovanni

0 — miles — 1/8

VIA VENEZIA
VIA DELLE RUOTE
VIA P.A. MICHELI
VIA S. REPARATA
VIA S. GALLO
VIA XXVII APRILE
VIA C. CAVOUR
VIA G. LA PIRA
VIA S.C. d'ALESSANDRIA
VIA SAN ZANOBI
Giardino dei Semplici
VIA NAZIONALE
VIA SAN ZANOBI

Chiesa di San Marco

Cenacolo di Sant'Appollonia

V.D. DOGANA

Piazza San Marco

VIA PANICALE
VIA TADDEA
V. S. ORSOLA

Biblioteca Marucelliana

VIA C. BATTISTI

Chiesa della Santissima Annunziata

VIA DEI GINORI
VIA GUELFA

Accademia

Museo Archeoligico

VIA SANT' ANTONINO

BORGO LA NOCE
VIA DELLA STUFA

Piazza Santissima Annunziata

V.D. COLONNA

VIA DELL' ARIENTO

(S)

Palazzo Medici-Riccardi

VIA RICASOLI

Spedale degli Innocenti

V. DE' GORI

Rotonda di Santa Maria degli Angeli

VIA DEI SERVI

Chiesa di San Lorenzo

Piazza San Lorenzo

VIA DEI PUCCI

Palazzo Niccolini

VIA CASTELLACCIO

VIA DEGLI ALFANI

VIA F.
Biblioteca Laurenziana

BORGO S. LORENZO
VIA DEI MARTELLI

Palazzo Pucci

CONTI
ZANNETTI

Santa Maria Nuova Hospital

VIA DELLA PERGOLA

VIA DEI CERRETANI

Battistero

Duomo

VIA BUFALINI

V. DEI PECORI

V. ROMA

V. DEI
TOSINGHI

VIA D. STUDIO

VIA FOLCO PORTINARI

VIA DELL' ORIUOLO

VIA S. EGIDIO

BORGO PINTI

Piazza della Repubblica

(F)

SPEZIALI

CORSO

VIA D. PROCONSOLO

BORGO DEGLI

ALBIZI

VIA D. STROZZI

VIA CALIMALA

V. DEI VECCHIETTI

VIA DEI LAMBERTI

VIA DEI CIMATORI

VIA DEI PANDOLFINI

V. DEI SEGGIOLE

VIA M. PALMIERI

N

Leaving the market, head down Via dell'Ariento. Veer left, passing the Chiesa di San Lorenzo (Church of San Lorenzo), begun in 1419 by Brunelleschi for the Medicis on the site of an older church. Some of the finest artisans of the time added to his efforts over the next 2 centuries. Michelangelo submitted plans for the unfinished façade (his original designs are in the *Casa Buonarroti*) to his Medici patrons, but they did not approve them. The Medicis did, however, accept his ideas for the Biblioteca Laurenziana (entrance through the cloister to the left of the church), a library that contains Cosimo de' Medici's collection of over 10,000 books.

At the corner of the piazza (note the statue of Giovanni delle Bande Nere by Baccio Bandinelli), Via del Canto dei Nelli becomes Via dei Gori. On the left is the impressive rusticated Palazzo Medici-Riccardi, a massive building that takes up a good part of a block. The Medicis lived here until 1540, when they moved to the Palazzo Vecchio (also see *Special Places,* THE CITY). At the corner of Via Cavour, be sure to glance up at the lantern by blacksmith Niccolò Grosso, who was known as "Il Caparra" (the "Deposit") because he wouldn't work without advance money. His work is found only on Florence's most important palaces.

Turn left onto Via Cavour and get the front view of the palace (No. 1), built by Michelozzo di Bartolommeo in 1444–64 after Brunelleschi's plans were rejected as being too showy for the conservative Medicis. (He later sold them to Luca Pitti for his Oltrarno palace.) The ground-floor arches originally were open, but were later filled in with "kneeling windows" based on Michelangelo's design. When the Riccardi family bought the building in 1665, they added more windows and their own crests. The tiny chapel upstairs is a gem, decorated with *The Procession of the Three Magi,* Benozzo Gozzoli's frescoes of the Medici family and friends riding on horseback through a biblical fantasy set in the Tuscan countryside.

Continue up Via Cavour, and if necessary, ask for information at the tourist office (No. 1r) or make a phone call at the *SIP* telephone company (No. 21r). Stop in at *Feltrinelli* (No. 12-20r) and peruse the art books. Note the writing instruments and accoutrements at *Casa dello Stilografica* (House of the Fountain Pen; No. 43). The sales staff is friendly and helpful, and the selection of pens — especially Italian models by Aurora, Ferrari, Omas, and Visconti — may prove irresistible. At least they don't take up much room in a suitcase. Change some money at the impressive Banco di Napoli (No. 24), and take a gander at the Biblioteca Marucelliana, the city's first public library, founded in 1703. Fans of modern furniture will be hard-pressed to pass by *Alivar* (No. 104r) without going inside to look at its stylish, columned interior, as well as its classic modern home furnishings for sale.

At the corner of Via XXVII Aprile, make a left and walk 1½ blocks to a former convent (No. 1) that houses in its refectory the *Cenacolo di Sant'Appollonia,* Andrea del Sarto's *Last Supper* painted in 1519 for the nuns of Sant'Appollonia. Go back to Via Cavour, make a left, and head past Piazza San Marco on Via Cavour to get a glimpse of the *Casino di San Marco* (No. 57), built by Bernardo Buontalenti on the site of San Marco's vegetable garden (now the Court of Appeals). Over the doorway a carved wooden monkey peeks out of a shell at those entering the building. Across the street, flanked by marble signs listing opiates for teeth, perfume, cosmetic vinegar, extracts, essences, and more esoterica is the *Farmacia di San Marco* (No. 146r), established in the 1400s. Ceilings are frescoed and the pharmacy's apothecary jars are antique, but the wooden cabinets are filled with modern pharmaceuticals.

Return to Piazza San Marco to see the Chiesa di San Marco (St. Mark's Church) built in 1452 by Michelozzo, where the puritanical Savonarola preached abstinence — a particularly difficult lesson for the Florentines of the late 1400s! Don't miss the spectacular *Museo di San Marco,* previously a monastery and now a museum dedicated to the mystical works of Fra Angelico, including the meditational frescoes in the friars' dormitory cells (also see *Special Places,* THE CITY). Across the Piazza San Marco, the *Accademia* (the museum entrance is a few steps down Via Ricasoli), tucked behind a 14th-century portico, is home to the original statue of *David* (which was moved from Piazza della Signoria in 1873) and to the *Florentine School of Fine Arts.* The statue had its toes damaged recently by a lunatic's hammer, but repairs were being made as we went to press.

Turn right to Via Cesare Battisti and amble down to the bright and airy Piazza della Santissima Annunziata, a beautiful Renaissance square. Although the piazza's structures were built over a period of 200 years, there is a feeling of flowing harmony. Brunelleschi's loggia of the Ospedale degli Innocenti (Innocents — a euphemism for illegitimate — Hospital) was built in the early 15th century to house the overflow of foundlings from the nearby Ospedale Santa Maria Nuova, and set the tone for later architects. The elegant loggia has archways topped with circular indentations, decorated with Andrea della Robbia tondos. Find the window, now covered with a grate, where abandoned babies were placed. Above it, a bust of Francesco I de' Medici appears, in a spirited architectural joke, wearing the "horns" of a cuckolded husband.

The Chiesa della Santissima Annunziata (Church of the Most Holy Annunciation), founded in 1234, was rebuilt in the mid-15th century by Michelozzo. Its portico sheltered pilgrims who flocked to the church from the countryside. In the middle of the square stands an equestrian statue of Ferdinand I de' Medici by Giambologna (his last work), flanked by two small green fountains. Note the unusual brick façade on the corner building belongs to the Palazzo Grifoni, designed by Bartolommeo Ammannati (a student of Michelangelo) for Cosimo I's courtier Ugolino Grifoni; it is now home to the regional government.

Detour, if you've got time, to Via della Colonna and the *Museo Archeologico* (Archaeological Museum; No. 38). Its Etruscan, Greek, and Roman paintings and artifacts are an important preview to an understanding of Renaissance art. Outside the museum, take Via della Colonna back to the Piazza della Santissima Annunziata. Head for Via dei Servi, a street built especially for processions from the Duomo, and dotted with important palaces. Brunelleschi fans should turn left at Via degli Alfani and stop at the Rotonda di Santa Maria degli Angeli (No. 15), an idealized temple that was never completed. It now houses the language program of the University of Florence.

Of interest on Via dei Servi is the Palazzo Niccolini (No. 15), a building with a checkered history. Designed by Baccio d'Agnolo, it was inhabited by a succession of wealthy Florentines, a Russian chamberlain, the Fascist Federation, and finally its present tenants, a government public works office. The graffito above the second-floor windows is captivating; observe it during a short respite on the building's stone benches.

On Via dei Servi, culinary aficionados will want to stop at *Dino Bartolini* (No. 30), a shop offering Italian housewares and some hard-to-find kitchen items such as molds for *colomba* and panettone cakes, chestnut roasters, polenta pots, and many other wares. On the corner of Via dei Pucci, look up to the right to spot the stately crest of the Medici Pope Leo X, carved by Baccio da Montelupo. Turn right to the Palazzo Pucci (No. 4), which is believed to have been designed by Ammannati and still is the home of the Pucci family (of fashion fame), whose ancestors Dante described as "newly arrived from the countryside." Its inner courtyard hides a few shops, selling not only the well-known Pucci designs, but wine, truffles, and olive oil from the family's country estates. Also note there the busts of famous Pucci ancestors, and numerous family crests — adorned with the head of a moor and a silver headband with three Ts: *Tempori-Tempora-Tempera* (Let things take their natural course). At the ground-floor boutique, admire the Pucci clothes and accessories with their distinctive avant-garde patterns from the 1960s, or whisk up the flight of stairs to the larger shop.

Once again, return to Via dei Servi and walk toward the Duomo, the Battistero (Baptistry), and the Campanile. This northeast approach gives the first-time (and return) visitor an excellent opportunity to appreciate the sheer magnificence of the complex — particularly its overwhelming size and polychrome stones. The Cathedral of Santa Maria del Fiore (the full name of the Duomo) was begun by Arnolfo di Cambio in 1296, but its dome, a masterpiece of Renaissance engineering, was built by Brunelleschi in 1436 and crowned by a lantern in 1461. The colorful pink, green, and white marble façade is from the late 1800s. A walk-through gallery on one side of the cupola's base was begun, but after Michelangelo scoffed at the notion — calling the structure a "cricket's cage" — the work ceased with only one side completed.

In front of the Duomo stands the Battistero (also known as San Giovanni), a Romanesque structure probably dating from the 4th century, which served as the cathedral before the Duomo was built. The bronze reliefs on its doors (reproductions) bridge the Gothic and Renaissance styles; the most famous are by Ghiberti, who won the competition for this commission over Brunelleschi. The Gothic Campanile was begun by Giotto in 1334; he died 2 years later, and the Campanile was not completed until the end of the 14th century. The relief panels, by Andrea Pisano and Luca della Robbia based on Giotto's designs, are copies of the originals now in the *Museo dell'Opera del Duomo* on the other side of the piazza (also see *Special Places,* THE CITY).

Take a well-earned rest at the *Scudieri* bar (on the corner of Via dei Cerratani) and contemplate the Battistero further; head down Via Roma to the Piazza della Repubblica for a break at one of the famous outdoor cafès, or make tracks back to *Nerbone* at the *Mercato di San Lorenzo* for lunch.

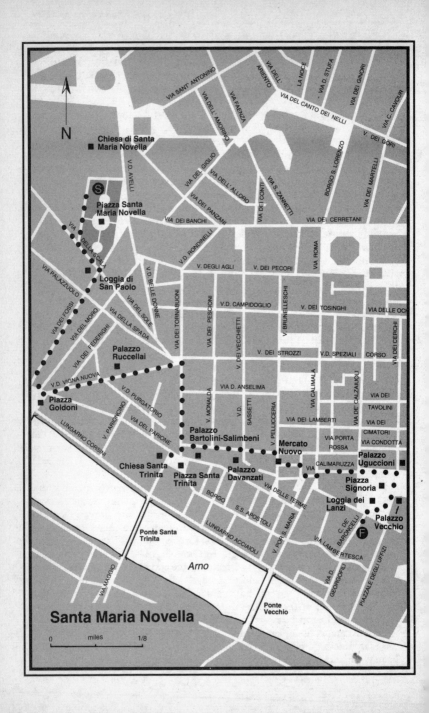

Santa Maria Novella

Walk 2: Santa Maria Novella

The Piazza Santa Maria Novella is considered by many to be Florence's most beautiful, perhaps because it seems removed from the rest of the city (although it is right behind the Functionalist train station, built in 1935). The itinerary starts and ends in two piazze, but in between it is a walk for shoppers — there is a wide variety of stores selling clothing, antiques, sporting goods, photographs, handwoven upholstery fabrics, perfume, essences, tassels, trimmings, and many other items to take home.

The piazza is dominated by a Gothic church — a masterpiece begun in 1246 by two Dominican monks. It was finished in 1360, except for the striped green-and-white marble façade that was added by Leon Battista Alberti from 1456 to 1470, and the sundial on the façade put in by Cosimo I's astronomer in 1572. The arches on the low wall to the right of the church are actually the individual tombs of famous Florentine families, each with its own heraldic crest carved in the stone (also see *Special Places,* THE CITY).

At the far end of the piazza are two marble obelisks supported by bronze turtles (made by Giambologna in 1608), markers for the chariot races once held here. Opposite the church are the elegant arcades and columns of the Loggia di San Paolo (1490), decorated with glazed terra cotta medallions of saints and a lunette of the meeting of San Domenico and San Francesco — by father and son Andrea and Giovanni della Robbia (specialists in glazed terra cotta reliefs), who are said to be figured in the half-moons at either end of the row. Before continuing, spend a few minutes enjoying the green grass in the middle of this lovely piazza.

Turn right down Via della Scala to *L'Officina Profumo-Farmaceutica di Santa Maria Novella* (No. 16 — watch carefully for the vertical sign on the front of the building), a well-preserved 17th-century pharmacy with frescoed ceilings, stone columns, and a patterned marble floor. Its wooden cabinets are crammed with jars, bottles of clear or amber liquids, and white boxes with old-fashioned labels, containing perfume, soaps, ointments, oils, essences, powders, digestive liqueurs, potpourri, bath oils, and after-shave, all made from formulas almost 300 years old. A unique, haunting scent accompanies this experience.

Continue on Via della Scala to *Giardino di Seta* (No. 26r), where silk flowers (complete with artificial aphids!) are hand-crafted by local artisans. Backtrack on Via della Scala, noting the bust of Cosimo I over the entrance to the 15th-century *Aprile* hotel (No. 6) and the frescoes under the hotel eaves, and the tiny Chiesa di San Sepolcro (Church of San Sepolcro; No. 9). Turn right at the loggia onto Via dei Fossi, a street studded with antiques shops. Of special interest are the etched graffiti designs on the bank façade (13 Piazza degli Ottaviani), and *Il Rifugio* (3r Piazza degli Ottaviani), a sporting goods store across the street featuring fine Italian athletic clothing and equipment, as well as American sneakers (whose prices may inspire horrified gasps). A medieval tower, redone in Florentine Renaissance style, houses *G. Lisio* (No. 45), a shop specializing in handwoven silk, velvet, and brocade upholstery fabric that can cost more than $3,000 a yard. Via dei Fossi ends at Piazza Goldoni, which is dominated by Palazzo Ricasoli (No. 2) on the left and a statue of Carlo Goldoni, the 18th-century playwright and father of modern Italian comedy. Notice the smile on his face.

From one of the piazza's benches, gaze out at the Arno and the Ponte alla Carraia. The original bridge (all of Florence's bridges — except the Ponte Vecchio — were destroyed by the Germans during World War II) was built in the 13th century by Ognissanti's monks to cart cloth across the river, but the present version dates from Ammannati's 16th-century design.

Turn left onto Via della Vigna Nuova, for some of the best shopping in Florence. The *Antica Setificio Fiorentino* (No. 97r), a silk factory owned by the Gucci family, has a shop here (closed mornings), but it's more fun to visit the showroom in the San Frediano quarter (see *Walk 4: Santo Spirito*). Among the street's other allures are *A. Biandi* (No. 86r) for knives and scissors; *Edizione & C.* (No. 82r) for stationery and stylish desk accessories, and at their tiny shop nearby (No. 91r), jewelry; *Cole Haan* (No. 77r) for shoes; *Baccani* (No. 75) for prints and frames; *Escada* (No. 71r), *Valentino* (No. 47r), and *Mila Shön* (No. 32r) for elegant women's wear; *Paoli* (No. 26r) for Florentine straw hats, placemats, and flowers; *Naj Oleari* (No. 37r) for fabric umbrellas, children's and women's wear, and gift items, all made with their distinctive cotton prints; two locations of fashion-forward women's clothes at *Alex* (Nos. 5r and 19r); and *Happy Jack* (No. 11r) for menswear.

Pause in the middle of the block on the stone benches outside the Palazzo Ruccellai (No. 18), considered a Florentine Renaissance masterpiece. At the end of the Middle Ages, after all the interfamily disputes were resolved, merchants added benches facing the street whenever they built new palaces so they could easily socialize and gossip with each other. Part of the building is home to the wonderfully restored *Alinari Photography Museum* (No. 50r), known for its constantly changing photography shows. The shop next door (No. 48r) sells catalogues for the shows, as well as *Alinari* photography books and prints. Across the street, for those who never can get enough, is *Ermengildo Zegna* (6 Piazza dei Rucellai) for the finest in men's clothes.

turn right at the traffic light onto Via dei Tornabuoni, the Fifth Avenue of Florence. Truly a royal shopping stretch, it has *Gucci, Armani, Ferragamo, Buccellati, Mario Valentino, Tanino Crisci,* and *Richard Ginori,* as well as *Cartier, Saint Laurent, Hermès, Louis Vuitton,* and *Celine* boutiques, all concentrated in a 2-block area.

Take a break from buying and enjoy the Palazzo della Commenda di Castiglione (No. 7), with its charming frescoed ceilings in the entryway painted by Bernardino Poccetti. Then meander to Piazza Santa Trinita. The Column of Justice in the center of the piazza was taken from the Baths of Caracalla in Rome. Admire the panorama looking toward the Ponte Santa

Trinita, then duck into the church of the same name to explore the Sassetti chapel (in the back on the right), noting the same view captured in the Ghirlandaio fresco.

Cross the street and enter the huge doorway of the Palazzo Bartolini-Salimbeni (No. 1) to view the columned courtyard's beautiful *sgrafitto*. Outside the palace, turn right to Via Porta Rossa, which is closed to most traffic. The 600-year-old *Porta Rossa* hotel (No. 19) is housed in an impressive building, with a wrought-iron lamp and overhanging arches. Nearby, the exterior of the Palazzo Davanzati (No. 13) still has some of its original iron adornments — rings for tying up horses, bars on the top 3 floors where banners and rugs were draped on holidays, and hooks for hanging tapestries. Inside is one of Florence's most delightful museums, the *Museo della Casa Antica Fiorentina* (also see *Museums,* THE CITY).

Worth a stop is *Valmar* (No. 53r), a shop that specializes in *passamanteria* — trimmings, cords, tassels, buttons, bows, belts, and other notions. Weary walkers can wet their whistles with a *frullato,* a frothy shake of fresh fruit, milk, and ice that can be made without sugar (*senza zucchero*) at the stand on the corner of Via Pellicceria.

Turn right, passing through the covered *Mercato Nuovo,* also referred to as the *Porcellino* after the bronze statue of a wild boar by Pietro Tacca (actually a copy of a Roman marble in the *Uffizi*). The statue's nose has been polished to a lustrous sheen by thousands of people rubbing it for good luck! Quality isn't high, but there are handbags, hats, and placemats made from traditional Florentine straw, and leather goods, scarves, lace tablecloths, and other souvenirs for sale. Note a cluster of locals at the nearby food stand on the corner who might be making short work of tripe sandwiches, a Florentine specialty.

Thread your way on the narrow Via Calimaruzza after perusing the selection of books at *Porcellino* (6-8r Piazza del Mercato Nuovo), and exit onto Piazza Signoria, Florence's outdoor sculpture garden, as well as its political and commercial center. Straight ahead is the equestrian statue of Cosimo I by Giambologna. Beyond it in this most Florentine of squares is Palazzo Uguccioni (No. 7), supposedly designed by Michelangelo, and the Tribunale di Mercanzia (No. 10), a commercial court built in 1308 with a row of crests above its second-story windows.

Cosimo I moved to the Palazzo della Signoria (also known as the Palazzo Vecchio) in 1540. It has been the seat of the Florentine government for over 500 years. Civil marriages are performed here (Tuesdays, Wednesdays, and Saturdays), and visitors so inclined may be able to shower a Florentine bride with rice. The *Neptune Fountain* by sculptor-architect Ammannati is known as "Il Biancone," or the "White Giant," and is generally disliked by Florentines; a local rhyme scolds the sculptor for having ruined such a beautiful piece of marble. A stone marker in front of the fountain commemorates the spot where religious reformer monk Savonarola and two followers were hung, then burned, in 1498. A copy of Donatello's *Heraldic Lion,* known as the *Marzocco,* and his *Judith and Holofernes* stand next to a copy of Michelangelo's *David.* To the right of the door of the Palazzo della Signoria, behind Bandinelli's unattractive *Hercules and Cacus* (almost on the corner of the building), is the outline of a man's head, carved into one of the flat stones. Michelangelo is said to have traced this "sketch" of a condemned prisoner behind his back.

Cellini's *Perseus* is the outstanding masterpiece of the Loggia dei Lanzi, built at the end of the 14th century for public ceremonies, and a fitting coda for this walk. Shop for postcards at one of the best-supplied stands in the city — the newsstand in the corner of the piazza — and have a well-deserved hot chocolate, coffee, or *aperitivo* at *Rivoire* (see *Florence's Best Cafés and Confections,* DIVERSIONS).

Walk 3: Santa Croce

The Santa Croce neighborhood is studded with huge palaces built in the 15th century for prospering cloth merchants. Its swampy lowlands (devastated in the 1966 floods) were convenient for dying cloth, as the name of the street Corso dei Tintori — Street of the Dyers — attests. This walk begins amidst the neighborhood bustle of the mornings-only *Mercato di Sant'Ambrogio* (Sant'Ambrogio Market) and travels past palazzi and prisons, a flea market, a relocated fish-market portico, and a piazza named after the first labor revolt, then stops for a taste of what's reputed to be the best gelato in town, and winds up at yet another beautiful square.

Make sure to start in the morning at the *Mercato di Sant'Ambrogio* (Piazza Ghiberti), a favorite with cognoscenti for its assortment of farmers, outdoor stands heaped with local (*nostrale*) vegetables, stalls hung and stacked with clothes, and an indoor perishables market in a smaller, but by no means less interesting, space than the *Mercato di San Lorenzo*. Many of the city's most exciting restaurants are in this neighborhood, well situated for the first choice of the best produce.

The far side of the piazza, a high, windowless expanse of cement that was once the perimeter of a prison, is covered with unattractive but colorful modern murals. Indoor cheese and salami stalls beckon with the fixings for an alfresco picnic. Sip a cappuccino or an intense black *caffè* at the *Caffeterria del Vecchio Mercato* in the center of the market, across from the lunch-only eatery *Da Rocco* (where vegetarians can sample some delectable fare), or hold out for breakfast at either the *Cibreo* or *I Dolci di Patrizio Cosi* bar (see below).

Leave the market and walk toward Via Verrocchio — peek into the tiny shop (No. 2) where a button dyer practices his craft. Next door, the *Cibreo* grocery (No. 4) sells Italian and exotic food and wine. Across the street is the *Cibreo* bar (No. 5), an excellent place to stop for a cappuccino and pastry breakfast. It's also a good choice for a light, inexpensive lunch, served from 2 to 4PM. (But be sure to save room for *Cosi,* a pastry shop coming up.)

Turn right at Via dei Macci past the third jewel in the *Cibreo* crown — the restaurant (No. 118r), where such delicacies as bell pepper soup and polenta with herbs and squid and swiss chard will please the palate. Proceed to the corner overlooking the Chiesa di Sant'Ambrogio. One of the oldest churches in Florence, it was probably founded in the 5th century. The church and a convent occupy the site where Sant'Ambrogio stayed while visiting Florence after he abandoned Milan during the visit of a pagan emperor. A Della Robbia terra cotta, on the corner of Borgo la Croce and Via dei Macci, depicts the onetime bishop of Milan blessing "the devout and humble inhabitants" who passed by. The green copper dome in the distance is the Moorish-style synagogue, built in 1882.

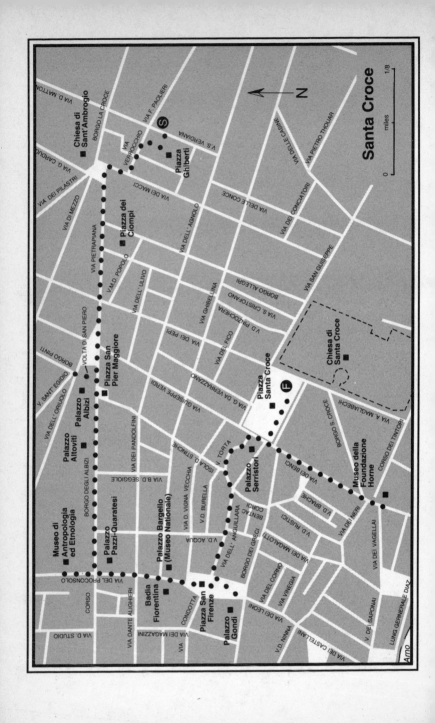

Santa Croce

N

0   1/8
miles

Chiesa di Sant'Ambrogio

BORGO LA CROCE

VIA D. MATTON

VIA F. PAGLIERI

VIA VERROCCHIO

V. S. VERDIANA

Piazza Ghiberti

VIA DEI MACCI

VIA G. CARDUCCI

VIA DEI PILASTRI

VIA DI MEZZO

Piazza dei Ciompi

VIA PIETRAPIANA

VIA D. POPOLO

VIA DELL' ULIVO

VIA DELL' AGNOLO

VIA DELLE CONCE

VIA DEI CONCIATORI

VIA DEI MALCONTENTI

VIA SAN GIUSEPPE

BORGO ALLEGRI

VIA S. CRISTOFANO

VIA GHIBELLINA

V. D. PINZOCHERA

VIA DEI PEPI

VIA DEL FICO

VOLTA DI SAN PIERO

BORGO PINTI

V. SANT' EGIDIO

VIA DELL' ORIUOLO

Piazza San Pier Maggiore

Palazzo Albizi

Palazzo Altoviti

VIA DEI PANDOLFINI

VIA B.D. SEGGIOLE

BORGO DEGLI ALBIZI

VIA GIUSEPPE VERDI

VIA G.DA VERRAZZANO

Piazza Santa Croce

Chiesa di Santa Croce

BORGO S. CROCE

VIA A. MAGLIABECHI

CORSO DEI TINTORI

Museo di Antropologia ed Etnologia

Palazzo Pazzi-Quaratesi

Palazzo Bargello (Museo Nationale)

VIA D. VIGNA VECCHIA

ISOLA D. STINCHE

V. TORTA

Palazzo Serristori

Museo della Foundazione Horne

VIA DEI BENCI

VIA DEI NERI

V.D. ACQUA

V.D. BURELLA

VIA DELL' ANGUILLARA

BENTACCORDI

CORSI

BORGO DEI GRECI

V.D. RUSTICI

V.D. BRACHE

VIA DEI MAGALOTTI

VIA DEI VAGELLAI

VIA DEL PROCONSOLO

CORSO

VIA D. STUDIO

VIA DANTE ALIGHIERI

Badia Fiorentina

CONDOTTA

VIA DEI MAGAZZINI

VIA

Palazzo San Firenze

Palazzo Gondi

VIA DEL CORNO

VIA VINEGIA

VIA DEI LEONI

V.D. NINNA

V.D. SAPONAI

V. DEI CASTELLANI

LUNG GERNERALE DIAZ

Arno

(S)

(LL)

Make a left onto Via Pietrapiana and go straight (*sempre diritto* as Italians always respond when asked directions to practically anywhere) to Piazza dei Ciompi, named in honor of the workers who revolted against the conservative government and the powerful wealthy woolmakers' guild that prohibited them from congregating. The workers rioted in 1378, incited by the Franciscan friars of Santa Croce, and won the right to form their own guilds. One side of the piazza is dominated by Vasari's Loggia dei Pesce, a portico decorated with colorful crests and tondos where fish vendors sold their wares. Florence's first fish market was originally next to the Ponte Vecchio in Piazza del Pesce, but was transferred to the attractive Vasari Loggia in the *Mercato Vecchio,* where Piazza della Repubblica is now, during the 1500s. The old market's narrow lanes and odorous garbage were considered an unhealthy eyesore by a later generation, and were torn down at the end of the 1800s to make room for the Piazza della Repubblica. The loggia was dismantled, and with the traditional Italian sense of haste, reassembled in its present location in 1955. Savvy antiques dealers stalk the flea market in the Piazza dei Ciompi, where some bargains can be unearthed by persistent shoppers.

Follow Via Pietrapiana, noting Palazzo Fioravanti (No. 32), designed by Ammannati. It has an intricate crest over the doorway. Stroll past the *Farmacia del Canto alle Rondine* (Nos. 79 and 81r), a 15th-century pharmacy that was moved here in the 1930s when its original location was usurped by urban renewal. Frescoed ceilings, wooden shelves, stained glass, apothecary jars, modern medicine, support hose, condoms, and aspirin coexist in this most Florentine of drug stores. Looming on the left is the unattractive post office designed by modern architect Giovanni Michelucci, possibly under the spell of the Italian postal service — lackluster at best. Concentrate instead on crossing the street, where Via Pietrapiana becomes Borgo degli Albizi.

Note the typical Florentine trompe l'oeil window shutters painted on the façade (No. 1). A few doorways down (No. 11r) is the bar *I Dolci di Patrizio Cosi,* easily recognizable by the crowds happily consuming some of the best pastry in town. (Another cappuccino and croissant breakfast may not be a bad idea.) Turn right at the 14th-century Palazzo Albizi and go through the Volta di San Piero, a shop-lined tunnel (both the sandwich and fried food shops are good snack possibilities) connecting the Piazza San Pier Maggiore to Via San Egidio. On the opposite corner is *Sbigoli* (No. 4), one of the city's best ceramic stores, and a must for lovers of rustic pottery.

Turn around to return to the Piazza San Pier Maggiore, where there are the remains of a once-thriving church, convent, and loggia — two of its three graceful arches are filled in with stores and shutters and topped with a balcony and apartments. Note the piazza's two medieval towers (de' Pazzi di Valdarno and de' Donati).

Head right to return to Borgo degli Albizi, once home to a Florentine family of note, made wealthy by the wool trade. An annual riderless horse race was held here in the 1400s, but the street is now closed to most traffic. The illustrious Albizi family, unlike George Washington, didn't sleep just anywhere, but owned the buildings at Nos. 9, 11, 12, 14, 18, 15, and 34, as well as the 14th-century building over the Volta di San Piero.

Note the Palazzo Altoviti or Visacci (No. 18), with its bust of Cosimo I presiding over the doorway. In the 1500s, Baccio Valori, a wealthy Florentine known for his culture and love of books, had the building's façade decorated with 15 square stone pillars topped with busts of famous Florentines, including Vespucci, Alberti, Guicciardini, Dante, Petrarch, and Boccaccio — the *visacci* (ugly faces) that earned this palace its nickname.

A Spaniard in the Medici court of Eleonora da Toledo bought four houses, demolished them, and had Ammannati design and decorate what is known as the Palazzo Ramírez de Montalvo (No. 26), with graffiti designed by Vasari and executed by Poccetti. The building is now languishing in a sad state of disrepair, but it's worth noting the ornate Medici crest above the windows of the second floor. Enter the innermost courtyard and look up for a lovely, private view of the Duomo.

Shoppers may be distracted by *Guardaroba* (No. 87r), a local designer discount shop with three locations in the city. Proceed to Via del Proconsolo and turn right to Palazzo Nonfinito (No. 12), begun by Buontalenti for the Strozzis and spanning Renaissance and baroque styles. The family hired a succession of architects, but exhausted their bankroll before the project was completed — hence its name, "Unfinished Palace." Legend has it that the dog-like monsters with wings hovering over the ground-floor windows symbolize a pact with the devil for which the Strozzis were punished by being left fundless with a partially completed palace. The building now houses the *Museo di Antropologia ed Etnologia* (Museum of Anthropology and Ethnology), Italy's first anthropological museum (also see *Museums,* THE CITY).

Across the street is the Palazzo Pazzi-Quaratesi, attributed to San Gallo, built in 1475 for Jacopo de' Pazzi, confiscated after the Pazzi family's conspiracy against their archrivals — the Medicis — in 1478, and later made into a residence of prominent Florentine families. Seek out the crest in the entryway by Donatello, and the peaceful courtyard with its strange but charming Resurrection fresco.

Farther down the Via dei Proconsolo is the Benedictine abbey Badia Fiorentina, founded in 987, enlarged by Arnolfo di Cambio in about 1285, and rebuilt in the 17th century. Dante first saw Beatrice at mass here. Its part-Romanesque, part-Gothic hexagonal campanile was completed in 1330. At the corner of Via Ghibellina is the somber Palazzo del Bargello, built in 1255 as the city's first Town Hall (or Palazzo del Podestà) and a civil and political center. A fine example of medieval architecture, it was also a prison, taking its name from the head of the police, the *bargello.* Prisoners who escaped were often tried in absentia and condemned in effigy, and their images were painted on the walls of the palace hanging by heels or throat and wearing the hat of a traitor. Although none of these paintings remains, there is evidence that Sandro Botticelli painted the Pazzi conspirators. Currently it houses an excellent collection of Florentine and Tuscan sculpture (also see *Special Places,* THE CITY).

Head down Via Proconsolo to where it widens onto the Piazza San Firenze. Here on the site of a Roman temple of Isis, the Law Court stands; composed of two churches joined with a convent in Florentine baroque style, it is topped with an imposing crest of the Strozzi family, flanked by angels with trumpets. Across the street is the impressive Palazzo Gondi (1 Piazza San Firenze), built after 1490 according to the plans of Giuliano da Sangallo. The southern façade was added in the 19th century, when part of the original was destroyed to widen the street. Enter the exquisite flower-filled courtyard, site of *Al Portico,* the wonderful florist. Cool off, listen to the fountain, breathe in the scent of greenery, and feel refreshed after the bustle and exhaust fumes of the city streets. Leonardo da Vinci once lived here.

Diagonally across the piazza is Via Anguillara. Make a right and drop in at the eatery at No. 70, where hungry strollers can indulge in a Florentine snack, a glass of wine, and a simple sandwich. Turn left at Via Torta, whose curve follows the lines of a Roman amphitheater. Stop at the Palazzo da Panzano (No. 14), which has changed ownership many times and is noted for the rather tame-looking lions flanking its doors. If a meal is in order, make a left onto Via dell'Isola delle Stinche, and stop in at *Pallottino* (No. 1r) to enjoy some hard-to-find Tuscan specialties, including stuffed chicken neck. Save room for gelato, and follow the trail of ice cream cups to *Vivoli* (No. 7). Sample some of what many feel is the city's best gelato (the fruit flavors excel).

Stroll down Via Torta and turn right to Via dei Benci. Head toward the river to the *Museo della Fondazione Horne* (Horne Museum; No. 6, at the corner of Corso dei Tintori). Formerly the home of Herbert Percy Horne, an English art historian, this 15th-century palace is now a museum with Horne's private collection of old kitchen utensils, Renaissance furniture, and paintings. Take Via dei Benci back Piazza Santa Croce, an elegant yet comfortable square, busy with children playing soccer, dogs chasing after pigeons, and babies being wheeled in strollers. Once the site of noble jousts, this piazza later was home to a violent soccer-like game — note the marble marker located on the Palazzo Antellesi, establishing the center of the field.

Palazzo Serristori (No. 1) is attributed to Sangallo, but was restored by Baccio d'Agnolo at the beginning of the 1500s; it now houses neighborhood municipal offices. Palazzo Antellesi (Nos. 21 and 22), one of the most attractive structures in the piazza, is actually two existing palaces combined with a unifying façade with frescoes painted by 13 artists in only 20 days — surely some kind of record. The crest of the Antella family and a bust of Cosimo II de Medici stand over the doorway. For visitors planning to stay in Florence for at least a week, apartments in this building can be rented (see *Best in Town,* THE CITY).

The first Church of Santa Croce was begun in 1228, though the present structure, designed by Arnolfo di Cambio for the Franciscans and considered a masterpiece of Florentine Gothic style, was started in 1294. The striped marble façade, the bell tower, and the statue of Dante to the left of the church all date from the mid-19th century (also see *Special Places,* THE CITY). Shoppers interested in leather goods might want to look at what's for sale at the *Santa Croce Leather School* (No. 16), the school and shop of the church's monastery. The stone benches around the piazza offer a well-earned rest for those who have completed the Santa Croce trek.

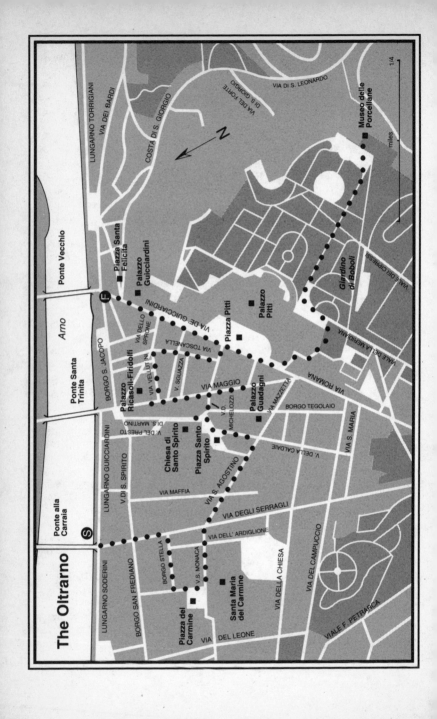

The Oltrarno

Ponte alla Carraia

Arno

Ponte Santa Trinita

Ponte Vecchio

LUNGARNO TORRIGIANI

VIA DEI BARDI

COSTA DI S. GIORGIO

VIA DI S. GIORGIO

VIA DI S. LEONARDO

VIA DEL FORTE DI S. GIORGIO

N

Museo delle Porcellane

miles

1/4

Giardino di Boboli

VIALE DEI CIPRESSI

Piazza Santa Felicita

Palazzo Guicciardini

BORGO S. JACOPO

VIA DELLO SPRONE

VIA DE' GUICCIARDINI

Piazza Pitti

Palazzo Pitti

VIALE DELLA MERIDIANA

VIA TOSCANELLA

VIA CHELLINI

Palazzo Ricasoli-Firidolfi

VIA DE' VELLUTINI

V. SGUAZZA

VIA MAGGIO

Palazzo Guadagni

VIA MAZZETTA

BORGO TEGOLAIO

VIA ROMANA

LUNGARNO GUICCIARDINI

V. DI S. SPIRITO

V. DEL PRESTO DI S. MARTINO

Chiesa di Santo Spirito

Piazza Santo Spirito

V.D. MICHELOZZI

V. DELLA CALDAIE

VIA S. MARIA

VIA MAFFIA

VIA S. AGOSTINO

LUNGARNO SODERINI

BORGO SAN FREDIANO

BORGO STELLA

V. S. MONACA

VIA DEGLI SERRAGLI

VIA DELL' ARDIGLIONE

VIA DELLA CHIESA

VIA DEL CAMPUCCIO

Piazza del Carmine

Santa Maria del Carmine

VIA DEL LEONE

VIALE F. PETRARCA

S

Walk 4: The Oltrarno

The area of Florence south of the Arno River, from Porta San Niccolò to Porta San Frediano (two of the city's gates, both built in the 1300s), is known as the Oltrarno, "the farther side of the Arno." Linked to the rest of the city by bridges, it is home to artisans, artists, fine frescoes, palaces, and piazze. In spite of its imposing royal palazzi, the Oltrarno is still known as a working class neighborhood and is considered the bohemian Left Bank of Florence. It also has some fine churches, museums, and a lovely garden.

Embark on the Oltrarno walk at Ponte alla Carraia, gazing upriver to Ammannati's graceful Ponte Santa Trinita, with its elliptically curved arches. The Ponte Santa Trinita is the only bridge in Florence conceived as a work of art, by Oltrarno mover and shaker Lamberto Frescobaldi with the backing of his noble neighbors and the monks of Santa Trinita. The bridge was to connect the aristocrats of Via Tornabuoni and Via Maggio. It collapsed in 1259, was destroyed by the flood of 1333, rebuilt in 1415, and destroyed again by a 1557 flood. The new Ponte Santa Trinita of Cosimo de' Medici was to be the link between his Oltrarno palace (Pitti) and the Palazzo Vecchio on the other side of the river, until Vasari built his connecting hallway. Michelangelo consulted on the project (a theory supported by the similarity of the curve of the spiral scrolls to that of his Medici tombs), but Ammannati got the credit. Ponte Santa Trinita was used by processions and carriages to make an impressive entry, and theatrical performances were held on special occasions. Statues of the four seasons were moved here from a nearby garden in 1608.

At the Arno's bank, have one of the city's best breakfasts of cappuccino and a tasty hot *cornetto* (as Florentines call croissants), fresh from the oven at the *Bar Marino* (19r Piazza N. Sauro). Then continue *sempre diritto* to the Palazzo Ferroni (8 Via Serragli), built in the mid-15th century. Peek through its iron gate at the baroque courtyard of arcades and columns. If it's open, explore the courtyard of the Palazzo Principe Aldobrandini (No. 9) for a look at a trompe l'oeil castle complete with crests painted on what were once the stables (now a garage). A stone stairway leads to the former greenhouse where lemon trees once wintered.

Turn right onto tiny Borgo Stella, noting the old-fashioned sign for the now-closed wine bar *Cantina Magnani* (No. 2). On the right side of the street, lofty treetops are just visible over the high wall of a secret garden. In a workshop (No. 17r), artisans restore furniture amidst a jumble of tools, tins, and antiques.

Make a left turn into the Piazza del Carmine, a lovely piazza that's sadly been reduced to a parking lot. Glance right for a view of the Cestello dome and bell tower. *La Dolce Vita* (No. 6) is the hip nighttime hangout for young Florentines, and boasts the most attractive crowd in town. It's also open till

2 AM for late-night strollers. Santa Maria del Carmine, a Carmelite church that dominates the piazza, houses the Brancacci Chapel with its recently (and splendidly) restored Masaccio frescoes (also see *Museums,* THE CITY).

Turn right down Via Santa Monaca, where even the youth hostel (No. 6) has a Madonna and Child scratched into a lunette over the portal. Palazzo Mazzei (No. 2) has an interesting crest above the doorway and charming frescoed ceilings that can be glimpsed through the ground-floor windows. On the corner of Via Santa Monaca and Via degli Serragli is a *Tabernacle of Virgin and Child* by Bicci di Lorenzo (1427). According to local legend, this corner was known as "Canto dell Cuculia," or "Cuckoo's Corner," after the cuckoo in the child's hand. Cross the street at the traffic light, to Via Sant'Agostino, which leads to Piazza Santo Spirito. The statue of Cosimo Ridolfi seems fitting for this piazza, since this promoter of agrarian reform presides in one of the last markets in Florence to host farmers selling their own produce, 6 mornings a week. The farmers are joined by merchants selling clothes, cosmetics, costume jewelry, and other sundries. The fountain in the center of the piazza was brought here from a nearby convent.

At Palazzo Dati (No. 12), the stone arches from its former doors are now built into the façade. Far more important is Palazzo Guadagni (No. 10), an elegant, early 16th-century palace attributed to Cronaca. Note the lantern on the corner of the palace, by blacksmith Grosso. On your way to the Chiesa di Santo Spirito (Church of Santo Spirito), with its austere, unfinished façade, stop in *Caffè Ricchi* (No. 9r) for a coffee and a peer around the small back room off the bar, to the right near the cash register. Its walls are covered with framed entries for a playful competition held to finish Santo Spirito's façade. (Postcards of the best works are available.) Among the entries, one poked fun at Gucci, whose offices are nearby; another proposed that the façade be a mosque; still another envisioned the façade as a chair with a cat on it! A few steps away is the workshop of *Alfonso Bini* (No. 5r), once specializing in hat forms, but now turning out a variety of items such as golf bags, shoes, Stetsons, bowlers, and more. Take a peek into *Morganti* (No. 3r), a *civaie* (legume shop) offering a cornucopia of seeds, beans, grain, and flour straight from their sacks, as well as licorice root and mushroom vermouth. If hunger pangs come on, sit in the piazza at *Borgo Antico* (No. 6r) and enjoy a Florentine meal, including fine pizza.

And now concentrate on the church, its stark simplicity and pleasant shape dominating the piazza. It was designed by Brunelleschi, begun in 1436, and finished (except for the façade) amidst great complications in 1487 after his death (also see *Special Places,* THE CITY).

Turn right to Via dei Michelozzi, which is overpowered for at least half the length of the street by Palazzo Capponi with its overhanging arches. Turn right again onto Via Maggio. Once known as Via Maggiore, this thoroughfare was formerly one of the most important streets of the city, as well as the site of a Renaissance building boom. Lovely palaces line the street; the family crests of the buildings' original owners are above the doorways. Many of the ground-floor shops now house antiques dealers.

Turn left to see the Palazzo di Bianca Capello (No. 26), which once belonged to the onetime mistress (later wife) of Grand Duke Francesco de'

Medici (both her husband and his wife died under somewhat mysterious circumstances). The palace was designed by Buontalenti as a residence for Bianca so she could be near her *amante*. Her family crest above the door depicts a hat with ribbons to tie under the chin — a reference to Bianca's last name, which means hat. Of far greater interest is the façade, covered with *graffito* work by Poccetti that is considered among the finest examples of this art form in the city. Enter the courtyard of the Palazzo Ricasoli-Firidolfi (No. 7) and feast your eyes on a beautiful space lined with busts of illustrious Ricasoli family members.

Leaving the palace, turn left, then left again onto Via Vellutini, a tiny lane banked on both sides with wide wooden doorways that hide cavernous workshops. Head for the laboratory of Fiorenzo Bartolozzi (No. 5), a world-famous woodcarver and extraordinary artisan. Wander through vaulted rooms — their high ceilings hung with lamps and chandeliers — filled with iron and wooden trim, posts, sculptures, frames, and bit and pieces of what most people thought was useless rubble left over from World War II. This clever artisan saved, rebuilt, and reworked these materials with the same skill and concentration he devoted to the restoration of the Abbey of Montecassino's woodcarvings. He continues in the same tradition today by making anything out of wood — from picture frames to full-size animals to table legs. Don't hesitate to ask for a tour of the shop — the craftspeople are enormously proud of their work.

After a visit with Signor Bartolozzi, turn right at Via Toscanella to discover more workshops, and at the end of the street go left onto Sdrucciolo de' Pitti, the "slippery" lane leading to Piazza Pitti. Luca Pitti had to buy up many buildings in the mid-1400s — which he then tore down to create the wide, sloping piazza crowned with his palace designed by Brunelleschi — in an attempt to keep up with the Medicis, who eventually bought the Palazzo Pitti in the 1500s. It's a typical merchant's home, equipped with ground-floor warehouses and wide doorways. The palace houses several museums (see *Special Places*, THE CITY).

Venture past the palace into the terraced Giardino di Boboli, one of the most exquisite examples of Renaissance gardens in Italy. When the Medicis bought the Palazzo Pitti, this large hillside tract of land was included in the deal. Boboli is a perversion of the name of the gardens' original owners — the Borgoli family. Niccolò Pericoli (known as Il Tribolo), a sculptor and architect who had worked with Michelangelo, was commissioned to design gardens out of what was a steep stone quarry. Subsequent changes were made by Ammannati, Buontalenti, and Parigi. It is a tranquil oasis offering not only a vast expanse of lawn, meandering paths, pine and cypress trees, fountains, and grottoes, but an amphitheater built for grandiose extravaganzas, a coffeehouse with a wonderful view, and many statues from the Medici collection of Greek and Roman art. There also are sculptures commissioned from 16th- and 17th-century artists, including many of shepherds, peasants, and animals, which lend life to the gardens. The *Museo delle Porcellane* (Porcelain Museum) houses a collection of French, German, Italian, and Austrian porcelains in a lovely pavilion. Head back down to the palace. Exit the front door and turn left.

At the corner of the piazza is the 15th-century *Casa Guidi* (8 Piazza San Felice), where Robert and Elizabeth Barrett Browning lived after their secret wedding in 1846 until she died in 1861. She is buried in the Cimitero Protestante (English Cemetery) in the northeast part of the city. Now an unfinished museum, the house has a small collection of the poets' memorabilia. Walk across the piazza to Palazzo Leader, also known as Palazzo dei Vini (15 Piazza Pitti), which houses a permanent exhibition on wines from the province of Florence. Frequent shows and wine tastings here will delight oenophiles, while *Pitti Arte e Libri* (No. 16) will engross bibliophiles with its extensive selection of guides and elegant pictorial books.

Palazzo Toscanelli (No. 18) was home to the cartographer who created the map said to have guided Columbus to the New World (a dubious distinction, as the explorer was seeking India!). And Dostoyevski lived at No. 22, where he wrote *The Idiot. Giulio Giannini e Figlio* (No. 37r), the most famous Florentine paper shop, sells exquisite handmade paper, address books, covered pencils, desk sets, and bill files; even window shopping here is a thrill.

Notice that Via Guicciardini seems to strangle Palazzo Guicciardini (No. 15) on the right side of the street. Birthplace of the 16th-century historian, Francesco Guicciardini, part of the palace was knocked down in the 1700s when Piazza Pitti was enlarged; it was then destroyed by German mines in World War II and eventually restored in 1950. Walk down Via Guicciardini toward the Ponte Vecchio, past American Express (No. 49) and *Menicucci* (No. 51r), a toy store with a large selection of stuffed animals and wooden Pinocchio dolls, which come equipped with an extra nose.

Piazza Santa Felicita is easily recognized by the granite column in its center — the statue that once topped it fell in 1732 and was never replaced. Wind up this walk at the Ponte Vecchio, where the works of many Florentine goldsmiths are for sale. Absorb the immortal sight of the bridge and the Duomo, with the mullioned windows of Orsanmichele's oratory in the foreground.

Walk 5: San Miniato and Piazzale Michelangelo

South of Florence are lush, green hills that offer a stupendous panorama of the almost fairy-tale city below; perhaps the most impressive is from Piazzale Michelangelo. There are several ways to get there: Bus No. 13 from the Piazza della Stazione, Bus No. 38 from Porta Romana, and walking up the Viale dei Colli from Ponte San Niccolò, but one of the most pleasurable is the climb up from the Ponte Vecchio along tree-lined streets. Along the way, take a look at the *Museo Bardini,* stop at a *latteria* (milk shop) for a gelato, at the 11th-century Chiesa di San Miniato al Monte (Church of San Miniato al Monte) with its lovely façade reminiscent of the Battistero, and at a Tuscan trattoria for a hearty Florentine meal.

From the Ponte Vecchio, turn left onto Via dei Bardi. Just before the street becomes Via San Niccolò is the *Museo Bardini* (1 Piazza dei Mozzi), constructed in the 19th century with pieces taken from older structures. The museum's collection of sculpture, tapestries, furniture, and paintings is just as diverse — it dates from the Etruscans to the baroque period.

If a pre-climb sustenance is needed, *Frilli* (57 Via San Niccolò) serves some of the best gelato in the city. After indulging in that quintessential Italian treat, make a right onto Via San Miniato. Leaving the confines of the city at the Porta San Miniato, take Via Monte alle Croci and make the first right turn onto Via dell'Erta Canina, a car-free road. It's a short hike to the top of the road. Make a left onto Viale Galileo Galilei and the Church of San Miniato will appear on the other side of an olive grove.

San Miniato's green-and-white marble façade is an excellent example of Tuscan Romanesque architecture. When the late afternoon sun strikes the façade, it is easy to see why the church is one of the city's most loved. With its romantic setting — high above the city with a wide panorama of Florence and the Tuscan hills, surrounded by olive trees, peaceful and tranquil — it is the perfect spot for a wedding — in fact, many Florentines get married here. And Gregorian chants are sung here daily from 4:45 to 5:30 PM. Stroll around the cemetery next to the church among the splendid collection of Italian funerary art or just sit and admire the view (also see *Special Places,* THE CITY).

If hunger strikes, head toward Viale Galileo Galilei, make a left and continue along the tree-lined boulevard to Arcetri, an interesting area with private villas and towers, and *Omero* (11 Via Pian dei Giullari), a trattoria

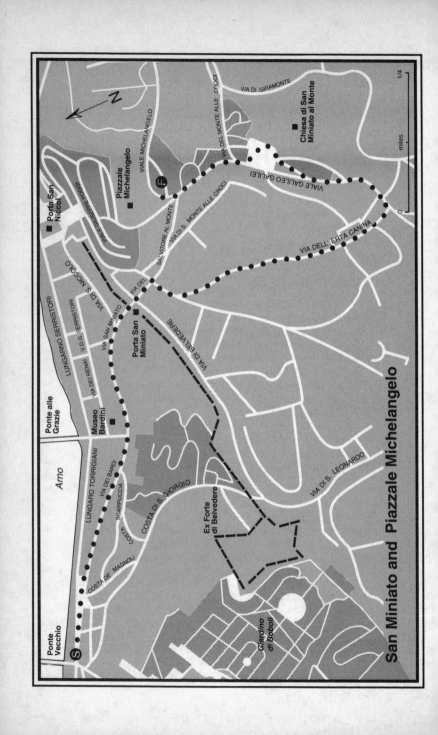

San Miniato and Piazzale Michelangelo

with a hidden terrace for dining in the summer that serves typical Florentine dishes, including *fettunta* (garlic bread). Backtrack on the viale to Piazzale Michelangelo.

The colors of Florence — terra cotta roofs, black, white, and green façades, and beige and brown buildings — all come together in magnificent miniature for viewers at the piazzale. Although the panorama extends to the countryside surrounding the city, it is Florence itself — with its many monuments, bridges, and the Arno River — that is the piazzale's main lure. At sunset, the colors mellow, and at night, the vista changes to one of sparkling lights against the dramatic buildings. In the piazzale itself are copies of Michelangelo's sculptures of *David, Dawn,* and *Dusk,* all set in the middle of a parking lot.

Head back down to the city, either retracing the same steps, taking the bus, or trying an alternate route.

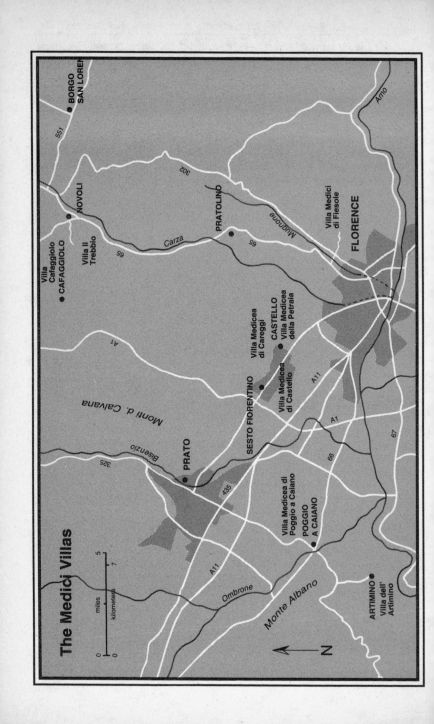

The Medici Villas

miles
kilometers

N

Drive 1: The Medici Villas

The Medicis seem to have had a thing about country homes, which they built with abandon throughout the Florentine countryside in the 15th and 16th centuries. Not only are the villas elegant, but in the true Medici fashion, the grounds are grandiose as well — gardens, fountains, grottoes, and statuaries abound. The view is always the quintessence of Tuscany — umbrella pines, cypress, olive trees, vineyards. In itself, it is well worth a drive through the country. The interiors of many villas are open by appointment only; to indulge in playing Medici-for-a-day, write the Soprintendenza per i Bene Artistici e Storici, Via della Ninna 5, Firenze, 50122 for permission to visit.

Take SS66 northwest 11 miles (17 km) to Poggio a Caiano, the site of one of the most splendid villas — the Villa Medicea di Poggio a Caiano. It was built for Lorenzo il Magnifico by Sangallo in the late 1400s. Medici Pope Leo X (Lorenzo's son) added the loggia with its glazed terra cotta frieze in the classical style, and twin curving staircases were a 17th-century addition. The villa was a favorite of King Vittorio Emanuele when Florence was the capital of Italy. It has recently undergone a much-needed restoration and now houses frequent art exhibitions. The villa is open daily except Mondays from 9 AM to 1:30 PM; the gardens are open from 9 AM to 4 PM in winter, 9 AM to 7 PM in summer.

From the villa, follow the signs for the medieval village of Artimino and a twisting, hairpin road through the lovely, rolling countryside to another Medici outpost, the Villa dell'Artimino. This magnificent 16th-century structure, sometimes called the Villa of the Hundred Chimneys (for obvious reasons) or La Ferdinanda, was designed by Buontalenti as a hunting lodge for Ferdinand I de' Medici. Its simple façade is adorned with a curving double staircase.

The villa sits atop a prominent hill overlooking elaborate gardens and olive groves, thick pine and ilex woods, and the vineyards that produce the famous red carmignano wines, lauded since the days of the Medicis. The grounds of the villa are open to the public. Delfina, a former cook at the hunting lodge of Artimino, who used to prepare the game brought in from the reserve by hunters, opened a small restaurant in the stables, then moved in 1960 to a rustic farmhouse down the road to *Da Delfina* (1 Via della Chiesa; phone: 55-871-8074), where she and her son Carlo prepare some of the best country-style food in Tuscany.

Take SS66 back to Florence and head 5 miles (8 km) northwest on the road to Sesto Fiorentino to the suburb of Castello, where there are three wonderful Medici villas. The Villa Medicea della Petraia (40 Via della Petraia) was built by Buontalenti in 1575 on the site of a medieval castle (which once belonged to the Brunelleschi family) for Cardinal Ferdinando de' Medici (later Grand Duke). Buontalenti kept the castle's original central tower, which offers an amazing view of the surrounding area, but the rest of the villa and the garden have been modified many times over the years. The courtyard was glassed in by King Vittorio Emanuele and transformed into a ballroom; its interior frescoes by baroque painter Volterrano celebrate the Order of Santo Stefano. The impressive garden is on three different levels — joined by stairs — and decorated with a fountain by Renaissance landscape architect-sculptor Il Tribolo and Giambologna's statue of Venus wringing out her hair. The villa is open daily except Mondays from 9 AM to 3:30 PM in winter, until 6:30 PM in summer.

The Villa Medicea di Careggi (Viale G. Pieraccini) was purchased in 1417 by the Medicis, and enlarged and remodeled by Michelozzo for Cosimo Il Vecchio, who made this one of Europe's most important intellectual centers. Sangallo added the loggia wings on the south side for Lorenzo. The fountain by Verrocchio, now in the courtyard of Palazzo Vecchio, originally was created for Careggi's gardens. Cosimo, his son Piero, and his grandson Lorenzo all died here. The villa is now part of the Careggi Hospital complex and is not usually open to visitors. For permission to visit, write to the Administrative Offices, Viale G. Pieraccini 17, Firenze 50139.

The Medicis bought the Villa Medicea di Castello in 1477, and Cosimo had it restored by architect-painter-chronicler Vasari in the 1500s, hiring Il Tribolo and Buontalenti to rebuild the villa and gardens. Also commissioned was Il Tribolo's fountain, which is topped with Ammannati's statue of Hercules crushing Antaeus and his allegorical statue of winter, dripping and shivering, arms crossed, with hands tucked under armpits. An original grotto is decorated with shells and stones in mosaic patterns, and exotic animals of great charm (including Giambologna's bear, monkey, rhinoceros, and even a giraffe) stand in a niche behind a marble tub decorated with fish. The garden is open daily except Mondays.

Return to Florence and take SS65 6 miles (10 km) north to Pratolino. In 1568 Grand Duke Francesco de' Medici hired Buontalenti to build a villa and garden for himself and his second wife, his former lover Bianca Capello. Situated on the crest of a hill, the Villa Pratolino-Demidoff was once one of Europe's wonderlands because of its splendid park and waterworks, but its grottoes, fountains, and villa were destroyed in the early 1800s to make room for an English garden. Only Buontalenti's chapel, the garden lanes, and Giambologna's majestic statue — the *Appennino* — remain to hint at the former glory of this Medici wonder.

Continue 9½ miles (15 km) north on SS65 to Cafaggiolo where the Villa Cafaggiolo is located. Once the preferred residence of Cosimo I, it was built by Michelozzo, who had already worked for the family designing various buildings in Florence. Head south on SS65 a few miles. Just before Novoli, make a right turn onto a country road and take it to another villa — Il Trebbio. Previously a medieval hunting lodge, Michelozzo restructured it in 1451. Il Trebbio's hilltop location affords splendid views of stately cypresses and silvery olive trees. Its simple square lines are a blend of Gothic and

Renaissance styles. A garden to the right of the villa is still in its original form, and a rose-covered pergola on the left uses brick columns from Cosimo's era. Lorenzo de' Medici, Alberti, Donatello, Brunelleschi, and Michelangelo all slept here.

Take SS65 back to Florence, stopping along the way at another villa built by Michelozzo (in 1458) — the Villa Medici in Fiesole (2 Via Beato Angelico). Possibly the first true Tuscan Renaissance villa, it was Lorenzo de' Medici's favorite residence and a center of famed European intellects. Tight rows of somber cypresses line the road that leads to the villa, which still maintains its basic lines and lovely terrace despite 18th-century modifications; pots of lemon trees stand in front and the view from here is breathtaking. Write for permission to visit, as it is now a private home.

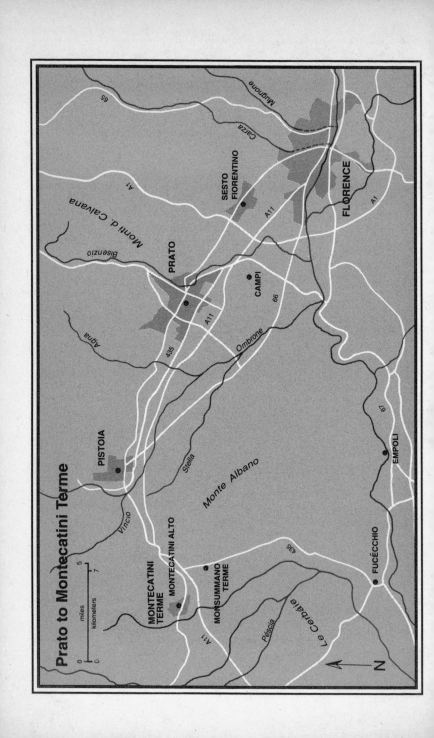

Drive 2: Prato to Montecatini Terme

West of Florence are three cities, each with a very different character. Prato, just 12 miles (19 km) away via the A11 autostrada, has been a textile center for many centuries, but it also has many medieval and Renaissance treasures. Pistoia is reknowned for its Romanesque sculptures, and Montecatini Terme is Italy's most famous and most fashionable spa. All three can be visited in a day, or stretched out over 2 or 3. Some recommended hotels and restaurants are given for those who wish to tour at a more leisurely pace.

Much medieval and Renaissance wealth went into the embellishment of the very prosperous town of Prato, which has been known for its high-quality textiles — especially its wool — since before the 8th century. Like all modern cities with ancient origins, however, there is an old and a new Prato. Bypass all the lifeless apartment buildings, textile factories, and peripheral reminders of the 20th century, and head right to the heart of the well-preserved historic center, following signs for the *centro storico*. The imposing 13th-century Castello dell'Imperatore (Emperor's Castle) is the principal landmark.

Medieval Prato was a staunch supporter of the Ghibellines (those favoring the emperor and opposing the temporal power of the pope), and in thanks for its loyalty, the flattered Emperor Frederick II built this massive fortification with crenelated walls, one of the very few examples of this type of architecture outside Sicily. A lofty view from any of its eight lookout towers is enchanting. Independent Prato eventually fell to the Florentine Guelphs (archenemies of the Ghibellines) in the 14th century, and the same Renaissance masters who lavished their arts on Florence were sent here to do the same. Witness the 15th-century Santa Maria delle Carceri (St. Mary of the Prisons), a fine Renaissance church by the noted Florentine architect Sangallo, just across the square from the castle. The magnificent interior is a study of harmonious proportions, highlighted with beautiful white-on-blue glazed terra cottas by Andrea della Robbia.

Undoubtedly the most renowned of all the Renaissance artists to work in Prato was Fra Filippo Lippi, who was himself a native *pratese.* An orphan, he was put in a monastery at the age of 15, but more suited to an unorthodox (and slightly licentious) life, he fled. He was captured by pirates, sold as a slave in Africa, and freed by the Saracens, who marveled at his artistic talents. Upon his return to Prato, he succumbed to the fair beauty of Lucrezia Buti, a young nun whose angelic face soon began appearing as that of the Madonna in most of his paintings. She gave birth to a son who would also become a prominent figure in Renaissance art; and Cosimo de' Medici had Fra Filippo released from his vows, freeing him to cover Prato's fine Duomo — and much of the rest of Tuscany — with his delicate frescoes.

The Duomo stands in Piazza del Duomo, on a site originally occupied by the 10th-century *pieve* (parish church) of Santo Stefano. One of the best examples of Romanesque-Gothic architecture in Tuscany, it has the typical green-and-white marble stripes adorning its façade, with a Della Robbia lunette over the entrance. To the right is an exterior pulpit, the work of Donatello and Michelozzo (1428–38); the *Dancing Putti* reliefs decorating it are copies of Donatello's originals, which are now in the *Museo dell'Opera del Duomo* (Cathedral Museum). Several times a year, on special occasions (including May 1, August 15, and September 8), the Holy Girdle of the Virgin Mary is put on display in the pulpit. Said to have been given to the ever-doubting Apostle Thomas upon the Virgin's ascension into heaven, this precious relic was brought to Prato in the Middle Ages by a Tuscan merchant who had a Palestinian wife. Ordinarily, it's kept in a chapel of the Duomo, where frescoes by Agnolo Gaddi tell the story. The frescoes in the chancel of the church — stories of the lives of St. John the Baptist and of St. Stephen — are of greater significance, however. These early Renaissance masterpieces took Fra Filippo Lippi 14 years to finish and are considered his finest work. Frescoes by another master, Paolo Uccello, are in the Boccherini Chapel, to the right.

The old civil law court building, the 13th- and 14th-century Palazzo Pretorio, is in picturesque Piazza del Comune. It houses the *Galleria Comunale,* one of the region's major collections of Renaissance, mainly Florentine, masters. Prato's tourist information office is at 48 Via Cairoli (phone: 574-24112).

Two recommended hotels are the *Palace* (230 Viale Repubblica; phone: 574-592841) and the *Villa Santa Cristina* (58 Via Poggio Secco; phone: 574-595951). Although outside the city, *Il Piraña* restaurant (110 Via Valentini; phone: 574-25746) is well — and widely — known for its specialties of fresh fish from nearby Tyrrhenian waters. Closed Saturdays, Sundays, August, and *Christmas* through *Epiphany* (January 6). Another good choice is *Il Tonio* (161 Piazza il Mercatale; phone: 574-21266), in the *centro storico* on the picturesque piazza where Fra Filippo Lippi was born (in a building that is no longer standing). It includes fish specialties on its extensive menu of Tuscan dishes. Closed Sundays, Mondays, and August.

Head west 12 miles (20 km) on SS435 to Pistoia. The treasures of this town are many, but since they were created by the roll call of artists who performed similar artistic feats in Prato and Florence, and because the creative inspiration is again equaled in the great city of Pisa farther west, most visitors give short shrift to Pistoia. That is a shame, because it is a town full of character, still girdled by a handsome set of 14th-century walls that were fortified by the Medicis and once accommodated over 60 lookout towers. Like its neighbor, Prato, Pistoia was a firm supporter of the Ghibellines, and it, too, eventually fell to that most puissant of rivals, Florence.

From a map of the city, it is possible to pick out a square plan (harking back to Pistoia's Roman origins) inside a trapezoid (the walls), right in the center of which is the Piazza del Duomo. The Duomo itself was built on 5th-century foundations during the 12th and 13th centuries, Pistoia's wealthier days. The Pisan-style façade has 3 tiers of arcades (as does the slim, adjacent bell tower, which was transformed, in the 13th century, from a Lombard military guard tower) and terra cotta decorations by Andrea della Robbia around the central door. The simple interior sets off an ecclesiastical masterpiece, the famous silver altar of St. James, housed in the Cappella di San Jacopo. Begun in the late 13th century, the altar contains more than 600 silver figures created by numerous artists through the mid-15th century — a compendium of Tuscan sculpture from the Gothic to the Renaissance. The Duomo's *Museo Capitolare* is worth a visit just for the dazzling array of antique gold plates, chalices, trays, and other treasures. The 14th-century green-and-white marble Baptistry, across from the Duomo, was built according to the design of Andrea Pisano, a name behind much of northern Tuscany's finest architecture. Two other buildings in the same square are the austere 14th-century Palazzo del Podestà, adjoining the Baptistry, and the 13th- and 14th-century Palazzo del Comune.

Not far away from Piazza del Duomo is the 13th-century Ospedale del Ceppo, which takes its name from the *ceppo,* or box, in which offerings were once left. The hospital's most striking feature is the beautiful multicolored terra cotta frieze decorating the early-16th-century portico, a splendid work by Giovanni della Robbia and the Della Robbia workshop. Elsewhere among this labyrinth of medieval streets are the city's two oldest churches — the 12th-century Sant'Andrea and San Giovanni Fuorcivitas, which dates from the 8th century but was reconstructed from the 12th to the 14th centuries. Each is the proud possessor of an elaborate pulpit, the former a masterpiece carved (from 1298 to 1301) by Giovanni Pisano (as with the Della Robbias, the skilled Pisano family of architect-sculptors spanned several generations — another pulpit by Giovanni is in the Duomo at Pisa and one by his father, Nicola, is in the Pisa Baptistry), and the latter by Fra Guglielmo da Pisa, a student of the Pisanos, finished in 1270.

It's hard to believe today, but thousands of Pistoia's buildings were damaged during World War II. The city's pride, and a timeless expertise, have re-created history, however. The tourist information office (Ente Provinciale Turismo, Piazza del Duomo; phone: 573-21622) provides all kinds of information about the city.

A nice place to stay is *Il Convento,* 4 miles (6 km) outside town (33 Via San Quirico; phone: 573-452651). It also has a good restaurant.

Meticulously groomed *vivai,* extensive nurseries of fledgling trees, from exotic palms to the ubiquitous cypress and everything in between, compose the outskirts of Pistoia. Just beyond them, following SS435, lies the elegant spa town of Montecatini Terme, less than 10 miles (16 km) from Pistoia.

What Vichy is to France and Baden-Baden is to Germany, Montecatini is to Italy. The resort's heralded mineral waters have had a salutary effect on many a stomach, liver, and intestine — including those of Giuseppe Verdi, Arturo Toscanini, and La Loren. To "take the waters" in Montecatini means to settle into a hotel, undergo an obligatory clinical consultation with a hydro expert, and make tracks each day, almost always in the morning and on an empty stomach, to one or the other of the town's *stabilimenti termali* (thermal establishments) to down the prescribed measure from any of the five springs — Tamerici, Torretta, Regina, Tettuccio, Rinfresco — that are used for drinking. About 2,000 immaculately clean WCs stand by, blending discreetly with the surroundings.

The waters of two other springs — Leopoldina and Giulia — are for mineral baths, and an eighth spring, Grocco, is expressly for mud baths. The *termi* were once the private property of the Medicis, who undoubtedly appreciated the restorative treatments for gout and an excess of *la dolce vita,* but it was not until the late 1800s that the waters' curative powers became well-known. Early in this century, all the various springs were taken over by the state, a massive building program was undertaken, and fashionable hotels were constructed to accommodate shahs, bluebloods, and Milanese industrialists. Now numbering well over 400, the hotels operate from *Easter* to the end of November.

A serious treatment should really last 12 days, so if you're here just a day or two, don't expect miracles (although it's possible to buy the bottled waters and schlep them home). But even for those who don't take the cure, a peek at one of the *stabilimenti,* all laid out in a vast green park, is enlightening. The most beautiful is the Stabilimento Tettuccio, built in 1927 in a classical style. Here, from early morning until noon, an orchestra plays under a frescoed dome, attendants fill cups at fountains spouting from counters of inlaid marble set before scenes of youth and beauty painted on walls of ceramic tile, and patrons stroll through the colonnades, peruse newspapers, or chat. The entrance fee is stiff because it includes water for those who are taking the cure (most who do, however, have a subscription), as well as the otherworldly atmosphere, and there is a lovely, conventional coffee bar inside. Off-season, only the less-impressive Stabilimento Excelsior, built in 1915 and with an ultramodern wing, is open.

Montecatini also has expensive boutiques, sports facilities, and seemingly endless flower gardens and forests of centuries-old oaks, pines, palms, cedars, magnolias, and oleanders. The tourist information office (66-68 Viale Verdi; phone: 572-70109, 572-78200, or 572-71284) has booklets on different walks through this luxurious vegetation, as well as walks up into the nearby hills. Spa information can be found at 41 Viale Verdi (phone: 572-75851). The Old Town of Montecatini, Montecatini Alto, is another excursion. Set on top of a hill that dominates the spa town, it is reached by funicular from Viale Diaz or by a road winding 3 miles (5 km) through olive groves and orchards.

For those who wish to take the waters, there are several places to stay in Montecatini — the *Grand Hotel e La Pace* (3 Via della Torretta; phone: 572-75801), the *G.H. Tamerici & Principe* (2 Viale IV Novembre; phone: 572-71041), and *Cappelli–Croce di Savoia* (139 Viale Bicchierai; phone: 572-71151). What the *Grand Hotel e La Pace* is to hotels, the *Gourmet* (6 Viale Amendola; phone: 572-771012) is to restaurants. An exquisite meal here is worth every calorie (there's fresh fish, however, for truly determined dieters). Closed Tuesdays.

Take SS435 to A11 to return to Florence.

Drive 3: Chianti Classico Country

In the region that stretches south of Florence almost to Siena in the heart of Tuscany, the lovely landscape of soft rolling hills, forests of umbrella pines and cypresses, and vineyards and olive trees is world reknowned. The chianti classico area (one of seven zones that produces the wine known collectively as chianti) is famed for its magical light, physical beauty, fine wine, and olive oil. After years of neglect, the area has undergone a transformation in the past 2 decades to country chic and boutique wineries, with many former farmhouses and castles restored by Tuscans, Italians from other areas, and foreigners (some of these buildings have been turned into hotels ranging from elegant to rustic). In fact, the English often refer to the area as "Chianti-shire" because of the large number of expatriates who have established a foothold.

A drive along La Chiantigiana (SS222) through Greve, Panzano, and Castellina is the easiest introduction to this area. The route then branches off east to Radda and south to Gaiole and Castelnuovo Berardenga, naming wineries along the way (with advance notice, many will arrange tours). Another way to explore this stretch is to drift from castle to roadside shrine, following the signs for *degustazione, vendita diretta,* or *cantina.* Also listed are some recommended hotels, if the mood to sleep among the grapevines and olive trees strikes.

Take SS222 17 miles (27 km) south to Greve, which stands between the Elsa and Arno valleys. It has a charming central square (Piazza Matteotti) surrounded by a shop-filled portico. On Saturdays the piazza is the site of a lively market, and an antiques fair is held the Monday after *Easter. Omero Casprini* (Passo dei Pecorai; phone: 55-850716), a rustic trattoria, serves homemade pasta and grilled meat; vocal Italian families fill this trattoria on Sundays (closed Wednesdays). A good hotel is *Fattoria La Loggia* in Montefiridolfi (phone: 55-824-4288). Two wineries are *Viticcio* (phone: 55-853210) and *Vicchiomaggio* (phone: 55-853003).

The campanile of the Church of Santa Maria can be seen from miles away, rising above the village of Panzano, 8 miles (13 km) south of Greve. The town has another landmark — the butcher shop of *Cecchini* (11 Via XX Luglio; phone: 55-852020), a local hangout with a 250-year-old history. Stop by for a taste of the splendid fennel salami known as *fiocchiona.* After that appetizer, dine at *Il Vescovino* (9 Via C. da Panzano; phone: 55-852464; closed Tuesdays). Two suggested hotels are *Albergo Villa Le Barone* (19 Via S. Leonino 19; phone: 55-852215) and *Albergo Villa Sangiovese* (5 Piazza Bucciarelli; phone: 55-852461). A winery to visit is *Fontodi* (phone: 55-852005).

Six miles (10 km) south via SS222 is Castellina, situated on a hilltop with

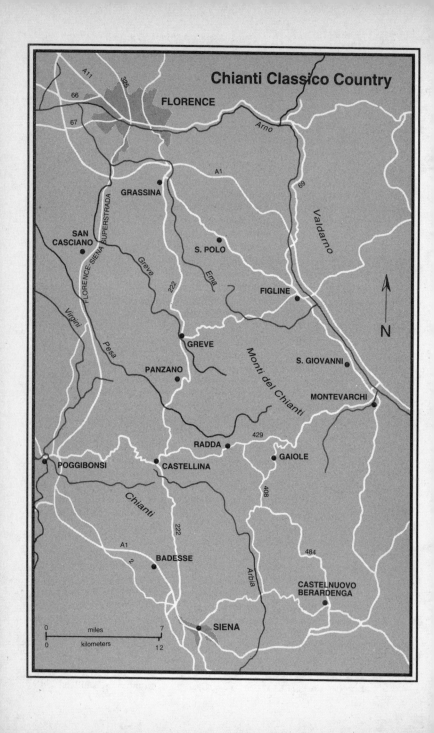

a wonderful view of the surrounding countryside, and dominating the Pesa, Arbia, and Elsa valleys. There is the 16th-century Palazzo Ugolini, the Rocca (a fortress dating from the 1300s), and an imitation Romanic parish church with a fresco by 15th-century Tuscan artist Lorenzo de' Bicci. Diners will enjoy the original Tuscan food and fine wines served at *Albergaccio* (35 Via Fiorentina; phone: 577-741042; closed Sundays). Two hotel suggestions are *Albergo Tenuta di Ricavo* (3 miles/4 km south of town on Via San Donato; phone: 577-740221) and *Albergo Salivolpi* (Via Fiorentina; phone: 577-740484).

Head east 6 miles (10 km) on SS429 to Radda, which was built on a medieval plan and has been the capital of the wine producers' Chianti League since 1415. Dine at *Villa Miranda* (in La Villa; phone: 577-738021) or *Le Vigne* (in Podere Le Vigne; phone: 577-738640). Both are closed on Tuesdays. Recommended hotels are *Albergo Relais Vescine* (in Vescine; phone: 577-740263) and *Albergo Relais Vignale* (9 Via Pianigiani; phone: 577-738300). A winery to visit is *Castello di Volpaia* (phone: 577-738066).

Continue on SS429 for 6 miles (10 km) to Gaiole, surrounded by vineyards and an important marketplace in the chianti classico area since the 12th century. The *Villa Table* (phone: 577-749498), famous for its wines, olive oil, and cooking school (see *Cooking Schools,* DIVERSIONS) has a restaurant (phone: 577-749424; closed Mondays) that serves traditional Tuscan food in a country setting. Other wineries in the area include *Giorgio Regni* (phone: 577-731-3005) and *San Polo in Rosso* (phone: 577-746070).

Take SS408 south to SS484 and head east to Castelnuovo Berardenga, the most southerly town of the chianti classico region, with two wineries to visit — *San Felice* (phone: 577-359226) and *Felsina* (phone: 577-355117). Dine at the nearby *Bottega del Trenta* (in Villa a Sesta; phone: 577-359226; closed Tuesdays and Wednesdays) and if so inclined, spend the night at *Villa Arceno* (in San Gusme; phone: 577-359066) or *Albergo Borgo San Felice* (in San Felice; phone: 577-359260).

Either backtrack to Florence on country roads and then north on SS222 or head south to Siena via the romantic La Chiantigiana or Via Cassia.

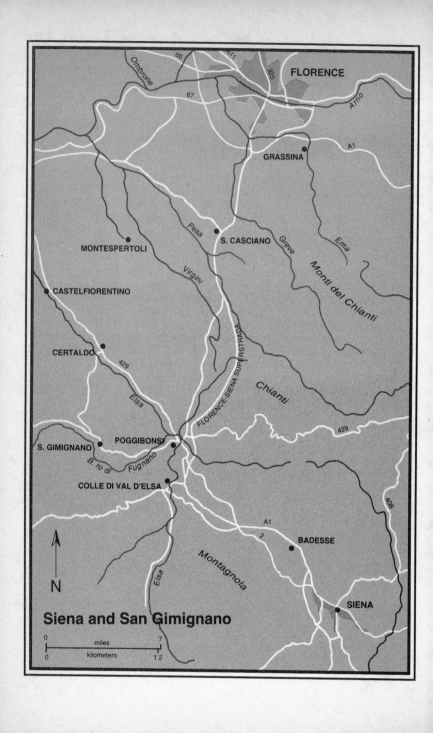

Siena and San Gimignano

FLORENCE

Ombrone

66

A11

325

67

Arno

GRASSINA

A1

Pesa

Greve

Ema

MONTESPERTOLI

S. CASCIANO

Virgini

Monti del Chianti

CASTELFIORENTINO

Chianti

CERTALDO

429

Elsa

FLORENCE-SIENA SUPERSTRADA

429

S. GIMIGNANO

POGGIBONSI

B. ro di   Fugnano

408

COLLE DI VAL D'ELSA

A1

2

BADESSE

Montagnola

N

Elsa

SIENA

miles
0   7
kilometers
0   1 2

Drive 4: Siena and San Gimignano

A visit to the picturesque hilltowns of Siena and San Gimignano (although Siena is really a city) is a trip back into the Middle Ages. Siena's two greatest buildings — the Duomo and the Palazzo Comunale — are both Gothic, and much of its art dates from that period. San Gimignano's walls and some of its structures are medieval, but the town is best known for its 13 towers. Although an excursion to both can be made in 1 day, for those who wish to become steeped in the medieval *ambiente,* a few hotels in each place are suggested.

Take the Florence-Siena *superstrada* 42 miles (68 km).

True to the traditional pattern of settlement in Tuscany, Siena sits on top of a hill or, rather, on top of three hills, enclosed within high walls — an age-old vision, the exact color of which everyone has known since opening the first box of crayons. Approaching these walls, it is easy to feel like a medieval traveler looking for access through a gateway or portico carved with the Sienese coat of arms. Inside, drawn into the labyrinth of narrow steets that snake through the medieval fabric of the city, the feeling does not dissipate. Few modern buildings disturb the illusion; it's as though medieval Siena were merely playing temporary host to modern life.

After Florence, Siena has probably the richest artistic heritage in Tuscany, but unlike Florence it remains more of a medieval rather than a Renaissance city, its overall 13th- and 14th-century Italian Gothic look is a result of certain vicissitudes of its history.

Florence was a menacing presence through much of Siena's history, and in a certain sense it was Florence that arrested Siena's development and caused it to remain the medieval gem it is today. One legend has it that Siena was founded by the Senes Gauls; another recounts that it was founded by Senio, son of Remus, one of the founding brothers of Rome, and hence the Roman she-wolf on the Sienese emblem.

Regardless of its origin, Siena was certainly an Etruscan city and then a military stronghold under the Romans until it finally began to flourish as a center of commerce, finance, and culture in the Middle Ages. At the same time, Siena's wealth and trade became the envy of her Tuscan neighbors, prompting continual warfare with the Florentine city-state in particular. By 1235, the mightier military strength of Florence forced Siena to accept harsh peace terms.

But that was merely round one. On September 4, 1260, the Sienese dealt the Florentines such a resounding defeat at Montaperti, a hill east of the city, that the battle is remembered to this day. Having exorcized Florentine dominance, good sense prevailed, and under a nine-member government of merchant families (Governo dei Nove), peace was made and Siena embarked on one of its most enlightened and prosperous periods. Some of the city's most noteworthy buildings, such as the Palazzo Comunale, the Palazzo Chigi-Saracini, and the Palazzo Sansedoni, as well as plans to enlarge the cathedral, date from this time. It was a golden age for painting, too — Duccio di Buoninsegna and Simone Martini were making names for themselves beautifying palaces and churches.

The good times lasted until 1355, when following a severe drought and then a terrible outbreak of plague in 1348, civil discontent brought about a rebellion of leading noble families and a series of short-lived governments. Would-be conquerors came from farther afield until, in 1554, a 24,000-man army of Spanish, German, and Italian troops (under the command of the Florentine Medici family) laid siege to the city. A year later, Siena fell. Cosimo I de' Medici became its ruler and Siena was taken as a part of the Grand Duchy of Tuscany, first under the Medicis and then under the French house of Lorraine, until it passed, with Tuscany, to the kingdom of Italy in 1860.

It was probably due to Siena's absorption by Florence that the city stayed as small and as resolutely medieval-looking as it is. What's more, it was probably due to their loss of independence that the Sienese invested their annual *Palio* — the reckless bareback horse race around the treacherous Piazza del Campo — with so much civic passion. There are two runnings of this madcap race, one on July 2 and one on August 16. Both originated long ago as the popular part of religious festivities, the former in honor of the Madonna di Provenzano, the latter in honor of Our Lady of the Assumption. The August 16 *Palio,* the more important of the two, has been documented as far back as 1310; the July 2 *Palio* was instituted in 1656.

Then, as now, the city was divided into *contrade,* or districts, which compete against each other with one horse and rider each. The city once had 59 *contrade;* now it has 17, with allegorical names such as Bruco (caterpillar), Tartuca (tortoise), Chiocciola (snail), Drago (dragon), and Leocorno (unicorn). Keep an eye on the corners of buildings when walking around town, the *contrade* are marked off with their symbols, just as streets are with their names. Each *contrada* has its own patron saint, a church where the saint is worshiped, and a feast day in the saint's honor, as well as its own fountain, outside the church, where its babies are baptized a second time.

A Sienese is born into his *contrada* and roots for it all his life, so when the day of the *Palio* rolls around, after months of preparation, spirits are as high as they are in a neighborhood *favela* in Rio during *Carnaval.* The day begins, now as then, with a mass in the Cappella di Piazza and the hanging of the *contrada* banners in either the church of Santa Maria di Provenzano or in the Duomo. Among the banners is the *palio* itself, the banner that goes to the victor. (A *palio* is a banner, but since it is one that is the prize of the competition, the word now also refers to the competition itself and has a double meaning, something like "stakes.") In the early afternoon, each horse is taken to its local *contrada* church to be blessed (it's considered a good omen if the horse leaves something behind). Then, later in the afternoon, comes the most magnificent historical procession in Italy — a parade of dignitaries such as might have taken place in the days of the Sienese republic, delegations from all the *contrade* in full 15th-century regalia, trumpeters, and *sbandieratori* (flag bearers) who wave, toss, and manipulate their flags in intricate synchronized routines.

The race takes 3 minutes at most, but it's hardly an anticlimax. While thousands of the spectators are tourists, the enthusiasm and joy shown by the winning *contrada* indicate that this is not merely an attraction staged for visitors but a deeply felt tradition. The victorious jockey is carried around town in triumph, and at the subsequent outdoor banquet in the winning *contrada*, the winning horse is treated as an honored guest. *Palio* time is definitely the time to visit Siena *if* you don't mind massive crowds and *if* you make all reservations and other arrangements well in advance. All the *Palio* pageantry may be only one expression of Siena's past, but it's the one that most vividly captures the imagination.

Tickets for the *Palio* are not easy to come by. Most of the grandstand seats on the perimeter of the course belong to the Sienese, almost by birthright. Remaining seats sell out many months in advance, and are expensive in the rare instances that they are available. Merchants in the town's better shops are the best source; ask around the Piazza del Campo. In 1991, the cost was about $180 per ticket. The demand for them is so great that spaces at the windows of homes around the Campo are sold, too, and scalping is rampant.

Non-ticket holders can stand in the mass of humanity in the middle of the piazza without charge, but early arrival (before noon) is imperative to ensure a view (pick a high spot near the Fonte Gaia). Another alternative is to buy a ticket for one of the *prove*, or rehearsals, that take place on the 3 days preceding each *Palio*, though this is becoming increasingly impossible as city officials usually buy up all the tickets. The regal pageantry is missing at these trial heats, but it's still possible to feel a bit of the spirit. Occasionally, too, a third *Palio* may be declared for some special reason (as in 1986, in honor of a local government anniversary).

A good introduction to the city is the bird's-eye view from the top of the Torre del Mangia, next to the Palazzo Comunale in Piazza del Campo, from which one can see not only all of the Campo below and across a sweep of red tile roofs to Siena's other major monumental complex, the Duomo, but also out to the surrounding hills. Another vantage point for bringing it all into focus is from the top of what the Sienese call the Facciatone, or big façade, actually the façade of the never-finished Duomo Nuovo (New Cathedral), which now houses the *Museo dell'Opera del Duomo*. Among other things, there's a good view of the Piazza del Campo and the Torre del Mangia from here. *Note:* Cars are not permitted in most of the downtown area.

A glance at the map shows that all of Siena seems to gravitate toward the seashell-shaped Piazza del Campo. In fact, since Siena's *centro storico* is no bigger than a large provincial town, almost all of its sights are within walking distance of this center of gravity. Be aware, however, that the town's narrow streets wind uphill and downhill, and sometimes turn into steps, so comfortable walking shoes are necessary.

Siena's main square, the Piazza del Campo, is certainly one of the most beautiful old squares of Europe. It's on a slant, and its brick paving is divided into nine sectors, a number that harks back to the 13th and 14th centuries, when the city was ruled by a government of nine men who did much to create the cityscape that remains today. The nine sectors converge on the piazza's lower side, in front of the Palazzo Comunale and the adjacent Torre del Mangia. Facing them on the higher side is the Fonte Gaia, a monumental fountain that was decorated with reliefs by Jacopo della Quercia (reproductions take the place of the 15th-century originals, which are now in the *Museo Civico* in the Palazzo Comunale). Its name — the "gay" fountain — alludes to the fact that the arrival of water in the piazza sparked no end of festivity in the 14th century. All around the semicircular edge of the piazza are medieval and Renaissance palaces, one of the most noteworthy of which is the Palazzo Sansedoni, with a curved façade. It dates from the 13th and 14th centuries, but became a single residence in the 18th century. At *Palio* time, the windows of the palaces are hung with ancient banners, the center of the piazza is stuffed with spectators, and the roadway all around turns into the route of the historical procession — and then the *Palio* racetrack.

The elegant façade of the Gothic Palazzo Comunale is slightly curved, in keeping with the unusual outline of the Campo. It is Siena's City Hall, as it has been since it was built between 1297 and 1310, but because part of it houses a museum, it is accessible to visitors. The adjacent bell tower, the Torre del Mangia, was added in the mid-13th century. It takes its name from a onetime bell ringer, Giovanni di Duccio, who was evidently a man of prodigal habits and better known to the Sienese as Mangiaguadagni (Spendthrift). The pillared and roofed structure at the base of the tower is the Cappella di Piazza, built from 1352 to 1376 to fulfill a vow made during the plague of 1348. Inside the Palazzo Comunale are beautifully proportioned rooms that give a sense of tangible authority rather than grandeur, and the frescoes with which they were decorated remain, although not in their pristine state.

The Duomo, a Sienese landmark, dedicated to Santa Maria dell'Assunta (Our Lady of the Assumption), is one of the most beautiful medieval churches in Italy. In many ways, it is a chronicle of the artistic and political history of Siena. It was begun in 1196, during the early stages of Siena's development as a city-state, and much of what is seen today was completed in the 13th century.

But in the 14th century, with a growing population and the example of Florence's huge Duomo, the city's plans for the cathedral also grew. It was decided that the existing church should form the transept of a newer, much larger church, so construction began again, in 1339. By 1355, money problems and the plague had put an end to the superchurch dream, but not before the façade of the new church had been built. (It is this piece of unfinished architecture, off to the right of the Duomo, that the Sienese call the Facciatone, or big façade.) Attention returned in the late 14th century to finishing the old Duomo, and the result is an imposing, if somewhat irregular, white marble basilica with characteristic black stripes. The lower level of the façade, largely Romanesque, is dominated by the stone carving of Giovanni Pisano, whose work decorates many Tuscan churches. The upper level, Siena's response to the magnificent façade of the Duomo in Orvieto, is full 14th-century

Gothic. The mosaics at the top, whose gold backgrounds catch the sun like mirrors playing with a beam of light, are from the 19th century. The interior of the church is rich in art treasures, not the least of which is the floor, done from the mid-14th century to the mid-16th century and divided into 56 squares, each recounting a different biblical story in inlaid marblework. Lovers of the Renaissance should look at the chapel, Cappella di San Giovanni Battista, which has frescoes by Pinturicchio (note the two portraits of Alberto Aringhieri). Pinturicchio also painted the lively, vivid frescoes recounting the life of Pope Pius II (Enea Silvio Piccolomini) in the Libreria Piccolomini, off the left side of the nave.

Siena's baptistry is down a flight of stairs to the right of the cathedral, behind the apse. A 14th-century building, it is best known for its baptismal font, designed by Jacopo della Quercia and considered a work of transition from the Gothic to the Renaissance. A collaborative effort, it has two bronze angels by Donatello, as well as bas-reliefs around the basin by Donatello, Lorenzo Ghiberti, and others.

The *Museo dell'Opera del Duomo* (Cathedral Museum), also known as the *Museo dell'Opera Metropolitana* (Piazza Jacopo della Quercia), contains mainly works that have been taken from the cathedral. Almost as interesting as the works themselves is their setting: the Duomo Nuovo, the unfinished extension of the cathedral that was planned and then abandoned in the mid-14th century. A visitor can only imagine its potential magnificence from the five huge Gothic arches that still stand and would have been the nave. Three of these have been closed off to form the museum. From the museum it's possible to climb to the top of the Duomo Nuovo façade — the Facciatone — for a splendid view of the town.

The *Pinacoteca Nazionale* (National Picture Gallery; 29 Via San Pietro) is housed in the beautiful 15th-century Palazzo Buonsignori, and a must for a clear understanding of Sienese art from the 12th to the 17th centuries. There are 40 rooms filled with Sienese masterpieces — from Guido da Siena, Duccio, Simone Martini, Pietro and Ambrogio Lorenzetti, Beccafumi, and more.

Palazzo Chigi-Saracini (89 Via di Città; closed Mondays), like many Sienese palaces and churches, was begun in the 12th century, finished in the Gothic style in the 14th century, and later altered and restored. Originally built for one of the leading families of Siena, it is now the seat of the Accademia Musicale Chigiana and a music school whose international summer students congregate around the carved stone well in the delightful courtyard. Concerts are held in the palace's music room, which is adapted from the noble apartments and is Siena's main concert hall.

In the midst of medieval Siena is the Palazzo Piccolomini (Via Banchi di Sotto), a mid-15th-century Renaissance palace that was once the home of the family of Pope Pius II and now houses the state archives, with a wealth of documents and statutes pertaining to Siena's turbulent history. Farther down the street are the Logge del Papa, three graceful Renaissance arches that Pius II had built in his family's honor.

One of Siena's oldest and best-loved fountains, Fonte Branda, stands at the end of Via Santa Caterina, not far from the sanctuary. There are references to it as far back as 1081, but it was rebuilt in the mid-13th century, when it was given its present triple-arched mini-fortress form with the emblem of Siena in the middle.

Besides the Torre del Mangia and the Facciatone, one other special spot in Siena offers a panoramic view of all the palaces and churches, the red-roofed expanse cut through by winding streets. This is the Fortezza Medicea (phone: 288497), also known as the Forte di Santa Barbara, a defensive fortress built in 1560 by Cosimo I of the Florentine Medici family shortly after his arrival in Siena as the city's conquerer. Now it's a city park, and although anyone standing on its battlements is no longer master of all he or she surveys, one does still survey quite a lot, both of the city and of the surrounding countryside, in all directions.

But the view is not the only reason to visit this well-preserved fort at the end of a long day's sightseeing. Inside, part of the space is given over to the *Enoteca Italica Permanente,* a showroom and outlet for all the best Italian wines, including the excellent chianti bottlings for which the province is famous. The most demanding restaurateurs do their shopping here, and so can the enthusiastic individual. Wine tasting is encouraged, for a small charge. With advance notice, a guided visit to a vintner's farm also can be arranged here for $35 and up a person; the price varies with the excursion. The cellars are open daily, 3 PM to midnight.

The city's tourist office, Azienda di Promozione Turistica (APT; 56 Piazza del Campo; phone: 280551) is an information office and travel agency.

Sienese shops are a mixture of extreme sophistication and rustic simplicity. While leading names in Italian fashion are in evidence in clothing and shoe stores, local craftsmanship can be found in the numerous ceramic and pottery shops selling original designs, as well as excellent copies of medieval and Renaissance Sienese items. The shops lining the main streets — Banchi di Sopra, Banchi di Sotto, and Via di Città — in the vicinity of Piazza del Campo are fertile ground for all of Siena's specialties, including the numerous culinary delicacies to be found in this area. Siena is particularly famous for *panforte,* a rich, spiced fruit and nut cake; *ricciarelli* (almond cookies); and salami. One favorite souvenir quest is the attempt to collect a set of flags, mugs, or plates that carry each of the crests of Siena's 17 surviving *contrade.*

There is a colorful outdoor market every Wednesday at Piazza La Lizza (near the Basilica of San Domenico) where everything from flowers to hand-bags, dresses, kitchenware, and pottery is sold.

Some recommended hotels are the *Certosa di Maggiano* (82 Via di Certosa; phone: 288180; fax: 288189; telex: 574221), *Villa Scacciapensieri* (a bit over a mile/1.6 km from the city center at 10 Via di Scacciapensieri; phone: 41441; fax: 270854; telex: 573390), and *Palazzo Ravizza* (34 Pian dei Mantellini; phone: 280462; fax: 271370; telex: 570252).

A few good restaurants include the one at the *Certosa di Maggiano* hotel (closed Tuesdays except to hotel guests), where such unusual fare as tortellini soufflé is served, *Al Mangia* (43 Piazza del Campo; phone: 281121; closed Mondays) for game and mushroom dishes, and *Da Guido* (7 Vicolo Pier Pettinaio; phone: 280042; closed Wednesdays) to indulge in typical Tuscan food.

Leaving Siena, take S2 north 20 miles (32 km) to Poggibonsi and head west on the picturesque country road for 7 miles (11 km) to the small hilltown of San Gimignano.

Ringed by three sets of historic walls, San Gimignano bristles with 13 (or 14 or 15, depending on exactly what you count) of its original 72 medieval towers, and thus is known as San Gimignano delle Belle Torri — San Gimignano of the Beautiful Towers. Each tower was attached to the private palazzo of a patrician family and was used partly for defense against attack from without, but also partly for defense against attack by feuding families from within the walls. As with today's skyscrapers, height was an indication of prestige, so "keeping up with the Dantes" is as old as the Tuscan hills.

The town's origins are Etruscan, but it takes its name from a Bishop of Modena who died here in the 4th century. It became a free commune in the 12th century, and life would have been tranquil had it not been for the destructive conflict between two families in particular, the Guelph Ardinghelli and the Ghibelline Salvucci (the city was predominantly Ghibelline). In 1300, Guelph Florence sent Dante as ambassador to make peace between the warring factions, but he was unsuccessful; internal strife grew so volatile that 53 years later, an exasperated San Gimignano willingly surrendered to the Florentines it had resisted for so many centuries.

Dante wouldn't be too overwhelmed by a return to 20th-century San Gimignano, so little have things changed. The two main streets of this perfectly preserved town, Via San Giovanni and Via San Matteo, feed into two splendid squares, Piazza della Cisterna and Piazza del Duomo. At the center of Piazza della Cisterna is the 13th-century well from which it takes its name. The piazza is paved with bricks inlaid in a herringbone pattern and surrounded by an assortment of medieval palazzi and towers. In the adjoining Piazza del Duomo, the 12th-century cathedral, known as the Collegiata, is flanked by more stately palazzi and seven towers. The Palazzo del Popolo, to one side of the cathedral, is the home of San Gimignano's small *Museo Civico*. It contains, besides paintings from the 14th and 15th centuries, the room from which Dante delivered his harangue in favor of the Guelphs, and it provides access to one of San Gimignano's towers, from which there is a view of the town and hills in all directions.

Stop in the 13th-century Church of Sant'Agostino at the far end of town to see the frescoes by Benozzo Gozzoli, and for another view out over the surrounding countryside — or back toward the town and towers — climb to La Rocca, a onetime fortress, now a public park (good pictures of the towers can be taken from the battlements here, but try to arrive early in the day to avoid direct sunlight). While away an hour at one of the sidewalk cafés with a glass of local *vino bianco* — San Gimignano's famous vernaccia is considered the finest white wine in the region and one of the finest whites in Italy. The tourist office is on the Piazza Duomo (phone: 577-940008).

If the mood strikes to stay in this medieval town, try the *Bel Soggiorno* (91 Via San Giovanni; phone: 577-940375), *La Cisterna* (23 Piazza della Cisterna; phone: 577-940328), or *Pescille* (Località Pescille; phone: 577-940186). *La Mangiatoia* (5 Via Mainardi; phone: 577-941528), a cozy and candelit trattoria, specializes in a variety of excellent homemade pasta dishes. Closed Fridays and January.

INDEX

Index

BIRNBAUM TRAVEL GUIDES

Order by phone, toll-free: 1-800-331-3761

Name_____ Phone_____

Address_____

City_____State_____Zip_____

Discover the Birnbaum Difference
More Details and Discounts Than Any Other Travel Guide

Get the best advice on what to see and do and where to stay while benefiting from money-saving information from America's foremost Birnbaum Travel Guides.

Country Guides—$17.00 Each

☐ Canada   ☐ Great Britain   ☐ Portugal
☐ Caribbean   ☐ Hawaii   ☐ South America
☐ Eastern Europe   ☐ Ireland   ☐ Spain
☐ Europe   ☐ Italy   ☐ United States
☐ France   ☐ Mexico   ☐ Western Europe

New Warm Weather Destination Guides 1992—$10.00 Each

☐ Acapulco   ☐ Bermuda   ☐ Ixtapa &
☐ Bahamas   ☐ Cancun/Cozumel/Isla   Zihuatanejo
  (including Turks   Mujeres (including Playa
  & Caicos)   Del Carmen

New City Guides 1992—$10.00 Each

☐ Barcelona   ☐ London   ☐ Paris
☐ Boston   ☐ Los Angeles   ☐ Rome
☐ Chicago   ☐ Miami   ☐ San Francisco
☐ Florence   ☐ New York   ☐ Venice

Business Guides 1992—$17.00 Each

☐ Europe 1992 for the Business Traveler
☐ USA 1992 for the Business Traveler

Total for Birnbaum Travel Guides	$
For PA delivery, please include sales tax	
Add $4.00 for first Book S&H, $1.00 each additional book	
Total	$

☐ Check or Money order enclosed. Plase make payable to HarperCollins Publishers.
☐ Charge my credit card   ☐ American Express   ☐ Visa   ☐ Mastercard

Card no._____ Exp. date _____

Signature_____

Send orders to:
HarperCollins Publishers, P.O. Box 588, Dunmore, PA 18512-0588